A 2021 Edgar Award Nominee for Best Critical/Biographical
An ABA Indie Next Pick • A PLA LibraryReads Pick

"This childhood memoir, though frank in its details of
postwar privation, is at heart a love story—her parents' love
for each other, and hers for them and the meaningful life they
gave her."—*The Wall Street Journal*

"I fell in love with Jackie Winspear almost at once, right there
on page 24 of her engaging, amusing and moving memoir of
growing up in the post-World War II English countryside."
—*The Washington Post*

"Heartfelt and humorous, poignant
and frank, and—as with the *Maisie Dobbs* books—
beautifully written."—Buzzfeed

"Evocative and unflinching.
Without a trace of self-pity, Jacqueline Winspear portrays
a childhood of rural poverty overcome by hard manual
labor, lifelong love amid emotional wounds, and a profound
understanding of how 'the gift of place' creates meaning
. . . An illuminating portrait of a time and place that is as
optimistic as it is deeply moving."—Sally Bedell Smith,
author of *Prince Charles: The Passions and
Paradoxes of an Improbable Life*

"Winspear's words are hopeful and bright, and imbued with
a resilience that will resonate with readers . . . The book will
appeal well beyond Winspear's fan base as a literary memoir
deeply linked to history and as a meditation on place and
family."—*Library Journal,* Starred Review

"An engaging childhood memoir and a deeply affectionate
tribute to the author's parents."
—*Kirkus Reviews*, Starred Review

Dad at seventeen,
just enlisted in the army

Mum and Dad aged
about 24. Dad holding Bess.

Dad in Germany,
riding Betsy and holding Roman

Mum & Dad
Just Married! July 1949

Mum at age 22,
and so beautiful.

Dad third from left, outside the oast house

Dad and Bess,
Black Bush Cottage

Mum and Baby Jackie

Jackie at The Terrace –
just moved in!

Dad and Baby Jackie,
Black Bush Cottage

Jackie age 9, John age 5

Mum and Dad on The Kent and
East Sussex railway, 2007

— THIS TIME —

NEXT YEAR

— WE'LL BE —

LAUGHING

Books by
JACQUELINE WINSPEAR

Maisie Dobbs
Birds of a Feather
Pardonable Lies
Messenger of Truth
An Incomplete Revenge
Among the Mad
The Mapping of Love and Death
A Lesson in Secrets
Elegy for Eddie
Leaving Everything Most Loved
A Dangerous Place
Journey to Munich
In This Grave Hour
To Die But Once
The American Agent

The Care and Management of Lies

Non-fiction
What Would Maisie Do?

— THIS TIME —
NEXT YEAR
— WE'LL BE —
LAUGHING

a memoir

Jacqueline Winspear

Copyright © 2020 by Jacqueline Winspear

All rights reserved.

Published by
Soho Press, Inc.
227 W 17th Street
New York, NY 10011

Library of Congress Cataloging-in-Publication Data

Names: Winspear, Jacqueline, author.
Title: This time next year we'll be laughing : a memoir / Jacqueline Winspear.
Description: New York, NY : Soho, [2020]
Identifiers: LCCN 2020019804

ISBN 978-1-64129-294-8
eISBN 978-1-64129-270-2

Subjects: LCSH: Winspear, Jacqueline, 1955—Childhood and youth.
Winspear, Jacqueline, 1955– Family. | Authors, English—21st century—
Biography. | Working class families—England—20th century—Biography.
Classification: LCC PR6123.I575 Z46 2020 | DDC 823'.92 [B]—dc23
LC record available at https://lccn.loc.gov/2020019804

Interior design by Janine Agro, Soho Press, Inc.

Printed in the United States of America

10 9 8 7 6 5 4 3 2 1

For my brother, John James Winspear
And in memory of our late parents,
Albert Frederick and Joyce Margaret Winspear

My heroes

Childhood is, or has been, or ought to be, the great original adventure, a tale of privation, courage, constant vigilance, danger, and sometimes calamity.

—Michael Chabon, *Manhood for Amateurs*

PROLOGUE

❧

It was our third visit to A&E, the accident and emergency department at the local hospital. The aggressive blood disorder that had been claiming my father's life day by day was bringing us to our knees. Months of regular transfusions were now wreaking havoc on every bone in his body. My mother was snappy, her temper breaking down faster than his veins—and I was doing all I could to care for them both, desperate to keep the ship on an even keel even as it was crashing against the rocks. My brother, John, was still trying to come to terms with what was happening—only a few months earlier Dad had hiked for hours with John in the mountains near his home in Ojai, California, and my strong, sturdy father had kept up a young man's pace, not even broken a sweat. His doctor had always said, "Mr. Winspear, you are one of the fittest men I see here in my practice, and I don't mean for your age." We had all felt quite smug—those Winspear genes were pretty darn good, weren't they?

Annette, the senior hematology nurse who had been our point person from day one, had called the house earlier that morning.

"How are you all holding up?" she asked.

"Not so great," I replied, feeling as if I were letting the side down. We didn't admit defeat in our family. I explained that Dad was being stoic, Mum was by turns sarcastic and argumentative, then compassionate and caring.

"And you?" she asked.

I shrugged, as if she were there with me. "I'm all right, Annette, but—"

"No, you're not, Jackie—I can hear it in your voice. You're exhausted. It's time you all had a break. Let's get your dad in for a transfusion and some pain meds, and I'll arrange for his transfer to the hospice for respite care—give you all a chance to draw breath. But you must tell him we're not packing him off to hospice to die—just for respite. The ambulance will be with you in about twenty minutes, and I'll be down there in A&E to meet you when you arrive."

I told my mother to get ready to leave, then went to my parents' room and knelt alongside my father's bed. "Dad, it's just for respite care—a bit of a break. You'll get a transfusion at the hospital—that'll perk you up—and they'll give you something stronger for that pain in your back. I'll be with you all the time, Dad. Mum's just getting dressed."

I helped my dad get up from the bed and steadied him as he made his way to the bathroom. I put out a fresh, ironed shirt, his best trousers and one of his favorite jackets. His leather shoes were polished. Dad was a dapper man, and unless he was working in the garden, he always wanted to be "well turned out." Even at seventeen, when he was first conscripted into the army, he took the uniform to a local tailor for alteration because he didn't like the cut. And now, though he could barely stand, he insisted upon dressing himself—no, he didn't want help from anyone, and certainly no one else could pull off that all-important Windsor knot in his tie.

At the hospital my father was wheeled to a cubicle, where

Annette took his hand and explained to us that they were just getting a quarantine room ready for him because "A and E is full of people coming in with all sorts of germs—and we don't want your dad catching anything." Then she said she'd like a moment alone with my father. I watched from a distance as Annette sat next to Dad, their heads almost touching while she spoke to him. I've wondered if this was the moment she told him, "Albert, it's almost time." I imagine it might have been.

In the quarantine room my mother and I sat on either side of Dad's bed. I watched as blood and platelets drip-drip-dripped into my father's arm, his shirtsleeves rolled up, his tie removed. He lay on top of the bedlinens, and I remember thinking, *He's such a smart, dear, lovely man.* The plan was that as soon as the transfusion was complete there would be a short wait and a cup of tea and a pastry for Dad before another ambulance would come to take him to the hospice. In the meantime, we waited. Drip, drip, drip, blood and platelets entering my father's body, giving us all a little more time.

We spoke of this and that for a while, ordinary things, subjects of no great import, then Dad turned and reached toward my mother, taking her hands in his own.

"Haven't we had a great life?" he said.

She leaned her head toward his, pulled back one hand and rested it against his cheek. He moved his head and kissed her palm. As quietly as I could, I stood up and crept away from my chair, my footfall silent as I left the room, turning the door handle without a sound so as not to interrupt their moment. Instead I stood in the hallway reading and rereading the wall-mounted instructions for evacuation in case of fire.

Haven't we had a great life?

And in that moment, as I turned and focused on the red-backlit exit sign, I felt my chest ache and my breath become short, and I wondered if I shouldn't be admitted into care without delay. My heart had swollen, and I felt a weight on my chest that took my breath away. I loved them not only because they were my parents—I loved them for who they were, for their resilience and capacity for endurance at the very worst of times. I cherished them for their love of each other, for their love of life—and of us. I would have moved mountains to keep them safe, together.

Haven't we had a great life?

1

About Me and Memories

∽

Memories appear in flashes of light, in short scenes, in reflec-
tions that can make us laugh or bring us to tears. They
might come in on a sneaker wave of grief, or be buoyed up from
our past by a certain fragrance in the air, or a sound from afar. The
essence of memoir, I suppose, is that it could better be described
as "re-memory." We don't just look back at an event in our past;
we are remembering the memory of what happened. It's a bit like
putting the laundry through two wash cycles.

The whine of a chain saw in the distance brings back autumn
days working on a farm close to our home in England's Weald
of Kent. Mist hangs across the land like a silk scarf—not quite
touching the earth, but not rising high enough to join a cloud.
Sunshine filters through, grainy, as the shades of gold change with
the waning day. And there it is, the whine of that chain saw. I
remember, once, walking with my father across the fields close
to their new home. Dad hadn't quite settled—it would take him
a long time to feel anything akin to the love he had for that old
house at the end of a Victorian terrace where he and my mother
had lived for over twenty-four years and raised two kids. As
we walked that day we found a hop bine growing through the
hedge, a leftover from the days when the field had been a hop
garden. (The hop vine is always called a "bine" in Kent and Sussex,

and hops are grown in a "garden" not a field.) My father pulled a couple of hops from the bine and crushed them between his hands, then brought his nose to his palms, his eyes closed. "My whole childhood is rushing before me," he said. Some thirty years later I watched as my brother threaded dried hops through the one hundred red roses atop my father's coffin. Our memories of childhood, too, were woven with the spicy fragrance of the hop gardens of Kent.

But the story really begins many years before, in London. And not the posh part.

We are, all of us, products of our family mythology. Stories are not only passed down, but nestled in every cell. When I thought about writing a memoir, I knew I had to write my parents' story—because I am of them. Everything that happened in my childhood—every household decision, every peal of laughter and every sharp word snapped across the table—was underpinned by my parents' attitudes to the world around them. Those attitudes were forged not only in their youthful experience of wartime London, but by a few postwar years, the years when they were uprooted from family and became—in the parlance of their time—gypsies.

But before I press the play button on that story, here's something about me and memories—my first memory is of something that happened when I was six months old, or thereabouts. I distinctly remember the scene, though it lasted perhaps only a couple of minutes. No one told me about it because no one else was there, so this was not a matter of absorbing other people's memories. The bird was there and I now believe he was a sparrow. It's a fair bet—there are a lot of sparrows about. My memory is of being in my pram. At the outer periphery of my vision I can see the edge of the hood to the left, right and above. In front of me is the handle—way out in front of me. The covers must have been close to my chin, because at the lower edge of my vision there is a white blurring, as if a blanket had been pulled up against whatever the weather was doing. Weather is always doing something in England, and in the mid-1950s, whatever it was doing did not deter mothers from putting their babies outside, even as far away as the bottom of the garden. It was deemed good for us. It was probably also very good for mothers who needed a bit of peace and quiet.

My attention had been drawn to a bird as it landed on the handle. I know I focused on it before I reached out to try to touch the bird. I remember feeling frustration because I could not control the hand, so the fingers kept going in and out of focus as I opened and closed them trying to reach the sparrow. I failed, because my hand came down and hit me on the forehead—my babyish lack of motor control. I had no words to think, nothing intellectual to trouble my new brain—but I remember the physicality of frustration at not being able to reach that bird. Then the sides of the hood seemed to close in and the outside world was pushed back.

After I wrote that paragraph, I went through some old photographs until I found one of me at that age, snuggled up in my pram, and there it is, that big fluffy white blanket tucked almost to my chin.

I have a long memory. I've thought about it a lot, and I believe it has something to do with the accident—it was as if the shock did something to me that left me with more than physical scars, and after I recovered it seemed that events I might have forgotten were locked into my memory bank. On the other hand, I find it funny that I can remember details from very early childhood onward, yet for the life of me I can never find my keys once I've put them down, or recall whether I remembered to give the dog her thyroid pill—strange that I should have adopted a dog with a dodgy thyroid, a family affliction that defined much of my childhood.

What I remember of the accident—which happened when I was about fifteen months old—is this: I was surrounded by grown-ups who were standing beside me around the kitchen table. I felt as high as their knees. We had company—my Auntie Sylvie, Uncle John, and cousins Johnny, Larry and Martine, who was younger than me by six months, so she was probably crawling, but not toddling. I was wearing my new nylon dress—it might have been bought in London by my aunt, as nylon dresses for little girls were all the rage because they could be washed and dried quickly. I doubt I cared about the dress, but I loved tea and I remember I couldn't wait to be given a cup of lukewarm, milky, sweet tea in my red mug. So I reached up to the table to grab the closest handle, which happened to be attached to my father's enamel one-pint army mug—he'd held onto it after his army demob years before, because he liked his tea scalding hot and the metal kept it that way. I can still see that handle above me and my hand stretching toward it, my fingers opening and closing as I reached up, just as I'd reached toward the sparrow.

That's the last I remember of the accident. My mother told me the tea was so scalding hot my nylon dress melted into my skin. My father tried to rip it off, then wrapped me in a blanket, and they ran from the cottage to the farm because the farmer had a car. We were living far off the beaten track, in a cottage in the midst of the Bedgebury Forest in Goudhurst, Kent. We had no phone, no car and no means of getting to the hospital. The farmer's car had to struggle through mud with my father and uncle pushing, I was told, and by the time they reached the main road I was in convulsions, screaming and screaming and screaming.

I still have some scarring across my chest where the dress was pulled away, taking a goodly layer or two of flesh with it, and another on my ribs from a skin graft of some sort. I was shot up with penicillin, which my mother always said saved my life. When I left the hospital weeks later, I started to remember almost everything that came to pass from then on, and a few things from before the accident. Hardly an event happened that was not catalogued in my mind unless I made an effort to forget it. At times I worked hard at forgetting.

This is my memoir of a time and place in a series of vignettes, screen shots, portraits and panoramas. At first, I wanted to call it *It's All Changed Around Here*, and here's why it came to mind. Imagine this: We are on our way from our home in Kent up to London. "We" comprises my parents, sitting in the front of the Morris Traveller, plus my brother and me on the back seat, likely arguing, perhaps even with fists flying. You might ask why my brother has built a wall of toilet paper rolls between us, and it would be fair to say no one could blame him. I suffered from severe motion sickness and he just could not stand me throwing up all over him yet again.

The car is grey with wood trim. It's our first family car, bought second-hand, and not only does it backfire with some regularity, but the vapor of exhaust fumes coming in through the back doors makes me feel even worse. My discomfort is compounded by the fact that my father is a terrible driver, so the car lurches sideways and forward every time he overtakes another car, usually yelling that the dozy bugger should get off the effing road. Dad had let his license lapse and he'd had to take a driving test again (or maybe that was it—he'd never had a license in the first place!), and now, not so long after he had finally passed the test on his sixth attempt, we were en route to visit our London relatives in what was supposed to be the comfort of our own car.

Fields and farms gave way to concrete and suburbia, then to an inner city still bearing livid scars of wartime bomb sites and blitzed broken houses—this in the mid-1960s. As the names of streets became recognizable to my parents, they would say to each other, "Look at that—do you remember when . . ." and a story was told about people we didn't know and a place we didn't understand. Finally, as we reached our destination—probably Auntie Sylvie and Uncle John's house in Camberwell—Dad would shake his head and say, "It's all changed around here." And Mum would agree and they would look about them and seem bewildered, as if a thief had crept in while they weren't looking and stolen part of their life, something precious never to be seen again. My brother and I teased them relentlessly. We mimicked them, and as we passed this or that street we'd call out names of places we didn't know, really, and I remember seeing my father and mother grin at each other and roll their eyes. How could we ever understand, we who had not lived in their world—a world they had left because they could not stay?

Change is woven into the fabric of my stories, probably because when I was a child the dueling senses of belonging and being out of place were ever-present, along with a fear that the rug could be pulled out from under us at any moment. But I loved the place where I grew up, despite the fact that—like a lot of kids—I couldn't wait to leave home, to travel, to see the world.

Last year I returned to Cranbrook, which you could say is my "hometown"—and isn't that such an American locution? I parked on the High Street and walked past the Indian restaurant where Palmer and White's, the haberdashery shop, used to be. I made my way past the Vestry Hall, where the ambulance station was located when I was a child, then up the churchyard steps and along toward the old primary school. I remember, once, waiting with my mother to watch a bride walking from a ribbon-bedecked car toward the church, her arm linked through her father's, her dress cascading silk atop a flounce of organza petticoats. As I reached out to finger the silk, she turned to me as if she'd felt my touch and she smiled. It was as if an angel had acknowledged my presence, and that I, too, could one day look so beautiful. I tried not to let my hand rest upon anything else for the rest of the day—my flesh felt sacred.

At the top of the churchyard I stopped by the old oak tree, the one where our class of five-year-olds, Infants 1, would sit and listen to Mrs. Willis tell us a story on a fine summer's afternoon. I remember the class walking in pairs from the classroom down to the churchyard. Mrs. Willis would bring a chair and once she was settled, the whole class of five-year-olds sat cross-legged on the grass looking up at her, waiting for the story to begin. I remember the shafts of light coming down through the trees, and feeling so gentled by summer's warmth and the rhythm of her voice. The old Victorian primary school has now been converted to accommodation for seniors, but the oak tree is there and will be there for a long time, I hope. I walked away from my past just in time to see a bride making her way along the flagstone path toward the church, her hand resting on her father's arm, her bridesmaids following, grinning, fussing with hair and tottering on high heels. I wanted to reach out and touch the silky fabric of her dress, but instead just smiled and said, "You look really lovely." And she smiled back. It made my day.

Time is a place and every place has a time, for each one of us. Almost thirty years ago, when I first came to live in California, I exercised horses for owners too busy to ride. One of those horses was kept at a private stable in the Marin Headlands overlooking the San Francisco Bay, so after riding and still clad in my breeches and tall leather boots, I would come down into Sausalito to buy a coffee at a little bakery close to the marina. The owner was originally from Iran—he told me he had been a "refugee from Persia." As he was making my latte, he asked what kind of horse I rode, and I told him she was a gorgeous Arabian. His eyes lit up, his smile broadened. I think it was what he'd hoped to hear. "My father bred the Turkoman Arab," he told me, holding his hand against his heart. And thereafter, several times each week as I sipped my coffee at the counter, he would tell me another story of the Arab horses he had grown up with, though he declined my offer to come to the stables—he said it would be too painful a memory.

I've thought about the Iranian man a lot over the years, and of the many people on the move across the globe. I've thought of the things that open the gates to that sneaker wave of nostalgia, reminding immigrants—and I am one—of the place of their first belonging. Their first love, I suppose. It could be the fragrance of a flower only grown in their country, or a familiar turn of phrase overheard. Perhaps it's the way dusk settles across the ocean, or even the image of a horse holding its tail high, nostrils flared as it gallops across headlands near the San Francisco Bay. And here, in California, in my house close to redwood groves and golden hills, I have a small hessian bag of hops, a tiny replica of the pokes our Kentish hops were packed into—sacks taller than a man to be taken to the breweries. Using a blanket stitch of thick string to secure the dried hops inside, my father made that small poke at the end of my first hop-picking season, when I was just six months old. He printed our last name in white chalk along the flank and added the year, as if claiming that season for me forever. I have a photograph of me that very September; I'm in my mother's arms as she's laying me down to sleep on a coat atop a mound of spent hop bines. The two dogs—working farm dogs, Bess and her daughter, Lassie—lay beside me, never to leave me, for they were my guardians. No one could entice them to move and no one dare approach me—only my father or mother could touch me. When I first read *Of Human Bondage*, by W. Somerset Maugham, I smiled when I came across a description of hop gardens in Kent and mothers laying their young down to sleep on mounds of spent hop bines covered by a coat or a blanket. I remember thinking, *That was me*. And it made me feel special; I felt as if that famous writer had walked by and caught a glimpse of me while I was a baby sleeping.

The writer Adam Nicolson, who comes from the same area in Kent, writes about the gift of place in his book *Sissinghurst: An Unfinished History*. Nicolson refers to place as "the roomiest of containers for human meaning." The land where I grew tall is filled with meaning for me—it's the land of hop gardens and apple orchards, of farms and fields, of trees to climb and streams flanked by pungent wild garlic and golden sun-reflecting celandines. This deep love of place is part of my family mythology, a delicate web across my heart.

I love thinking about place, wondering how places change, or don't, and I like looking at what place does to people and people to place. I'm fascinated by what it means to be held in place, and how place gives our lives meaning and how we assign meaning to a place. I live some six thousand miles away from the land of my growing, and even from such a distance I can feel my roots in that soil. Take me there blindfolded and I would know I had come home. The air's texture and fragrance, the sounds, the sense of light even though my eyes are closed—I would know I was where I belonged, once. And perhaps it's truly where I belong now—writing memoir is a way of discovering something about ourselves, so perhaps there's something to be revealed to me. But time has marched on, and so have I—and if truth be told, even as a child I always felt as if I were on the outside looking in, so it's comfortable for me to live in a country where I am not expected to be like anyone else, because I come from a different place. Perhaps the early years when my parents were considered outsiders has something to do with it.

2

A Wartime Evacuation

❧

Should we name names, we writers of memoir? Should we tell a tale that exposes another in a poor light, decades after that person has hurt us? No, I won't name the girl who in primary school would punch me on the shoulder while surrounded by her little coven of fellow tormentors, who would call me "Gypsy, Gypsy, dirty Gypsy." I was neither a Gypsy nor was I dirty—my mother prided herself on her whites and made sure every stitch of my school uniform and underwear was fresh and laundered. If I was run over by a bus, she wanted the doctors and nurses to gasp in wonder at my sparkling white knickers as they ripped off my clothing to save my life. Years later, when my brother was rushed to the hospital fighting for *his* life following a burst appendix, one of the nurses commented on his white underwear, and it pleased my mother no end.

But there was a grain of truth in the bully's words, because my parents had lived alongside Romany travelers before I was born— and it had been the making of them. And though my grandmother said my father had whisked my mother away to the country so another man wouldn't make eyes at her—she was a looker, that's for sure—I have come to believe the truth has much more texture and strength to it. I wonder at how intuitive he was, even at a young age; how instinct informed him that my mother had to get away from the city streets, from the bomb sites and out to the country where they could both let go of what had come to pass in the years of their growing into adulthood. They were twenty-two years of age when they married in 1949, and I believe their dislocation from family gave them the strength, work ethic and initiative that would drive them forward into a life well-lived, hard though it was. But somewhere along the line, my mother had to tell her stories, had to get them out from inside because they were dark, festering and painful. So she told the person who was around her all the time. She told me.

My mother's history became my history—probably because I was young when she began telling me about the war, about her father and his drink, and about the different houses they lived in during her childhood. I was a willing listener even as a small child, for my mother was a very good storyteller. She spoke to me as if I were an adult—there was never baby talk in our house—and I hung on her every word. Looking back, her stories—of war, of abuse at the hands of the people to whom she and her sisters had been billeted when evacuated from London, of seeing the dead following a bombing—were probably too graphic for a child. But I liked listening to them. I liked being with her, and I liked the bits about everyone singing in the air-raid shelters, about how she'd saved up to see *Gone with the Wind* at the cinema and when the air-raid warning sounded, the film kept playing and she was one of the people who refused to leave until it ended. The trouble is, at this point in my life I am haunted by her stories. I am haunted by the sad spirits of experience that trailed behind my mother, dictating her every word, every decision, every single thing she took on in life. "Took on" is a good description, because my mother seemed to have her fists balled all the time, ready to do a lot of taking on.

"Tell us about being down evacuation." It was another bad weather day away from the farm. Another day in the kitchen, by the Rayburn—a solid fuel stove, a smaller version of the better-known Aga stove—while my mother stopped for a cup of Camp Coffee, a bitter drink with chicory, all they could afford and my mother's one treat. I'm not sure what task she had paused, because my mother hated housework, hated the dusting and sweeping and everything that went into keeping an old house going without any labor-saving devices. She liked to tell a story, though, and was always ready with a new one. She'd make her coffee, light another cigarette, blow her first smoke ring, and she was off, back into the past.

My mum was evacuated on September 1, 1939, when she was twelve years of age. Along with her was an older sister, Rene, who would only be evacuated for a short while, until she was fourteen, the school-leaving age—after that you were brought home and sent out to work. There were two younger sisters evacuated, Sylvia and Ruby, and two brothers, Charlie and Joe. Until she was old enough to be evacuated, Rose—the baby of the family—would remain behind with my grandmother, who also had three older children, Ada, Dorothy and Jim, all of whom would soon be in the services. One of my aunts told me that the war was a liberation for my grandmother—her husband was away in the army and almost overnight she relinquished any responsibility for all but one of her kids.

Perhaps this is where I mention that my grandmother had ten children, seven of whom were girls. A small herd of tall headstrong females. I often think our get-togethers were more like elephant families on the move, with maternal leadership firmly established. The "girls" would line up, six of them—Ada, Dorothy, Rene, Mum, Sylvia and Rose (Ruby had emigrated to

Canada)—then they would link arms and high-kick their way across the room, singing, "Sisters, sisters. There never were such devoted sisters." My uncles would roll their eyes. Uncle Charlie said that his sisters were "formidable." You didn't dare argue with them, and while they might argue with each other, woe betide an outsider who went up against one of the siblings, because the whole pack would come down on them.

"Tell us about when you were down evacuation." I asked about evacuation as if it were a place, because my mother talked about being "down evacuation" as if she were saying, "We went down the lane." Evacuation wasn't just an experience, an escape from the threat of bombing and Nazi invasion—it was a destination, albeit an unwanted one. In that place so many children felt trapped and were abused, while others, the lucky ones, landed at good homes with caring foster parents.

The evacuation of children from Britain's cities had been planned since the closing days of World War I, when it was understood that any future conflagration would include an air war and civilians would be targeted. The order to evacuate was given on August 31st, just days prior to Britain's declaration of war on Germany, on September 3rd, 1939. Almost one million children were evacuated in anticipation of the immediate threat—sent away from home to live with strangers, who received payment for each child fostered. According to my mother, she and her siblings were among hundreds of children shepherded onto a long train bound for the perceived safety of Kent, though at the time they had no idea where they were going. Each child had a label attached to their coat with their name and school. Following a stop-and-start journey—passenger trains were required to pull into a siding to give trains carrying troops right of way—they reached the first of several overnight stops in different places before arriving at a destination outside Westerham in Kent. Following a long walk the youngsters were herded into pens used for cattle and sheep on market day. The town had nowhere else to put so many children, so they waited there in the pens until the locals came along to claim a child or two to take in, many pointing to their choices and saying, "I'll take that one and that one" or "I only want boys." Farmers liked boys because they could be put to work. Some only wanted girls. As she saw them off on the train with hundreds of other children, my grandmother told my mother to make sure the family remained together at all costs, but the boys and girls were split up.

Children were evacuated along with all the pupils in their school, unless the parents had decided that they were keeping their children at home and the whole family would die together when London was bombed. For the evacuees there was a level of continuity and comfort to have friends, siblings and teachers all going to the same place. The irony for the contingent from my mother's school was that at the supposed safe location, their teachers were assigned classrooms at an empty school—and those rooms had been made available when the local children and their teachers were evacuated to Wales a couple of days earlier. Given the risk presented by being so close to Biggin Hill aerodrome, which was to become one of the most important air stations during the war, the local authorities had decided to err on the side of caution with regard to the safety of their young. My mother said it felt as if the London kids were expendable—though it gave them a bird's eye view of the Battle of Britain as it raged overhead during the summer of 1940.

For Mum and her sisters especially, evacuation was hell. The girls were billeted with a man who, they came to know, "interfered" with little girls. I think my older aunt dealt with it by going into denial, into a safe place in her imagination. This is only conjecture on my part—I just know my mother felt her sister Rene didn't do anything to stop it, whereas my mum, with her fists balled and—let it be said—a bit of a mouth on her, did everything she could to fight for her siblings. That was a grief she held until her dying day—that she could not stop the abuse, despite weaving dressmaking pins into her pajamas and sleeping on the outside of the bed shared by the sisters, so that when the man put his hands under the covers in the dead of night, he would feel that first sharp round of defense nipping into his fingers.

In her sixties, while she was having an ear exam, the doctor asked Mum what had happened to her, to break her eardrum. "Oh," she said, "that was when I was evacuated in the war. The man who took us in brought back his hand and hit me around the head, slamming me into the wall when I talked back to him about putting his hands into the bed where my sisters and I were asleep." She began telling her story to the ear doctor. But she was also suffering from painful trigeminal neuralgia, possibly also caused by the same beating around the head. She recounted the conversation to me later in a telephone call. It was as if she just could not help herself telling the story again, and to a stranger. When I put the receiver down after the call, I remembered reading Aldous Huxley's novel *Island*, and the scene where a child makes Will Farnaby tell the story of his wounding time and time again until it doesn't hurt any more. I wondered if every time my mother told her story, it released some pain. Apparently the ear doctor hemmed and hawed and then referred her to a neurologist for the trigeminal neuralgia.

My Aunt Ruby says she felt like an orphan until she was ten, due to being evacuated. And the aunts who were there at the time have spoken of Aunt Rose's terrible screams when she was three and old enough to join her sisters. Uncle Joe, who was eight years old, tried to run away from the abusive farmer with whom he was billeted. He began walking back to London, and because he was thirsty and hungry he took a pint of milk from a doorstep. Joe was caught and sent to a reform school. But we're a fighting family; you never saw photographs of a prouder man than when, decades later, his grandson graduated from the University of Oxford.

The memories of her evacuation were something akin to terrorists in my mother's life. It was as if they held her hostage, and I know every single story. Mum told me of the day she and Auntie Sylvie were so desperate and unhappy that they made a pact to kill each other, a joint suicide using their scarves. They agreed that they would both pull at the same time and that would be it, their unbearable life would be over. They each stopped pulling when they saw the other go blue. And I know about that summer of 1940, during the Battle of Britain, when they were walking along and saw a Luftwaffe Messerschmitt aircraft coming down after being hit, black smoke and flames pouring from the tail. But the aviator's trigger finger still worked, because, as he flew low over a field of women and children strawberry-picking, he took aim and fired until he crashed in a neighboring field.

A platoon of Canadian soldiers had been marching along the lane and had seen everything. Some began running toward the Messerschmitt as others helped the women. My mum and aunt followed the soldiers toward the downed aircraft, just to see what happened. And what happened was, I suppose, the justice of the moment, as women lay wounded in a strawberry field in Kent. The Canadians took the still-alive pilot into the church, where they slipped a rope over a beam and hanged him until he died. I doubt anyone ever knew about it other than those who saw it happen, which amounted to some young Canadians far from home and two evacuee children. Any knowing villagers said nothing. For all intents and purposes, the pilot died when his plane crashed to earth, while a Royal Air Force pilot in a Spitfire high in the sky above did a victory roll.

During a conversation with Aunt Sylvie at her ninetieth birthday party last year, she recounted her memories of that time. The only point of difference was that my aunt remembered the killing of women working in a strawberry field and the hanging of a Luft-waffe pilot as two distinct events witnessed by the sisters that summer, and that they had taken place on different days. But the wounds my mother took to her grave were very much present in my aunt's heart—wounds inflicted by bearing witness to war. On the day I left to fly back to California, my aunt said, "I love talking to you, Jackie—you've got all your mum's memories, and it's as if she's here with me."

My mother was brought home to London to work as soon as she reached fourteen, the minimum school-leaving age at the time. Her mother had let out rooms to lodgers—places to live were becoming fewer and fewer in London due to the bombings—so Mum had to sleep on two dining chairs pushed together. In prep-aration for her homecoming, my grandmother had secured a job for my mother. She was told she had to start work the very next day at the laundry, which was so sad, because Mum cherished her education, loved learning, and at the age of twelve had won a full scholarship to a prestigious private girls' school that her parents would not allow her to attend. As the story goes, there was only one scholarship place available, and the teacher's daughter was the "runner up"—so the teacher persuaded my grandparents not to send my mother, underlining that with ten children, they could ill afford the uniform or the books.

Going to work at the laundry broke my mother's heart, but

she enrolled in evening classes instead, because she had no intention of staying put in a laundry. "Night school," as it was known, had been popular in British towns and cities since the Industrial Revolution, and many institutions had been purpose-built for the continuing education of adults. Those classes held the promise of advancement for ordinary working people, and without doubt my mother had set her sights on advancement.

As much as the experience of evacuation was terrible, I believe it was the bombings that affected my mother—and so many people—more than they would ever admit. After all, this was life with a "Keep Calm and Carry On" attitude. You just got on with it. If a bomb dropped on the house and you were in it, then under it, and were lucky enough to be pulled alive from the rubble—as was my mother—you just brushed yourself down and carried on. My mother told me about the beautiful Hungarian embroidered blouse she had saved money and clothing coupons to buy. She brought it home, and as she was ironing out the creases, she looked out the window and waved to the little girl who lived opposite, the one who had a crush on Uncle Charlie. She was playing hopscotch in the street. Mum finished ironing her new blouse, and the last thing she remembered was laying it across the top of the piano before reaching to fold the ironing board. Then the street outside the house was hit by a bomb. She remembered not being able to breathe because her ears and nose were plugged with dust. She could not open her eyes. Then she felt rubble being pulled away, and a big policeman leaning over her. "Don't worry, love, you'll be all right," he said, as he took off his greatcoat and wrapped it around her, then picked her up and began carrying her toward the church, where survivors had begun to gather. And as she was being carried away and rubbed the dust from her eyes, she saw two things: The strips of material from her blouse, shredded by shards of wood from the piano, blowing away in the wind, and the air raid precautions men with sacks, collecting the remains of the little girl who had been playing hopscotch outside the house opposite. "Don't look, love," said the policeman. "Keep your eyes closed." When he handed her over to the Women's Voluntary Services at the church, she realized the blast had ripped away every stitch of clothing she was wearing. She never knew that policeman's name, but she could remember his number, which was on the shoulder of his greatcoat.

When I was a child, long after my parents' war, I would lie in bed at night terrified that bombers would come and we would all be dead by morning. I would often hear a light aircraft in the dark distance—I have no idea where it came from or where it was going, for we lived in a rural area—but as it came closer, my fear grew, and I would roll out of bed and crawl underneath. No one ever asked why I would emerge from under the bed when called to get ready for school. Perhaps they thought I was just being a kid.

"So, can you tell me about any other times you've felt this kind of fear?"

At sixty-three years of age, I had finally decided to do something about fears that would come out of nowhere to paralyze me when I was riding my horse. Yes, I'd had my share of accidents, but I'd been riding again as soon as I could get back in the saddle, and I was training in the equestrian sport of dressage four or five times a week. But this new, paralyzing fear was something else. It had started in a small way after my mother died, and was escalating fast. First I'd be aware of every rustle in the bushes that might startle Calvin, my big Dutch Warmblood—but Cal is a good lad, nothing much upsets him. Then the fear of cantering emerged and soon I was close to tears every time my trainer asked me for something more, or to try something new. That was when I went to see the sports psychologist who, I was told, was great at getting people back on track, no matter what their sport. And I love riding.

"Jackie? Can you tell me about any other times you've felt this kind of fear?"

My mind had wandered. It was our third session and I was miles away, wondering if I was throwing good money after bad, though I was feeling the fear, I guess, and trying to avoid it.

"Jackie?"

"Yes? Um, yes, I can."

Another pause.

"Well?"

"Well? Oh, yes, well . . . tomorrow I have to go to an event where I'm a guest speaker and there will be almost three hundred people there."

"It's natural to have some anxiety about that," he said.

I shook my head. My throat was dry, and I could feel rivulets of sweat rolling down my back. "Oh no, I'm not worried about the speaking—not tomorrow anyway. I'm just terrified of the drive." I began to pick at the skin around my fingernails—another habit that was getting worse. Sometimes I would pick until I bled. "I've been avoiding freeways because I've become scared of them, and I'm worried I'll make a mistake and cause a terrible accident and cars will crash and people will get killed." I blurted out the words and was left breathless.

He looked at me. "Have you felt like that at any other time?"

I told him about being scared of bombs.

I told him about being afraid I would not be able to keep my brother safe—fine when we were kids, but he's now pushing sixty, and I'm really getting on his nerves.

I told him about my mother's stories.

"How old were you when you first heard these stories?"

I shrugged. "About three. Maybe three and a half."

"And you write about war—in your work."

"Um, I suppose—well, yes, I do. It's a theme—people getting through war."

He nodded. It was a sage sort of nod, a knowing. If he weren't so tall, I'd say he reminded me of Yoda. "Jackie—you have secondary PTSD."

I shrugged. Laughed a bit. I thought he was making it up. I'd never heard of it. Then I consulted Dr. Google as soon as I arrived home.

Secondary traumatic stress is the emotional duress that results when an individual hears about the firsthand trauma experiences of another . . . the essential act of listening to trauma stories may take an emotional toll.

I looked away from the screen and considered—not for the first time—a review of one of my novels. It had remained with me because the reviewer had spoken of "the wartime period that continues to haunt her." That was a review of a novel about the Great War, my grandfather's war. I'd felt exposed by the reviewer's words. She had seen inside me. She knew I was haunted. And sixty years is a long time to put up with ghosts.

3

Country Boy

એા

My father, born in South East London, was a city boy who
always loved the country. His family were among the great
exodus of people who left London in late summer to go to Kent
for the picking of hops. This was in the days when London was
enveloped in the toxic yellowish green "pea-soupers" that looked
as if they could be cut with a knife, hence London's nickname—
"The Smoke." This killer phenomenon was described as "the
noxious blend of smoke and fog" in 1905 by Dr. Henry Antoine
Des Voeux, who used the word "smog" at a public health congress held in London—though the *Los Angeles Times* in 1893 had
already attributed the use of "smog" to a "witty English writer."
He would have to have been witty, to make light of those killer
London smogs.

Hops have been grown in Kent, in England's south eastern
corner, since the 1500s. By the nineteenth century the industry
had grown so much that the hop-picking season demanded more
workers than were available in rural Kent, so each year whole
families would come from the poorest areas of south and east
London, in particular, to pick hops. Ordinary working people
couldn't afford not to work, so hop-picking provided a few weeks
away in the country without losing money. It was their summer
holiday. My paternal grandparents, aunts, uncles and cousins,

all Londoners, came to Kent for the hop-picking, and as a child my father picked hops along with his family. It was not simply a working holiday, but a time when working-class city folk could inhale deep breaths of fresh country air—and my father loved that clean, clear air.

My grandparents and their parents before them came for the hop-picking, so the tradition ran deep in my family. Nan and Grandad kept a separate set of whitewashed furniture to bring to Kent, just enough pieces to make their "hopper hut"—simple shed-like accommodation provided by the farmer—a little more comfy. Special trains were laid on to bring the workers to the country and many came by bus, the head of the family holding a letter in a brown envelope, confirmation from the farmer that they had the promise of work and a roof over their heads. My father told me that when he was a boy, he was never happier than when he saw the oast houses hove into view as the family trudged several miles from the station to the farm, pushing a barrow with their furniture and household belongings secured on top. Hops were dried in an oast house, that distinctive farm building hallmarked by a cone-shaped kiln and a white cowl resembling a witch's hat, which drew the warm air up through the hops. The oldest known oast is just outside the town where I grew up and dates back to the seventeenth century. Now most oast houses have been converted into upscale homes; the hop gardens that were spread across the land of my growing are no more, for England's hop industry began to die after the war. Prices were undercut by cheaper European hops, and a growing consumer desire for a milder beer than the English hops would provide.

Of course, the finer points of agricultural economics were not on my mind out in the hop gardens when I was a child—and until I was eleven I was part of that tradition. Instead my memories of hop-picking are of the camaraderie, of people calling out to one another, and of someone starting a song and everyone joining in, so it was as if a rag-tag choir had given full voice across the land, London songs echoing across country fields. In my memories there's color, laughter and noise, and people shouting that you should see what's over in the next hop garden—the bines are hanging so heavy with hops they're touching the ground. I can hear the farmer calling, "Get your hops ready!" as he makes his way along the rows, plunging his wicker basket into each family's bin, counting out the bushels of hops picked and marking up the workers' tally books. Before he arrived at the bin, my grandmother and mother would push their hands deep into the mound of hops to fluff them up, which in turn might yield an extra bushel of hops counted on the tally book. I can almost feel my flesh pucker at the biting sting along my bine-scratched arms as I lathered them with soap and water at the end of the day—a hop bine could give you a nasty cut if you weren't careful. You slept well during the hop-picking season.

Amid the memories, there's the ever-present fragrance of those spicy hops. I remember, once, reading a novel in which the author—who did not come from Kent or indeed from the United Kingdom, but had set her book in the county—had described the smell of hops as being like beer. I shook my head and put the book aside. Beer may smell like hops, but hops do not smell like beer. Even as a small child, I looked forward to hop-picking season for the spice-laden fragrance in the air, and loved every single morning when I left the house and that peppery atmosphere seemed to envelop me. Chill mornings and warm days heralded hop-picking, a season that could last from mid-August to late September, dependent on the crop. The new school year started halfway through the hop-picking, so for me there was always a sense of moving on and moving up, of untouched exercise books waiting to be filled as I stepped up to the next rung on the ladder to wherever I was going. I remember leaving the house with my mother early one day in September. "It feels like a real hop-picking morning, doesn't it, Mum?" She laughed and agreed, leaning her head back to take the air. But we were loading the car for my return to college, and by then my mother was a senior government executive working in prisons' administration, while my father had his own business. Time had marched for all of us, and the hops were long gone.

The truth is, I think my father liked the country for the quiet. He hated loud noises, though would make an exception for a good swing band when he and my mother went dancing, a hobby they took up in their late forties. And oh, could they dance! I was a child when I worked out the reason for my father's need for quiet, and as if experience is filtered into our cells even before we're born, I have found that I, too, like to be quiet. My songwriter-musician husband waits until I leave the house before he turns up the amps and starts to play a song he's been working on. My dislike of loud noises, of sudden unwanted sounds, is rooted in my grandfather's shell shock, I am sure, for my father had grown up in a quiet house, a house where a man wounded in the Battle of the Somme in 1916 went on with his life despite injuries to his legs, his lungs and to his soul. In his book *War Child: Children Caught in Conflict,* Martin Parsons, founder of the Research Centre for Evacuee and War Child Studies at the University of Reading, England, suggests that it takes three generations for an experience of war to work its way through the family system. I can believe it.

To be honest, most people would not have known about the shell shock—Grandad was a good man, a man who loved his family, who cherished his grandchildren, and who worked hard. He was kind and gentle. But I witnessed the effects of his trauma, and it's something I will never forget, though I have wondered what my father might have seen in the years of his growing.

My father was born in 1926, ten years after my grandfather was wounded as he ran from a trench across no-man's land toward the enemy. He was cut down by machine-gun fire and had already sustained gas damage to his lungs. Grandad had first enlisted in 1914, and when most of his battalion was wiped out during the First Battle of Ypres—at what the soldiers called "Plug-street Wood"—he was required to reenlist with a new regiment. In the interim period, he was on stretcher-bearer duty.

My grandfather was a costermonger by trade, a man who sold fruit and vegetables from a horse-drawn cart. This was in the days when a man had to fight for his turf, and as a young man my grand-father had a reputation as a spry featherweight with a demon of a one-two punch. Before I started school he taught me how to protect my eyes in a fight, while landing a left hook on the chin of my aggressor. I'm still wondering why he thought I might get into a fight, because I hate any form of conflict. When I was twenty-one and working for an airline, I'd tagged along with a gaggle of aircrew to a bar and in conversation one of the pilots happened to mention that his grandfather had been a costermonger. "Mine too," I said, and I told a story about one of Grandad's horses. "Oh, your grandad must have been a successful man—he had horses. My grandfather only had a push-barrow," said the pilot. I was at once very proud, perhaps even more so because I understood Grandad's struggle.

The damage to my grandfather's lungs was so invasive that at least once each year—usually in winter—he suffered congestion severe enough for the doctor to send him away to the coast. The ambulance would come and take him to a place where other gas-damaged "old soldiers" from the Great War who fought to breathe could regain some semblance of health. My father and his brother would struggle to keep the business going, boys trying to do a man's work. But the horse and cart had to be sold, and the family survived on the meagre soldier's pension my grandfather received from 1924 onward—eight years after his wounding and six years after the Armistice—following an assessment of his disability. The boys earned money before and after school with paper rounds, running errands and delivering messages for shopkeepers. Then my grandfather would come home from the seaside, procure a barrow and start his business again, pushing the barrow miles to Covent Garden market in the early hours to stock up with produce, before returning to Camberwell to complete his rounds. Soon there would be money enough to buy another horse, so the barrow was sold to buy a cart, and life would tick along until he could barely breathe again. The basic subsistence offered by his war pension didn't amount to much, but Grandad managed to keep his family clothed and fed.

There's a story about my grandfather that my dad loved to tell—I think because it said something about his father's spirit. One of Grandad's customers, a well-to-do lady who lived in a mansion in a wealthier part of the area, asked Grandad if he would be so kind as to move some furniture to her daughter's house when he'd finished his round. He agreed—it was extra money, after all. Moving the furniture meant the horse had to walk at a steady pace up an incline, but when they reached the top, my grandfather was stopped by a policeman who questioned where he was going with such fine furniture—the unspoken message being, "And you, a simple costermonger—it's probably all been stolen." The policeman insisted my grandfather return to the woman's home, so he could check Grandad's story. The woman was furious with the policeman, informing him that of course Mr. Winspear was acting on her behalf. So the policeman told Grandad he was free to go on with the delivery, but then he saw him unhitching the horse. "What do you think you're doing?" asked the constable. "You'll block the street." My grandfather turned to the policeman and said, "My horse went all the way up that hill once, and all the way back down again because of you—so I'm going to take him up there without a load, while you put your mind to how you're going to bring my cart up to meet us." It was sometime later that my grandfather, resting with his horse—who had enjoyed a drink from a trough and a nosebag of oats—saw a cluster of policemen hauling his cart and its load up the hill. Telling that story, I wonder about a time when there were troughs of water in London for horses to take their fill.

My dad was a sprinter. He was fast—really fast—and like many boys from ordinary working-class homes, he imagined a better life opening up through sport. If it hadn't been running, there was always the boxing gym on the upper floor of the Thomas à Becket pub on South East London's Old Kent Road. My dad's teachers told him he might even have a chance at the Olympics, so they were coaching him for competitions beyond the school. But those Air Raid Precautions men had different ideas. They went to the schools in London, picking out the fastest boys to be message runners as Britain prepared for an invasion or sustained bombing. The Blitz came soon enough, and my thirteen-year-old father was running through streets of burning buildings taking messages from one post to another.

The strange thing is that I never knew any of this until I lived in California. My parents were visiting and we were sitting in my kitchen with a group of friends who had dropped by to meet them. I was telling the assembled company about my father's aptitude for speed, and how my brother and I were probably a disappointment because we were not sprinters—we were both pretty good long-distance runners, but it was speed my dad was interested in. One of my friends turned to Dad and asked, "Were you a message runner during the war?" And my father said, "Funny you should say that—yes, I was." I was shocked. How could I never have known this about my dad? In fact, I don't think even my mother knew. He recounted the story of being chosen, and how his teacher had said how sorry he was, because the war was ruining the chances of boys like him—boys who had something amounting to opportunity because they were good at sports. It made me wonder whether he was relieved to be apprenticed to a painter and decorator when he turned fourteen in October 1940. It wasn't until he was in hospice care in 2012 that I discovered more about Dad's apprenticeship, and again I wondered, "Why didn't I know this?" Unlike my mother, my father kept stories to himself, but I believe the work involved in that apprenticeship— and the exposure to toxic materials that were likely not tested for human tolerance—was at the root of the illness that finally took his life.

4

Before They Began

∽

My parents were married in the summer of 1949, in a wedding ceremony that kicked off three days of celebrations. As my mother told me, "We were so broke after the parties, we had to take all the bottles back to get the deposit money." Though she was already qualified as a bookkeeper, my mother had joined the Civil Service and was working on the secure government telephone exchange. My father was employed as a painter and decorator, having returned to his original trade following army demobilization in 1948. He met my mother soon after leaving the army and was in the process of reenlisting when their paths crossed—but he changed his mind about what might come next. His reason for planning a return to the service was simple—he had been offered the chance to train at the army catering college. Though some might not believe this, the army knew how to train a chef for the officers' mess and the many dinners and dances officers enjoyed. My dad loved to cook and it would have been his chance to do something he could give his heart to. So perhaps it's time to tell you more about how a young soldier who had become an explosives expert at the age of eighteen came to the attention of the army cook in Germany. We have to join that young man just as he's beginning his apprenticeship at fourteen years of age in October 1940—this boy who hated loud noises, but had been tasked with running through the Blitz to deliver messages.

I heard the first part of this story when I was eighteen, and the most important part when my father was in the hospice, just days before he died. So much became clear with the telling. My father meted out his stories with care, as if he had squirreled them away to season with time.

His first employer won a lucrative contract to paint the buildings of every Royal Air Force depot, airfield or decoy airfield, inside and out, with a fire retardant. Airfields had been targeted by the Luftwaffe, so to save people and buildings from the spread of fire, the retardant had to be applied—and the RAF was building and rebuilding aerodromes at a fast pace. So my father, the apprentice, joined a crew and was sent from place to place, living in billets in country towns and small villages, wherever the government found room and board close to an airfield. There was an advantage to the job—it was a "reserved profession." That meant my father would be protected from enlistment because he was employed on essential government work. But he was also working with highly toxic materials, so his steady hand was an advantage.

In one area Dad was billeted on a farm, walking along country lanes each morning to meet the crew—he was older by now, sixteen going on seventeen, I would imagine. He loved that farm. During his stay—a long one, because there were several airfields within traveling range—the farmer taught my father how to work with sheepdogs, and Dad began training two of them before and after work. These were Old English sheepdogs, not collies. My father loved those dogs. But the painting job had begun to wear on him, and he wanted to go home to his family—he'd hardly seen them since starting the apprenticeship. In 1943 he gave notice.

His boss told him he was a fool, warning that he'd be called up and that would be him in the army. But he was young, and he thought the war would be over soon—how long could it go on, after all? The previous war had lasted four years, so they were probably close to the end—or so he told himself. He also thought it would take a few weeks for the authorities to find out he'd left his reserved profession; he would have some time. The farmer was sorry to see him go, and as a gift gave him the two sheepdogs, Tiny and Tiger. When I first heard the story, I wondered what the heck he thought he was doing, taking two big working dogs to a house in South East London. But my father believed he would soon return to the land with his dogs and stay there forever as a farmworker—and he was only seventeen, after all.

The government had other plans. My father received his call-up papers within twenty-four hours of officially leaving his job. He was instructed to report to barracks without delay. He left the two dogs with his parents, organized a local lad to take them for walks in the park—he told the boy he wouldn't be away for long—and joined the army. Following the usual medical and tests, together with an assessment of his previous work, it was discovered that my father was one of those people who remained very calm under pressure. He was an unassuming, thoughtful person. So they sent a young man who had grown up in a quiet house—who had lived with a man suffering shell shock—to train in explosives. In the meantime, though he was sending home most of his pay to keep the dogs, it wasn't long before my grandparents wrote to tell him they'd sold them. It broke his heart. I would never have told my father this—and no doubt it crossed his mind—but I believe the dogs were euthanized, because people in Blitz-hit areas were instructed to take their dogs to be put to death humanely given the extent of the bombings. It was hard enough saving human lives and dealing with the dead without having to account for household pets.

It was in Germany, before the war's official end, that my father ended up working in the army kitchens. Germany had yet to surrender, and the armies of Britain, the United States and Russia were moving in. My father was with a unit blowing up German communication lines, bridges and roads, and at the end of one long day they were instructed to pitch their tents for the night on the banks of a river. My father looked at the river and realized the best place to get a good night's rest was on the other side—he'd watched the flow of water and believed, correctly, that the location his commanding officer had chosen could easily flood. Ever resourceful, Dad found a place to cross the river and pitched his tent. He woke up the next morning surrounded by Russians in their tents. His commanding officer was shouting at him from the opposite bank that he was being put on a charge for disobeying orders and would be peeling spuds for a very long time if he didn't get right back over that river. My father's fellow soldiers were on the British side of the rushing water, wringing out their sopping wet clothes.

It wasn't such a long time in the kitchens, as the telling goes, but it was enough to persuade one branch of the army that the young soldier with a steady hand on the detonator had a gift when it came to preparing food. He was offered a place at the army catering college, but turned down that first offer because, in his words, "I didn't want my mates to laugh at me." In the meantime, despite having marched him to the kitchens, his commanding officer missed his "calm under pressure" demeanor, because there were still bridges to be demolished. And there were horses to ride, because as the soldiers worked their way across enemy territory, and as the war came to a close, Dad's unit moved into a barracks abandoned by a German cavalry regiment. The groom had remained behind to look after the horses. My father could tack up a horse and stay in the saddle—as a child he'd trotted along the streets of London on his father's cart horses—but the German taught him to ride like a gentleman. In truth, my father really wanted to ride like a cowboy, which probably has some bearing on the fact that my brother and I both ended up in California. It was Dad's tales of the Wild West that did it—but that's another story.

We talked about all these things when my father was in the hospice. He told me about his dog, Tiger, how he would walk under the kitchen table and lift it up with his back, and how my grandmother would complain and his father would laugh. He told me about that job where he was exposed to the powerful fire retardant used to protect the airfield buildings. One of his first tasks was to mix the emulsion and pour it into buckets for the painters. Then he had to test it after each wall dried. The testing amounted to lining up a series of blowtorches along the floor, with only a couple of inches between the searing hot flame and the dry fresh paint.

"Then we'd leave the torches right there for three or four hours," said Dad.

"Wow—didn't that leave a burn?" I asked.

"Not a mark. Not a mark," he replied.

"What was that stuff called?"

"Oh no name, love. It just had a number."

I knew then that the viscous emulsion had probably never been put through tests for human tolerance. Such things happen in wartime—consider the effects of Agent Orange on a later generation of soldiers.

My father had been diagnosed with a serious blood disorder

categorized as "idiopathic." That means there is "no known cause." When I recounted the circumstances of my father's passing to my doctor in California, she told me that when she was in medical school one of her professors maintained that idiopathic really meant that the doctor was an idiot and couldn't figure it out. But I think I figured it out—of course with the help of Dr. Google. While my father's illness is known as "idiopathic," research has revealed a link between exposure to toxic substances and the condition, which leads to a breakdown of the red blood cells; the young cells—the blasts—die at birth, and if they survive, they don't enjoy a long life, so the blood's clotting ability is diminished. In the end you simply bleed to death. Fortunately—though in truth there was nothing "fortunate" about it—that bleeding is, for the most part, internal.

At a vulnerable age he'd been exposed to a powerful fire retardant with no name. Then explosives, followed by the paint he used as a master craftsman, from the days of lead through to polyurethane. And of course there were the years he worked on the farm where I was born, which meant exposure to the powerful insecticides and fertilizers that came into use in the 1950s to increase food production in a country still subject to wartime rationing. As they say in America: Go figure.

Dad hated painting airfield buildings, and wasn't thrilled about explosives, or the noise. He loved the farm, though. The land was our special place. We'll go there soon. But first—more about my mum.

According to my mother, my grandmother told her that when she was a baby, she'd tried to kill her by putting a pillow over her head as she was sleeping, but my mother wouldn't die. Nanny Clark—we added her last name to differentiate between the two grandmothers—confessed to my mother that by the time she was born, she'd had enough of children and didn't want any more.

Something must have gone wrong, because my mother was in the middle—number five in the family of ten. I remember commenting to my mother that during her childbearing years my grandmother probably hadn't seen her feet for a good fifteen years. Mum had laughed and said, "We'd be in bed at night, all squashed together, and then we'd hear a wail and someone would say, 'Oh no, we've got to make room for another one.'" Apparently, Nanny Clark "carried small" when she was pregnant.

My mother's father worked in the printing industry; he was a lead compositor for the *Daily Express*. This was in the days when the journalists, copy boys, compositors and anyone who didn't have to work into the night would gather in a Fleet Street pub as soon as the afternoon edition was put to bed. And they would drink. And drink.

When I first came to California and decided to become the writer I'd wanted to be since childhood, I signed up for a journalism course at UCLA. The instructor was a freelance US correspondent for London's *Daily Express*. I told my mother about the course and my instructor, and she said, "Oh, you should tell her that your grandfather was a drinking buddy of Lord Beaverbrook's." (Beaverbrook had owned the *Express* during the war and later became one of Winston Churchill's most favored advisors.) I responded, "Let's face it, Mum—your father was a drinking buddy with anyone who would drink with him."

If I had asked any of my mother's sisters and brothers about my grandfather, they would have all described his drinking, and each would have a story to tell. But the aunt closest to my mother knew the truth, that my mother was the old man's "whipping boy." Mum often repeated the story of something that happened one evening after the old man returned from work. I never heard anyone refer to him as "Dad." He was always "the old man." He had come home at about five o'clock in the afternoon. It was long after lunchtime last orders, and more likely the landlord had pulled down the blinds so the regulars could remain for a while. My grandfather had enjoyed a few too many and had gone straight to bed.

A couple of hours later, Nanny gave my mother a plate of food to take up for him. Now, what my grandfather didn't know was that his family never had enough food. My mother was hungry, and as she walked up with the plate, the food slid toward the edge and she could not resist hooking her finger into the gravy to come out with a lump of mashed potato. She smoothed over the dent and knocked on the door. The old man opened the door and looked down at his plate. He took the plate and dragged her into the room, where he removed his leather belt and beat her until her buttocks and legs were striped with welts. Her mother told her it served her right for touching his food—he was the breadwinner, after all.

To be fair, in that day and age looking after the breadwinner was paramount in any home—the man who brought home the money came first, so the fact that my grandfather was not allowed to go hungry would not have been unusual. But the question lingered—why didn't he know his children weren't getting the same sort of food on their plates? He was a man who earned a very, very nice living, given his position, and he drank a good deal of it away. But Mum said he gave my grandmother sufficient funds for their keep. Yes, that was my question—where did the money go? As she entered her seventies, my mother began to question it too—though she also blamed herself, admitting to me that "I could be a saucy little cow when I wanted."

But there was no getting away from the fact that Grandfather Clark knew how to throw money away. "I was coming out of school when one of my friends said, 'Quick, come on, down the road—there's a man throwing money into the street!'" Mum looked at me as she recounted the tale. "So I ran down the road, around the corner, and there were all my school friends running around picking up florins and half-crowns and pound notes, and screaming that there was more to come. But I just walked away so no one could see me. I went straight home and then to the toilet outside. I sat there for a long time crying. My dad was throwing all his money away because he was drunk."

Whenever my mother talked about her father, she looked up as if she were viewing a statue of someone revered on a pedestal. On some level she adored her dad and I believe that, despite everything, she saw the best in him. She saw the man who believed in education, who loved to recite poetry and who loved his wife very much—to the extent that he couldn't keep his hands off her, or she him.

Years later, I was emailing back and forth with my cousin Jim—named for his father and our grandfather—who had fallen down a never-ending rabbit hole when he began tracking the family tree via an ancestry website. I told him about the only time I remember meeting our grandfather. My mother hadn't seen him since she was eighteen, since she had given evidence during her parents' divorce. Her brother—cousin Jim's dad, the eldest boy in the family—had given her away at her wedding. The next time she saw Grandfather Clark my mother must have been thirty-three, because my brother was a babe in arms, and I was five years old. I'd arrived home from school and was in the kitchen having a cup of tea while Mum prepared vegetables for dinner. Dad wasn't home, so it was about half-past four. There was a knock at the back door. My mother grabbed a tea towel, wiped her hands and ran to the door, but as fast as she opened it, she drew it almost closed again so only she could see who was there. I'd managed a brief glimpse of the visitors and I'd heard the voices, so I knew it was my Uncle Jim with another man. I tried to squeeze my head into the space between her skirt and the door, but she pushed me back.

"I don't know why you brought him here, Jimmy—he's not seeing her. He's not seeing her, and he's not seeing my boy."

"Oh come on, Joyce—come on, love. He's not getting any younger."

She was adamant. I was worried and my brother began to cry. I had never heard her speak to anyone in the family like that, even if there had been a row.

I'm not sure how long it was before my mother relented and allowed her father into the house, but I remember him sitting in the armchair next to the television, my baby brother on his knee. John was wearing the blue romper suit she'd knitted before he was born, in the days when she would lean over the kitchen sink and retch while holding the bump in her middle and I would ask if I could help her because she was scaring me.

The thing I remember most is my grandfather's big nose. It seemed enormous to me. He was still wearing his flat cap and he hadn't taken off his overcoat. My father had come home from work and was being polite. My mother made a pot of tea; her face was dark, and she was shaking. Was this when I first started to notice the shaking? When I became aware of her wide eyes, a hallmark of the Graves' Disease—an overactive thyroid—that would affect her for years and require many treatments with radioactive iodine? I know I clambered into her lap and felt her bones digging into me, so I went to my father instead, who put his arms around me, as if knowing I was scared.

"He scared me, too," cousin Jim told me, and recounted the times our grandfather would visit them. "I always ran to my room because he frightened me, but my dad would call me down and I'd get into trouble because I didn't want to go."

Was it the stories our parents had told that made us scared? And when did my uncle forgive the old man? My mother always told me that one of the most heart-wrenching things she'd ever witnessed was her older brother raising his hand to his own father to protect their mother. But there was that other side to the story.

"When they had a row," my mother explained, "Mum would pick up a vase to throw it at the old man, so one of us would grab the good vase and put a milk bottle in her hand instead. And then we'd get Rene to have a nosebleed. That would stop the fighting." My Aunt Rene had a delicate nose, apparently, and could spike a bleed just by thinking about it. My brother was the same. The first few times blood began spurting from his nose, I was always blamed and given a "what for" slap by my mother—even though I hadn't laid a finger on him. It took a while for them to realize he had a sensitive nose, which later required a procedure to cauterize a blood vessel.

Reflection came to my mother later, when we were talking one day about those early years of her childhood. I was almost forty and had a desire to confirm my own memories of her stories. "You know, I've remembered Clara liked a drink too," she said, talking about her mother. "She'd send one of us along to the pub with the money for a Guinness. She'd always have a bottle or two tucked away behind her chair." She looked out of the window. "And in the war, when the old man was away in the army, guarding Italian prisoners of war, he'd come home on leave and there was nowhere for him to sleep, so he'd just sit there on a chair in the kitchen, nodding off."

Maybe that was just one night, because another aunt recounted being brought home from evacuation when she was fourteen and sleeping in the dining room on a chair while her parents were bedded down on a mattress in the same room. "It was terrible," she said. "They were 'at it.'" I tried not to laugh—there was something amusing about the way she said they were "at it"—though I know it wasn't funny at all. Perhaps I was embarrassed by her candor.

All those girls married good men—local boys who weren't drinkers or abusers. My father would never have raised a hand to his wife or children, and my mother's weapon of choice was usually her tongue, which she could use to devastating effect. My cousin Larry has a different perspective on the family dynamic— with all those uncles and aunts, I also have a whole busload of first cousins, each one with memories of our parents' stories. His father told him that when he was growing up in the same neighborhood, their family felt sorry for my grandfather because my grandmother turned her children against their father and he was never welcome in his own home. During her final years, my mother told me her parents had decided to get back together again after being separated, and though their children were all grown, they told her not to do it, not to go back to him.

My mother's father died alone and was apparently dead for three days before his body was found. A man with ten children died alone. Despite all that had happened, and all those family stories, I find that so very sad and now I wish I had known him. My mother could not stop laughing when informed of his death— I can still see her bent over laughing, tears splashing down her face—and she didn't go to his funeral. I have no idea if he was buried or cremated, or where his remains were laid to rest—if they were. My brother has no recollection of him at all, and I wonder how many of my cousins knew him. We all know he liked a drink, though.

5

Just Kids

❧

Stop. Rewind. No, a bit more. Stop—there it is. Now play.

Before we move on, let's look at my grandmother—my mother's mother. Clara Frances Clark, née Atterbury. She'd fallen in love with my grandfather, James William Clark, and sent a Dear John letter to her fiancé, who was at that time serving on the Western Front. I wonder if she was still working in the Woolwich Arsenal at that point. The vision in her right eye was compromised following an explosion at the munitions factory—a disaster that had taken the lives of several girls working nearby. Her sister, stationed next to her, was also injured.

Perhaps that less than perfect vision affected Clara in all sorts of ways, because I have seen a photo of my grandfather in those days—courtesy of cousin Jim and his research—and cannot imagine what she saw in him, though Auntie Sylvie has told me that he was a snappy dresser, a very smart man. But maybe it was his love of literature—according to Mum, the only time he seemed pleased with her was when she recited poetry for him. My grandmother loved books, too. She could read a novel a day and still keep a house with ten kids in it—she would read into the night, apparently, though obviously given the number of children she was easily distracted from a story. Clara passed on that love of books to her children, especially the girls—my mother and aunts have all been passionate readers. I could imagine them rushing en masse into the library on Wells Way in Camberwell and there not being any books left on the shelves by the time they left. Well into her eighties, my mother was reading five books each week and was always ready to discuss them. My aunts have all been the same.

My grandfather had enjoyed a good education paid for by two maiden aunts, and set stock by his children's schooling—which makes it more unbelievable that he allowed himself to be talked into refusing my mother her chance. Could it have been spite? A sort of payback for the time my mother had her *Loneliness of the Long Distance Runner* moment with her father? Remember that scene in the film? Tom Courtenay played the teen, Colin Smith, who was sent to a reform school after he was caught stealing money. The governor—Michael Redgrave—believes in the restorative power of sport, and pins his hopes on Colin, the talented runner, to win a race set up against boys from a local private school. The young offender understands Redgrave's manipulative ways, but bides his time, waiting until the closing moments of the race—he is well ahead by this point—where he can be seen by every spectator when he just stops and stands and watches as all the other runners go past. It was an "f-you" moment. My mother did that to her father, in a way. He was proud when she was selected to recite a poem at a school event. He might have even come home with a new pair of cheap canvas plimsolls for her to wear—usually he cut off the heels of charity-shop women's shoes for his daughters, which is why they all suffered with bad feet later in life. Hard to believe that when he and my grandmother had only two children, before the other eight came along, one every eighteen months like clockwork, there had been new clothes for the two older girls every week. Or were there? I've wondered about that story.

He'd coached my mother on her performance, but instead of reciting the assigned piece, she surprised everyone when she stood up on the stage, gave a wink and launched into the lyrics from the old music hall song "MacNamara's Band": *My name is MacNamara, and I'm the leader of the band* . . . She was eleven at the time and delivered the performance as if she were a drunk, causing the audience to break into laughter at her comic timing. I think it might have been a song my grandfather would sing when he was in his cups. He left his seat and walked out of the hall with my grandmother in his wake. My mother caught the stinging end of his leather belt later.

Mum seemed to idolize her mother, spoke highly of her—until later years, when the odd comment was passed, as if she had begun to doubt herself. There was that reconsideration of Clara's liking for Guinness; and my mother would sometimes say to me, perhaps when we were talking about her childhood evacuation from London at the outset of war, "I don't know how she could have done it, how she could have sent us away." I was helping my mother to the bathroom at the hospice where she was spending her final days—she would be dead within twenty-four hours—and was assisting her in a most intimate way when she said, "I wish I could have helped my mum like this. I wish I'd been there for her." Several very obvious aspects of their relationship began to dawn upon me, to the extent that I surprised myself because I had never thought about it before, and I was well practiced in having to think about everything in my family, always alert to any looming disaster that might come in like a rogue wave and sweep us unawares into a sea of chaos.

When I was a child we'd go up to London on the train or the coach a couple of times each year—perhaps Easter, or Christmas—and I'd go to spend a week with my father's parents in the summer, a treat I loved. Nanny Winspear would order a small bottle of chocolate milk, a "Milky," to be delivered every day, because she knew I loved it and it wasn't something Mum would ever have bought, even if we could get chocolate milk, which we couldn't. And Nanny let me drink anything through a straw, even my tea. My parents didn't have enough money to go to London more often and I don't think they would have anyway, and in time my fortnightly visits to the Kent and Sussex Hospital ophthalmic department, plus my mother's appointments for her thyroid checkups, all took a lot of fare money. During those London visits we'd go to Nanny and Grandad Winspear, and we'd see Auntie Sylvie and her husband, Uncle John, or Auntie Dot and her husband, Uncle Pete. But we'd never visit Clara. After my mother died, I asked Aunt Rose about it, and she told me that, when my grandmother had gone to live with her, she'd call whichever aunt or uncle we were staying with to find out if my mother was coming round to see her own mother, and Mum would always make an excuse. Aunt Rose said she didn't know why, but, "Your mother probably had her reasons." I asked Auntie Sylvie about it, and she said, "Oh you know, your mum was busy."

Why did my mother avoid her own mother? Clara came to stay with us just once in Kent. She came down on the motor coach. I remember her showing me how to light a fire; I knew already but I liked to watch the way she rolled the paper. She made us hats out of newspaper, and water lilies which we floated on puddles, and she listened to me read—every day I had to read to her. I know she thought my brother was a holy terror—and let's face it, he was.

I was seventeen and in the first year of my A-level studies at Cranbrook School when I was called to the office—my instinct was to wonder what I'd done wrong, so I was somewhat relieved to receive a message that my mother had called to let me know she'd had to go up to London. I knew then that it was probably Clara who had died. At her funeral we all clustered in her kitchen, where Auntie Dot filled a half-pint Guinness mug with fresh water from the tap and all the grandchildren drank from that mug, each of my cousins waiting their turn, looking a bit nonplussed but accepting the unexpected ritual anyway. When the funeral cortege approached The Arrows, the pub along the road, the locals were lined up outside and raised their pints of Guinness as the hearse bearing my grandmother's body passed by.

It was my first trip to North America. I had just turned twenty and was bound for Toronto to stay with my friend Jenny for the summer—she had emigrated the year I turned fourteen, and we'd written every week or so since then. Jenny's parents were planning to take us on a trip up to Ottawa and Quebec, then across to Vermont before looping back into Canada. I was beyond excited— I had been saving for a trip to Canada since I was four years old, when I'd been told about my Aunt Ruby who had emigrated "over there." Even as a small child I was fascinated by travel, by the mystery of other countries.

"Just you watch out for those American boys, Jack," said my mother.

"What?" I was packing my suitcase for the trip. I couldn't afford to buy anything new, though I'd made a matching skirt and blouse set to travel in. It would be my first ever flight in an aeroplane.

"The Canadians are all right, but watch those Americans," she said. "They flash around the nylon stockings and Hershey bars, and then they think they've got you."

"It's not the war, Mum!" I carried on packing.

☙

My mum didn't date American soldiers during the war, though I think she was amused by them. Of course, you could get a reputation if you went out with American servicemen. It was okay to bring one home if you had family around to keep an eye on you, but a girl wouldn't want to go out with too many of those boys alone. One of my aunts fell in love with and was engaged to an American officer, but she broke off the engagement because she thought that if she went to America she would never see her family again. He called her his "Red" for her rich deep coppery hair. They exchanged cards every Christmas, first just the two of them, and then from one family to another, and years later he and his wife came to England and met my aunt and uncle for dinner. Apparently, as he saw her approach with my uncle, he said, "There's my Red," though by that time her hair was white.

My mother and her friends had a favorite trick they played while on the bus to work, when they saw American soldiers on the same bus. They'd sing this song:

> The Stars and Stripes fly high over Germany
> High over Germany
> High over Germany
> High over Germany
> The Stars and Stripes fly high over Germany
> UNDER THE UNION JACK!!

Fortunately, the Americans had a good sense of humor, and laughed along with the locals. And three of them made a young girl's seventeenth birthday so memorable in the summer of 1944.

My mother had gone to Hyde Park with two friends, a day out in the park to celebrate her birthday. While they were walking along, talking and giggling as girls of that age will, they noticed three young American airmen coming toward them. The Americans weren't going to pass up an opportunity to chat up the girls, so they began walking with them, asking their names and making jokes.

"You should have seen them," said Mum. "They wore their caps at an angle to one side, and they called us 'Honey' and made us laugh."

Mum's friend told the boys that it was her birthday, so one of them asked what presents she'd received.

"I just laughed," Mum explained. "I told him, 'Don't you know there's a war on? We don't get presents! No one gets presents—it's just a birthday. Nothing more than that.'"

The young airmen looked at each other, and one said, "Meet you back here in an hour—right here." And they ran off.

One hour later, the girls came along, expecting the airmen to have stood them up. But there they were, with a big bouquet of flowers and a box of chocolates for Mum, and cigarettes and nylon stockings for each of the girls.

"Oh, you should have seen them," said my mother. "They were running along, arms out, pretending to be aeroplanes. They were jumping on and off the park benches, shouting, 'Look at me, I'm a B-29!'"

And then it was time for them to leave, to go back to their base.

Later, in the air raid shelter as bombers flew overhead, my mother offered the chocolates to her family and other people nearby, but no one would take a chocolate because they were American, and if you had gifts from American servicemen they thought you were "that kind of girl." So my mother ate every single chocolate one by one, while giving a running commentary on how lovely this one was, or that one, and what flavor she'd eat next. "And I blew smoke rings so it upset the people who really wanted a ciggie but didn't want to take one."

I remember her laughing when she told me the story, then her expression changed and she looked wistfully out of the window, as if she could see through the glass into the past. "But we were all just kids. It was wartime in the park, and we were all just kids."

6

A Gypsy Life

಄

My parents met when Dad's friend started going out with one of Mum's friends. My dad thought my mum was a "a very nice young lady." That's what he told me years later. He probably also thought he'd hit the jackpot, because she was stunning, bright and fashionable I believe my mother saw his kindness and soon appreciated his very dry sense of humor. My mother's wit was in-your-face funny, though often at someone else's expense. Dad's was subtle—he'd say something and just wait for you to get it, and when you did, you laughed until your sides hurt. I know his proposal of marriage was along the lines of "We've been going out a year, Joyce, so we might as well get engaged." A year later, on July 31st, 1949, they were married.

Once wed, there was no choice but to move in with my father's parents. Housing was at a premium in London and rooms hard to get for a very long time—six years of Luftwaffe attacks had left bombsites where homes used to be, and families needing a roof over their heads were joining a very long list to get one of the temporary prefabs erected to relieve the housing crisis. The 1950s and '60s urban tower blocks of flats designed to rectify the situation had yet to go up—many have been demolished now, the architect who designed them admitting his error because people aren't meant to live in anthills.

Living with my grandparents was hard on the newlyweds, and it must have been worse for my mother, who was used to being surrounded by her siblings. Mum and Dad hated the lack of personal privacy, and in particular that my grandmother would linger outside their bedroom with her ear to the door. My grandmother was always the last one in the house to go to bed, because she liked to mop the kitchen floor and make sure everything was tidy to come down to in the morning. It was her habit to put away her mop and bucket and then have a cup of tea and a thick cheese sandwich, a quiet moment to herself before turning off the lights and making her way upstairs. My mother would hear her stop outside their bedroom door, and finally one night could stand it no longer—she nudged my father awake, who said in a very loud voice, "If anyone's listening outside this door, I'm going to get up and give them a piece of my mind." They dissolved into giggles when they heard my grandmother scurrying along the landing.

My parents were soon applying for every flat or rooms they saw advertised and still couldn't find a home of their own. The final straw came when they lost the chance to move into the first-floor rooms of a Victorian house just along the street. The elderly man who lived there had been taken into hospital and was not expected to emerge breathing. Though my mother worried about seeming heartless, ready to move into the old boy's home before he was cold, she knew that time was of the essence, so she put on her best suit, her best shoes and she went to see the landlord. She explained that she was very sorry about the tenant's health, but just in case the accommodation became vacant, would he let them have first refusal? The landlord laughed. "Not really, love—there's thirty names on that list already."

My mother came home and wept, but soon after the disappointment they saw an advertisement in the classified sales section of the local newspaper that piqued their curiosity: *Gypsy caravan for sale*. The price was fifty quid. This was their chance to get away. This was their chance to leave the Smoke, put the war and the bombsites behind them and build a different kind of life.

They hadn't quite enough savings to buy the caravan, so they borrowed the rest from Auntie Dot and Uncle Pete, and wrote to the farmer at Forge Farm, where Dad's family had picked hops every year. He offered them a place to situate the caravan and the promise of work as and when it came up. If they could get down there before hop-picking, they would have a job to last at least a month, and to follow they'd have more work when apple-picking started. So they packed up and left as soon as they could. They were going to Kent, to an area where at that time of year it would not be unusual to see pubs bearing signs outside warning, *No Hoppers, No Travellers or Gypsies*. By default, "Hoppers" meant Londoners. My parents already fell into one category and were about to fall into another.

The change was harder for my mother than my father. She was definitely a woman of the town, a city girl. She wore the latest fashions with clothes tailored to her specifications. She was the first young woman in her neighborhood to wear the New Look, with its rationing-be-damned lower calf length hem. She wore good shoes and her long dark chestnut hair was styled in a Rita Hayworth bob. I remember Phyllis Cooke, who ran the shop at the end of the road with her husband, Fred, saying to me, "When I first saw your mum, I thought, 'She won't last five minutes in the country.' But she did—and your mum was a worker. Worked her fingers to the bone."

Dad was equally dapper, but he was just as happy in old jeans, a leather bomber jacket and Wellington boots. The caravan's former owner towed their new home down to the farm and they settled in, with my mother embroidering curtains and soft furnishings for their eight-foot-by-five-foot living area, while my father repaired and painted the caravan. They soon procured a tent to attach to the caravan, enlarging their living space. In summer they would pull a mattress into the tent, but in winter they would move back into the van, and the snug heat of the pot-bellied stove. The tent was most likely a traditional "bender tent" of the sort made by Romanies to live in alongside their caravans. Traveling folk would make their tents from six or more lengths of hazel, which were then bent over into a dome shape to support tarps. They were cozy, like igloos made from wood and tarp.

Their caravan had been set close to those of a family of Romany gypsies, and a cordial relationship developed. There was a nod to signal good morning and evening as they passed going to and coming from work. Nowadays the word is more commonly spelled "Romani," though at the time most of the traveling folk would have preferred "Gypsy" to the other word used to describe them: "pikey," a term that denotes someone of low birth. In Kent and Sussex, the word "Diddakoi" (or "Diddikoy") was more likely to be used by local house-dwellers to describe nomadic workers—the derogatory name refers to people of mixed Romany and other Gypsy or traveler blood.

When I delivered the eulogy at my mother's funeral, I was proud to share the story of my parents' early days living alongside Romany families, recounting the bond that formed between them. After the service, one of my brother's old friends approached him, grinning, and said, "I never knew you were a pikey, John." For a second I thought my six-foot-two-inch brother was going to deck his best friend since childhood, but he just turned away. My parents only ever referred to the family respectfully as "travelers"—in their way they were all travelers, folk living a simple life while making a living from the land.

It's often assumed that "Romany" refers to people from Romania, however that is not the case. Instead it is derived from the Romany word "rom," which means "head of house" or "husband" or even "king." Romany travelers were first recorded in the British Isles in the early 1500s in Scotland and England before spreading across into Wales and Ireland, and in each place the language took on elements of local dialect. There is also a distinction between the travelers then and contemporary Roma who have entered Britain from Eastern Europe in recent years.

For most traveling folk the late 1940s and '50s were a very different time. There were no "big fat Gypsy weddings" in those days, though a funeral was a sight to be seen. You never saw a whole tribe settle on a cricket pitch in very fancy caravans, only to become British tabloid fodder within hours. In fact, you never saw those colorful caravans of children's tales—instead they were often plain and towed by lorries, though some owners liked gold fittings, or horseshoe embellishments. Many travelers descended from the wave of Romany immigrants who escaped Eastern Europe in the early 1900s, seeking a place of safety in Britain after having been caught up in the anti-Jewish pogroms that bled across the Russian empire and into other parts of Eastern Europe. The same thing happened in World War II when Romany families were rounded up along with Jews and sent to concentration camps.

Romany travelers often had darker skin—possibly a genetic link to the first Romany people, who are believed to originate in the Rajasthan region of India, where there are many similarities in the Urdu spoken there and the Romany language. When the new influx of Romany immigrants entered Britain in the early twentieth century, the women, in particular, seemed exotic, with their jet-black hair tied back by silk scarves. They wore colorful wide skirts, embroidered blouses and shawls, and seemed like a breath of fresh air to a certain strata of privileged young London society. Artists, writers and philosophers who felt constrained by the lingering Victorian mores began to adopt those vibrant colors and what they thought was a freewheeling lifestyle, and as a result became known as "Bohemians," reflecting an Eastern European influence. The word had already taken root in France some years earlier among the artists and musicians of Paris. The irony is that no Romany would have tolerated the promiscuity and experimental behavior of those London or Parisian Bohemians—they would have been beyond ashamed and anyone not living by their strict codes would risk exile from their family. I find it interesting that today's "Boho chic" has its roots in the history of a dispossessed people who traveled far to escape persecution for their way of life.

The winter of 1950 came in frosty and dark, and there was no work. My parents would take on any farm job and walked miles to other farms to earn money, then they came back to Forge Farm. The winter became harder, and at one point they were living on boiled turnips, perhaps a little rabbit if my father borrowed a shotgun. But there would be no returning to London to the echo of both families' saying, "We told you so." They had already been omitted from the invitation list for one family wedding because the bride's parents said they didn't want any gypsies in the congregation.

It was during one of the cold, dark days of winter that my mother literally worked her fingers to the bone. They were on a woodland job, cutting back something—I'm not sure what, but

I know they were using bagging hooks. Maybe they were coppicing, a process in woodland management in which the young shoots are cut away from a tree stump so that in a few years the tree will grow up again. A bagging hook is a fierce looking implement, akin to a scythe with a short handle. You get into a rhythm moving it, one hand taking hold of whatever it is that needs to be cut out, and the other wielding the bagging hook in a low swooping movement. I've used a bagging hook, and was always relieved when the job was done and I could clean the tool, rub the edge of the blade with a stone to keep it sharp, apply oil to prevent rust, then wrap it in sackcloth and put the thing away. On this day my mother was working at a pace, doing a job they weren't familiar with but had to take on because they were broke. Then it happened—she lost her rhythm and sliced into her fingers right down to the bone. She called out to my father, who gave her a large clean white handkerchief, and said, "You've got to keep working, love—we need the money." My mother tried to do more, but couldn't, so she just walked away toward the long meandering lane that led to the farm. I don't think my father even saw her go, he was concentrating on the work.

As she walked, the village doctor was coming down the lane on his rounds. He drew his car to a halt and asked Mum if she wanted a lift. She declined, said it was all right, she could walk, her boots were muddy anyway and she could see he was busy. Then he noticed her left hand swaddled in a red handkerchief, blood dripping through and splashing onto her boots, and he realized she was in shock.

"Get in the car now, Joyce." He opened the passenger door, helped her in, and drove straight to the farmhouse.

The farmer's wife was probably used to all manner of worker

injuries being treated in her kitchen, but it might have been the first time the doctor had performed an operation on the table, injecting my mother with a local anesthetic, then a tetanus shot, before disinfecting the deep cut and finally stitching the flesh. It left a scar, needless to say. When I was born some years later, it was with a small scar across the first two fingers of my left hand, as if the bagging hook's blade had inserted itself into my mother's DNA. Or into her soul.

That same winter, while my mother was at home in the caravan and my father had gone to the woods to gather more fuel, the Gypsy matriarch knocked at the door. Her name was May.

"You'll never get through until spring like that, girl," she said to my mother, hands on hips. "I know you two are going hungry for want of work. Come with me."

That's all she said. She took my mother to her own warm caravan—her "vardo," in the Romany tongue—and she taught her how to make flowers from tissue paper and wire, how to gather them into vibrant bouquets and place them in a large wicker basket to sell door to door. Soon my mother was wearing gold hoop earrings, her hair protected by a colorful scarf. She'd already perfected her neighbor's dialect, and became fluent, using both Romany words and the inflections of speech when conversing in English. It was not a stretch, as many Romany words had been adopted by working class Londoners over the years, because travelers often wintered in London's parks when work on the land tailed off, so there was an intermixing of language. But all traces of my mother the city girl vanished for as long as it took to sell a basket of paper flowers.

A life on the move meant that many travelers could not read or write, and as my parents became trusted friends, so my mother would be brought official letters received via the farm to read out and advise on what to do next, which often meant writing letters on behalf of the families. She helped children with their reading and enchanted them with her own stories, and found herself in demand when, after she permed her own long dark hair into a mass of curls, a group of teen girls begged her to perm their hair in just the same way. Knowing that traveler parents were very strict with their daughters, she told the girls she would not do a thing to their hair unless their fathers came to the van to give permission. She earned a good deal of respect for sending the girls packing back to their parents before she would touch a hair on their heads.

Life began to look up. Then, to add to their fortunes, along came Bess, the lurcher.

The lurcher—known as the "Gypsy's dog"—was originally a first cross between a sighthound, perhaps a greyhound or whippet, and a collie. Not a purebred Border collie, but a collie of the type you found in the country then—a sandy brown long-haired dog that was a bit of this and a bit of that, all those bits herder and retriever of one sort or another. Today the lurcher has become a trendy dog, often bred from lurcher to lurcher, and not the whelping of a first cross between two different breeds. They may also have been infiltrated by an "oodle" of some sort. You'll see them featured in magazines for city folk who go to the country in their Range Rovers at weekends and wear green Hunter wellies—minus the mud—to ivy-clad gastro pubs with Michelin-starred chefs. The true lurcher had all the speed of a greyhound along with the smarts and nose of a collie. "Lur" is the word for thief in the Romany language.

Bess was the lurcher my father found tied to the back of a vardo on another farm. Her bones were sticking out and there was hunger in her eyes, so without being seen, my father began sharing his sandwich with her each day. If she was untied, she'd run off to find him. Wherever he was, anywhere on the farm, she would seek out my father. She had chosen him and he had chosen her, finally giving up a hard-earned few bob to buy her after her owner had told him, "You might as well take that thing off my hands—she's no good to me."

Bess would go out with Dad every evening to find their dinner—she could catch a pheasant as easily as a rabbit, without him even lifting his gun. In time, Bess had garnered a reputation for being a great hunting dog. Travelers and farmworkers alike came to the caravan wanting to buy her, but my father's answer was always the same. Pointing to the sky, he would say, "When you can buy that moon up there, you can buy my dog." Albert Winspear loved his dog and she loved him back until the day she left home to die alone. Dad searched for her for days that became weeks, tramping through woodland and across fields for miles upon miles calling her name. But in his heart he knew that Bess, too, was a Gypsy and she'd decided it was her time. My parents had other dogs over the years, but there was never an equal to Bess. Even in his later years Dad talked about hunting with her as if it were yesterday. "She'd see the rabbits across the field, and off she'd go, like the wind," he would say. "The rabbits would run under the fence wire, but before she reached it, Bess would go over on her side—" He would slice the air with his right hand. He had knobby hands, worker's hands that my brother and I have inherited. "She'd slide under the wire, and the next thing you know, she'd be up on her feet again with a rabbit in her mouth. She'd bring me back our dinner, that dog, but we never left the field until we had one in the bag for her too."

I created a canine character, "Jook," based upon Bess for my novel *An Incomplete Revenge*. The dog's name was a twist on one of the Romany words for dog, which is "jukel." It was a delight to watch my father read that book and his smile as he came upon the part about the lurcher, the Gypsy's dog.

It's only when I think again about those stories of the caravan, of the traveler family they held in high regard, of Bess and the farms they worked, that I remember just how young they were, my father sometimes foolhardy and my mother tempestuous. If I look at photos taken of that time—small square black-and-white images taken with a Brownie Box camera—it appears that the more "Gypsy" my mother became, perming her hair so she had a cascade of mahogany curls, wearing colorful clothing far removed from those city girl suits, so her carefree attitude to life grew with the sheer space living on the farm afforded her.

As a child, listening to those stories, I could feel the wildness in them—there was a lack of boundaries I didn't recognize from the tight rules laid down for me, and though I was mesmerized by the telling, the sheer craziness sometimes scared me. To be fair, I think our London relatives probably thought my brother and I were like children raised by wolves, for as soon as I'd finished my after-school jobs in the house—and I always had a lot of jobs in the house—we were free to wander across the fields to build camps in the woods, or dams across streams, or to fish for sticklebacks, or gather wildflowers to bring home, where they would be placed in jam jars to grace the table. Sometimes I look back and think it always felt like summer, even when snow was falling.

My mother collected colorful old china plates and ornaments, bought for a penny or two as they went from farm to farm in Kent, stopping in junk shops and flea markets. She would hang her treasures around the caravan and in the tent, decorations to make the place more like home. One summer's morning, it was getting late and my mother was languishing in bed. She hated getting up early, and it was probably a Sunday. My father, an early riser, had already been out with Bess and was cooking breakfast. He went into the tent and said, "Time to get up, Joyce."

But she turned over and ignored him.

He went out, came back a little while later, and tried again.

She told him to get lost.

He tried once more, anxious to enjoy the best of the day. It was getting nigh on half past ten, after all.

She gave him the two-finger sign that in Britain means, "F-off."

He crept outside, returning with a paraffin can, and said, "If you don't get up, I'm going to burn you out of bed."

She laughed.

So he began slopping paraffin around the bottom of the mattress.

She laughed again. "You wouldn't dare," she said.

Oh, but that's the thing. My dad would dare. And he did—though he thought, when he lit the match, that there would just be a little fire, enough to scare her, and then he'd put it out. But the bed erupted, burning rapidly with flames almost to the ceiling. My mother rushed from the tent while my father extinguished the blaze, but she came back with a sledgehammer and chased Dad around the outside of the caravan until he and Bess ran off into the woods. Such was her temper that she lifted the sledge-hammer and smashed every single plate she'd collected and hung with care in that tent. Then she sat down and laughed until she hurt. My father came back and they made breakfast together while working out what to do about the scorched mattress.

The truth of the matter is that my mother was always a creature of highs and lows. She had compassion and kindness, humor and a good line in hugs. But she had a temper and a cutting wit to go with it, a devastating combination if she had you in her sights and let loose a volley. If she wanted to burn you, she never had to pick up a can of paraffin, or light a match.

I'm not sure when Mum and Dad moved from the caravan into what they always referred to as "the little black hut"—but I know from their stories that it was uncomfortable, cold, damp and brought them to the edge of despair one Christmastime. I suspect their vardo had to be sold, or perhaps another traveler handed them an amount of folding money they could not ignore. Since they were now homeless, the farmer offered them a small wooden hut with no insulation. It was about twelve feet by twelve feet at most, but my father found some old planks and made a divider so there was a living space and a sleeping space. He put in a pot-bellied stove he'd found on a dump, and with some end-of-line wallpaper—he didn't need more than one or two rolls —he made their new abode a little more pleasing. Despite the fact that it was only a hut, Dad did his best work, so no one could see where one length of wallpaper met the next, and the hut was kept spotless.

Even with the stove going full blast, the chill air would go right through them as winter set in. Life was far from "kushti"—the Romany word for "good" or "lovely." At this point, after more than three years of farm living, my mother was down to a couple of dresses, a pair of men's trousers worn on the farm and held up with a belt of string, her jacket and a pair of rubber boots.

"I was always afraid to take my feet out of my boots because they'd stink," said Mum, recounting life in the hut.

Christmas came in with a severe cold snap that first year in the hut. Snow was on the ground and a wet vapor seemed to envelop every ounce of space. As they sat at the tiny table eating a meal that didn't amount to much, my mother burst into tears.

"If I had the money," she said, "I'd go back to London."

"And if I had the money"—said my father, pushing aside his plate—"I'd bloody well send you back there."

It was at that low point as my mother wept even more, that they heard a car in the distance. They opened the door and looked along the farm track through the driving snow. It was Auntie Dot and Uncle Pete in their small car, slowly making their way over the ruts and puddles, fishtailing to a halt outside the hut. Mum ran into her older sister's arms.

"Come on, Joyce," said the ever-doughty Auntie Dot, pushing my mother away. "Pull yourself together—we've come for Christmas."

Uncle Pete brought in a box of food and soon a new festive feast was on the table.

"It turned out to be one of the best Christmases ever," said Mum. "We had everything we needed, just the four of us."

It was on one of our long walks on a summer evening when I was twelve and John eight that we ambled along the track toward Forge Farm. Mum and Dad were pointing out landmarks from the early years of their married life, when we came to an old dilapidated hut where the farm dogs were kept. Dad approached the hut, the dogs barking and growling as he came closer. He held up his hand as he reached the half-door and looked in, rendering the dogs silent, sitting on haunches and staring up at him as if waiting for his next command. Dogs always paid attention to my father, probably because he expected nothing less of them.

"Well, look at this, Joyce," said Dad.

Reaching into the hut, Dad tore a strip of wallpaper from the slats of wood and held it up for us to see. I took the paper from his fingers and stared at the pattern of trellised red roses. My father reclaimed the paper from me, scrunching it up and throwing it back into the hut.

"Never be wed to the past, love," he said. "Never be wed to the past."

My parents smiled at each other, and we walked on.

7

Moving Back the Veils

∽

When I was a child I used to have a recurring dream that came to me as if it were an otherworldly visitation. The dream became less frequent as I entered my teen years, though to this day I have occasionally woken in the night in the midst of that same dream. The dream begins as I enter what at first seems like a tunnel, but is really a series of arches—it's akin to an edifice constructed for a deity, although sometimes it's like being in a long tent, a never-ending marquee. Before me are a series of drapes made from thin gossamer-like fabric hung on either side of the tunnel. The ground is not firm, but instead strewn with vibrant silk cloths. I'm searching for something, or I'm on a journey—it feels like some sort of quest. I touch first one of those drapes, pushing it aside to pass through, then the other, and then another—from right to left I am pressing aside veil after veil, almost as if I am swimming through silk. I know I will keep going in this way until I arrive—but I never get to the end and I don't find what I'm looking for. I have seen such arches in places where the Moors left their mark—in Portugal, Morocco, Gibraltar, Spain—and I have wondered if I might find the dream's purpose in the Middle East. In Oman, in the Sultan Qaboos Grand Mosque, I stepped into a corridor of arches and had to take a photograph—I felt almost as if I were walking into my dream. Now I find that writing memoir is so much like that quest into the tunnel of veils, drawing back one after the other, peeling back the years as I wonder, "Is this how it happened?" "Is this how I felt?" And more recently, "Have I clutched that memory to my heart long past a time when it should have been cast aside?" I'll let that thought sit for now, because it's time to go to Black Bush Cottage, a tied dwelling on Forge Farm, near Goudhurst in Kent. It's the address listed on my birth certificate.

It is only since beginning to write this memoir that I've wondered how my parents thought they could bring a newborn babe home to that tiny hut. There was barely enough room for them, let alone a growing child. My mother had already suffered a miscarriage a year earlier—and no, there was no hospital, no visit to the doctor. It was just what happened, and like many women in similar circumstances before her and to follow, she had the miscarriage and got on with what came next—though in later life she talked about that lost child, whom she identified as a tiny, tiny boy.

When the farmer learned that Mum was "expecting," he came to the hut to speak to my parents. "This is no place to bring a baby," he told them, in no uncertain terms. He offered them Black Bush Cottage, a tied dwelling that had just become available— accommodation tied to the job and the land, as had been the way of farming for centuries. My father was given the job of managing the livestock in place of a retiring worker, and my mother's bookkeeping responsibilities soon encompassed all four farms under the farmer's tenancy.

Imagine this—a thirteenth-century cottage set on a hill above the farm it served, with the railway line running along the edge of the property, surrounded by fields and woodland. This is the world I was born into. My mother was admitted to the maternity ward at Pembury Hospital before she began her long labor and my father went back to work having accompanied her there on the bus. This was the same hospital I would be rushed to some fifteen months later, screaming as my skin peeled away from my body.

At about four o'clock on a spring morning, the farmer woke my father by throwing stones up at the bedroom window of Black Bush Cottage, and when my Dad, still with sleep-filled eyes, threw open the window and looked down, the farmer shouted up to him.

"You've got a girl, Albert. The hospital just phoned. You'd better get down to the bus."

As the telling goes, when he walked into the ward the nurses knew exactly whose father he was. The very same thing happened when Dad was admitted to the Conquest Hospital in Hastings, following a relapse during his final illness. I arrived at the nurses' station and was about to ask where I could find Mr. Winspear—he'd been moved to another room that morning—but before I could speak, the nurse said, "Well, no prizes for guessing who you're here to see—Albert's in a room along the corridor, to the right." It's a memory I hold close to my heart.

Black Bush Cottage had no electricity, no indoor WC, no bathtub and certainly no shower. There was an "earth closet" at the end of the garden, which meant my father had to dig a new trench on a regular basis, then move the shed-like structure atop the trench, along with the wooden "throne" inside. When that was done, the old trench was filled in. That is how these things worked. To compare, my cousins in London all had upstairs bathrooms and indoor toilets, plus hot and cold running water, though my cousin Sue can remember the hissing of gas lamps in the flat where they lived when she was a child. Our water was heated in a cauldron atop an ancient black cast-iron stove and poured into a tin bath set in front of the fire. Lighting was by oil lamps.

As I grew from a baby to a toddler, the farm was my whole world. I would run on unsteady legs into the garden each morning to choose my breakfast—I was a small child who knew exactly where to look for a big brown egg. My mother continued to keep the farm accounts in good order, and while Dad loved his work in charge of livestock, at certain times of year it was all hands on deck to bring in the harvest, chiefly hops, apples and barley.

What do I remember about Black Bush Cottage, apart from the accident and that frustrating moment with the sparrow? I remember going with my mother to meet my father as he came across the fields from work during the lighter months. I remember seeing his silhouette crest the hill by the two big plane trees and then his arms stretch out ready for me to run to him.

Years later, long after I'd emigrated to the United States, I was staying with my parents at their home in Sussex. Having spent the afternoon in a neighboring village visiting a friend, I had to return my rental car to the local garage. I'd called my mother to let her know that I would walk home across the fields, declining her offer to pick me up. In truth, I wanted this walk alone, because the following day I would be boarding a flight bound for San Francisco.

It was late afternoon on a warm May day as I set off, taking the path that led from the road, through a wood, then onto the farmland that ran close to my parents' house. I had just leaped over the stile from one field to another when I saw my father in the distance walking to meet me. As he caught sight of me, he held out his arms wide, and in that moment I felt my heart swell. I began to run, waving to him, and as I caught up and put my arm through his, he spoke my name—his special name for me, the only one he ever used. There are times when I would give anything to hear his voice say my name just once more.

Later, I told a friend about that day, and he said, "Your dad gave you a moment, Jack—one of those very special moments."

Much of the fuel for the stove at Black Bush Cottage came from the railway lines. We'd go for walks along the tracks whenever our supplies of coal ran low. Buckets in hand—mine was a small rubber pail—we'd collect coal dropped from the steam trains as they passed. Later, after my mother had saved a good part of the forest from a fire sparked by a train, not only was she given a reward of fifty pounds for her swift action in raising the alarm— akin to winning the lottery when set against their income—but from then on, as trains passed the house the engineer would throw a bag of coal over the fence at the bottom of the long, steep garden. The railway's management was very grateful not to have to forfeit a large sum in compensation to the landowners, so, heated by Welsh boiler fuel powerful enough to drive a steam engine up a hill, the cottage was always toasty to the point of tropical.

Our rural idyll, this world where I chose my own egg for breakfast, where I would toddle boldly through a field of cattle, swatting them away with my little hand so I could pass, where I ran into my father's arms as he came over the hill by the plane trees, came to an abrupt end. I was about two years old when my parents arrived at the sudden decision to move from Kent back to London. They made the journey in their old car—probably another Morris, and probably a model from, oh, I think 1937. My dad liked a Morris. This one was dark red with a big radiator at the front and running boards along each side. If they had kept it, they would have made a fortune loaning it out for gangster movies. This Morris had a string bag on the underside of the roof where you could store additional luggage during the journey—a blanket, or your picnic. The root cause of that pilgrimage back to London, late at night, was a blazing row my father had had with the farmer. "I've had enough," he said, "we're going back to London." So, like the *Beverly Hillbillies*, they packed up the car with the belongings they could move, and set off late at night.

Dad ran every traffic light because the car had no brakes— this was the car he had bought after my accident because I had almost died for want of immediate transport. When we arrived at my grandmother's house, my mother set me on the ground and I keeled over. She had been gripping my little legs so tight that she had cut off the blood supply to my feet. Mind you, she had left all the furniture behind, everything they owned except clothing and immediate necessities. Those were the days when my father—my kind, calm father—could still be a bit hot-headed when asserting his independence. In later years, I asked my mother about that evening, when she'd left the cottage she had come to love. She just shrugged and said, "Well, it was a laugh, really." In truth, I don't think it was a laugh, because I think going back to London was the last thing she wanted.

Living in an urban area turned me into a child who screamed with joy and relief as soon as my mother came home from work and took me straight to the small park close to my grandparents' house. I would douse my head in the water fountain and run around like a banshee, screaming inside and outside with the sheer frustration of being where there were no green fields, only old bombsites and noise, my pent-up country girl energy so at odds with what had come to pass. Both my parents knew this and it was my mother who finally called the farmer—at this point she was once again working for the government telephone exchanges in London, so making the odd personal telephone call wasn't out of the question.

In addition to the fact that neither parent was happy living in London—and with my father's parents because accommodation for a young family was still hard to find—two things happened to hasten their departure. The first involved me and my grandfather—Jack Winspear, my namesake.

My father and mother left for work early in the morning, and I was left with my grandparents until my mother came home at about five o'clock. I know my mother hated leaving me, because as soon as she left the house she would walk to the confectioners on the corner and buy me a Milkybar, a small bar of white chocolate, or perhaps a handful of sweets, and as she passed the house again on the way to the bus stop, she would push the treats through the letterbox for me to catch. The minute the door closed behind her in the morning, I would sit underneath that letter box, my hands cupped and at the ready. She always made sure I could touch her fingers as she called out, "I love you" before going on her way.

On this day, after we'd had lunch, I asked my grandmother if I could leave the table. As soon as she nodded, I clambered down from my chair and began running around and around the table, squealing and then screaming as I waved my doll in the air. She was my favorite, not really a doll but a stuffed toy with a soft red body and a head made of some sort of hard material onto which was painted a face, with dark eyes, long lashes and a sweet red tulip mouth. Round and round I went, and I remember not being able to stop, even though I saw Grandad becoming agitated, his whole body shaking while his eyes widened and began to water. Then it happened. He grabbed the knife from his plate, pulled the doll from my hand and repeatedly stabbed her in the forehead, uttering a cry that seemed to come from deep inside his body. Then he threw her along the passageway that led to the front door.

I remember running to pick up the doll, turning to look at him, and feeling a great weight in my chest. I wanted to go to him, throw my arms around him and take away the pain, because that's what I could see—someone I loved in pain. My grandmother acted quickly, taking my hand to lead me into the kitchen, where she opened a box of Elastoplast and made much of poking the white stuffing back into the doll and then sticking the adhesive patch across her forehead to make her "all better." Then she returned to my weeping grandfather, who I so wanted to see all better.

When my mother arrived home, I rushed to tell her all about what had happened to my doll. She wasn't angry, but told me that Daddy would mend the doll when he came home. I remember asking why Grandad was so upset, and she told me it was because of his war wounds. Years later, watching a documentary that included a reenactment of soldiers in the Great War undergoing bayonet practice, I recognized my grandfather's guttural cry. My childish screaming had unleashed dreadful memories for that dear man. My parents understood this and knew that, much as Grandad adored his grandchildren, a home where an elderly man who had endured physical and emotional war wounds was no place for a small girl with an overabundance of energy.

It was something that happened at my mother's workplace that tipped the balance, making the plan to move even more urgent. This was the late 1950s, a time when the nuclear threat loomed, and following the 1946 speech in which Winston Churchill had declared that a "Cold War" existed between the then USSR and the rest of the Western world, arrangements had been made at the highest levels for nuclear attack. A crucial element of any preparation for war is communication, and soon after taking up her former work, my mother was involved in what were then secret drills. I was about twelve when she described the underground bunker that had been built below her place of work—it was a whole series of rooms strong enough to withstand nuclear attack. As she told it, there were dormitories, a cafeteria and cinema, but of more crucial importance, there were stations identical to those the operators were using on a day-to-day basis. During the drills operators left their regular positions and moved at speed down into the bunker to take up exactly the same place and thereby be at the ready to maintain international government communications during a time of war. The massive steel doors would slam shut behind them and they would be on lockdown. It must have been following the first of those drills that my mother asked her supervisor what she was supposed to do, after all, she had a small child at home—she wanted to know if she could return to her family. Would there be an "all clear" like there had been after a Luftwaffe bombing raid during the war?

"Oh no, you have to stay here, at your station. It doesn't matter who you've got at home—this is your job," said the supervisor. "There's no going home. You take up your position, and you stay there to do your job."

I can imagine her beginning to panic—remember, this was a woman who suffered claustrophobia following that bombing during the war when she had been trapped under the rubble of her house. Just being below ground must have terrified her. She asked again what would happen if she just wanted to go home.

The supervisor took a bunch of keys from her pocket and selected one, then unlocked a cupboard and pointed to the firearms inside.

"This is what happens, Joyce," said the supervisor.

That afternoon while at work, my mother placed a call to

the farm manager at Forge Farm, who told her that since she'd returned to London, it had only taken a matter of weeks for his accounts to become a mess across all four farms—and just by chance another tied cottage had just become vacant, and it would be theirs if they wanted it. It would be attached to her job, not my father's. Mum was reminded that the farmer was not one to forgive and forget, and even if my father came on his knees, he would not get his old job back.

Of course I didn't know the details, but I do remember her coming home from the telephone exchange, hurriedly putting on my coat and hat and taking me by bus to find my father, who was with a crew painting a tall building. We stood at the foot of the scaffolding and my mother called his name. He was high up near the roof and didn't hear, so she filled her lungs and called again. Then I saw a tiny figure in white overalls stop, look over the scaffolding and wave.

"Alby—we're going home!" yelled my mother, her hands cupping her mouth. "We're going back!"

I watched as that white figure in the distance ran along the scaffolding, then down a ladder, and along more scaffolding, then down another ladder; a human marker growing larger on the snakes and ladders board as he came closer to the beginning of the game. And it was the beginning—the start of a journey back to our home, our real home, because even though everyone my parents loved was in London, the years of living close to the land had marked them. They were country folk through and through now, and they were drawing back another veil, and moving on.

8

Back to the Land

❧

I was at the airport in Houston, heading toward the gate for a flight to Phoenix, the next destination on my book tour, when I passed my father. His silver-grey hair, royal blue blazer, crisp white shirt and navy blue tie, finished with the all-important Windsor knot, were instantly recognizable. I spun around, ready to run after him. But he was gone. There was no man in a royal blue blazer. No silver crown in the distance. And my father had been dead for nine months.

I sat down on the nearest seat and called my brother, who said, "Oh, Jack . . ."

I heard a catch in his voice. There was no teasing on his part. No "Oh for goodness sake, Sis." He understood. We talked a little more, but soon I had to board the aircraft. And I remembered, then, a comment my cousin had made years before. "Oh, you Winspears, you're all a bit fey," she'd said. I had to look up the original meaning. *Otherworldliness. Magical.* But I knew what I'd seen, and John knew it too. So, perhaps we were a bit fey. Perhaps we did believe in that which could not be explained.

When I look back, living at Brown House Cottage was magical. On the day we moved in, as we walked along the sloping path at the side of the cottage, past the big red water pipe, and as we entered the small scullery kitchen and the low-beamed sitting room, I felt cocooned. I remember the narrow staircase that led up to two small bedrooms, one of which would be mine. Everything seemed magical in the sixteenth-century cottage—even the fact that someone had dumped a load of sand against the five-bar gate leading to the field opposite seemed fortuitous; my mother told me it belonged to the sandman, because he had to keep his sand somewhere and wasn't it lucky it was so close to our new house, because we'd all sleep so well. Oh yes, now we were away from London, we'd all sleep well—indeed, hadn't the Prime Minister, Harold MacMillan, told everyone in the country just that year that they'd never had it so good?

Every day Mum and I would walk down to the farm so Mum could work on the accounts. I always had a toy or two, a coloring book and my pencils, and a story to read. We'd often detour through woodland on the way home, perhaps to collect a treasure—a fallen chestnut, a perfect red leaf, a posy of wild-flowers—or we would look for fairy doors, those places at the base of a tree where the bark had grown away from the trunk, and which seemed for all the world like a little door to another world. Mum would knock first and listen, then I would knock and she would shake her head and tell me that fairies were shy. Or perhaps they were just not home that day. Dandelion seeds caught on the air would always be fairies, on their way to help any bees that were weary as they went about their day's work. There was magic everywhere when we lived at Brown House—even a wishing well in the middle of Bedgebury Forest, "Crown Lands," which surrounded the farm and were owned by the monarchy.

I remember our walks into Goudhurst to do the shopping, and I remember the lady we passed every day as we made our way down to the farm. Hands in pockets, she seemed to be stepping out for the exercise rather than having a destination in mind. I was almost three years of age, and I recall her wearing a dark raincoat, and always a hat pulled down over her eyes. At first she didn't reply to my mother's cheery "good morning" but then she softened and smiled, at last responding with her own greeting and sometimes a "How are you?" One morning, as she passed, my mother leaned down and whispered to me, "She's one of those women who parachuted into France during the war—Mrs. Mackie told me." It was probably only when I asked what a parachute was that she remembered my age, and that it was perhaps a story that could wait until later, when I was older, though I returned to my questions about the woman again and again as I grew up, fascinated by the notion of secrecy. She lived in a "grace and favor" house on the edge of the forest, which was the property of the Crown. Her home was a dwelling given to a person to use for the rest of their lifetime, by the grace and favor of the monarch, in recognition of their service to the country. The image of that woman has been tucked away in my bank of memories for a good number of years, waiting to be drawn out and explored.

While living at Brown House Cottage I had two accidents— and I'm now beginning to see something of a pattern here. The first was a fall when I refused to hold my mother's hand. Instead I ran ahead along the rough track to the farm, whereupon I lost my footing and tripped face-first onto a large, sharp stone that tore into the flesh across my forehead—I still have the scar. I didn't feel a thing due to lingering shock from the scalding, and I remember looking up into my mother's face and giggling as she wiped my forehead with her handkerchief. Once again the farmer was enlisted to rush me to the doctor, this time for stitches.

The other accident happened while Auntie Rene was staying at the cottage with her husband, Eric. I would not have known this at the time, but the visit came when she had just lost her first and only child as she was being born; the umbilical cord was wrapped around her neck. My aunt must have been devastated, but I can only remember her smiling and playing with me. We walked into Goudhurst on a bright morning—it was a good two miles along the road—and one of the first stops was the butcher's shop, which was situated at the top of the hill next to the Star and Eagle hotel and restaurant, where in my mid-teens I would spend Saturday nights washing dishes.

To get to the door of the butcher's shop, you had to climb a flight of stone steps that must have been there since the Middle Ages. We had both dogs with us—Bess and her daughter, Lassie— so while my mother went into the shop, my aunt waited outside at the top of the steps. The pharmacy was just across the street, and there was something my aunt needed urgently. I remember her saying, "I'll just nip over the road," before wrapping the leashes around my little hand and telling the dogs and me to "wait there." But these were farm dogs, as familiar with hand signals as my father's whistle. Upon reaching the other side of the road, my aunt decided to wave to me. I remember her smiling as she raised her hand. The dogs launched themselves down the steps with me in tow.

Everything went black, then I looked up and saw faces staring down at me. Someone lifted my head because I was coughing up blood and a big red stain was appearing across the front of my cardigan. My mother heard the screams from inside the butcher's shop and ran down the steps, pushing through the onlookers to pick me up. In another shop someone had already called the ambulance and I was rushed to the Kent and Sussex Hospital, emerging some days later with only three or four baby teeth remaining in my mouth and deep grazes on my face, arms and legs. That accident would cost me many sixpenny pieces I never received from the tooth fairy. Later, after I'd started my education at Cranbrook Primary School, when it came time for the annual school photograph my mother always instructed me to, "Keep your mouth shut. We don't want everyone to see your gums."

Only now in writing about these events do I realize I was probably quite accident prone from early childhood. And I always thought my brother was the one to keep an eye on.

We didn't stay long at Brown House, probably just over a year, all told. Within about nine or ten months my mother was pregnant with my brother and my father had landed a job as foreman with Abnett's, a firm of painters and decorators in Hawkhurst, so we needed to live on the bus route because we no longer had a car—it had been sold soon after we arrived back in London. I know I felt safe at Brown House Cottage, though on the day we moved I was so terrified of being left behind that I clambered aboard the removal lorry and hid behind a wardrobe. My mother found me snuggled there with Lassie, the dog—Bess had gone on her way to die alone by then. Soon the back doors of the lorry were closed up and we all sat alongside the driver. We were on our way to our new house in the tiny hamlet of Hartley, on the bus route between Cranbrook and Hawkhurst. I remember looking back at Brown House and feeling sorry for the cottage—to this day I hate to see empty houses; homes from which the soul of family has taken flight.

I sometimes drive past the cottage when I return to Kent, though now it is a much larger country home, having years ago been remodeled together with the neighboring dwelling. It has a posher name, too, though to me it will always be Brown House. Living there marked the end of those years when we were never truly settled. Now we were moving to the home where

John would be born and that my parents would eventually buy. They would live in the house at the end of The Terrace for some twenty-four years, before moving to Sussex in 1982. Their Gypsy days were truly over. But those peripatetic years had marked us all, becoming part of our family story—perhaps the most magical part for us fey Winspears.

9

We Four

ॐ

The Victorian terrace house my parents rented was at the end of a row of three-story dwellings built in 1878 to accommodate the families of men working on construction of the railway and the new branch line station that would link Cranbrook not only to the bigger towns of Tonbridge, Paddock Wood and Tunbridge Wells, but to London. When we moved in, the row of houses was still painted in the olive green and cream livery of the Southern Railway. Ah, but this house had electricity, although the wiring was dodgy. My brother still laughs when he talks about Dad rewiring the house, bit by bit, and the day he gave him one end of a wire and, pointing to the dark space under the dining room floor, said, "All right, son, just crawl under there until you see my hand poking through, and pass that wire up to me." The wire was live and my brother was five years of age at the time.

There was no bathroom—there wouldn't be a bathroom until I was almost fourteen, the same year America put a man on the moon. But we had a proper outside WC with a tall rusting iron cistern high up on the wall and a chain for the flush. There was no mains drainage and it often fell to my father to unblock the septic because the access cover for the system that served the whole street was just outside our kitchen window. Oh, those Victorian builders were a clever lot!

There was a fireplace in every room and the cast-iron stove in the kitchen also heated our water via a "copper" at the side of the inglenook. A copper was a sort of wide and deep cylindrical copper sink embedded in sandstone cement. A tap above the sink was used to fill the copper with cold water, and another miracle of Victorian engineering heated it. When it was hot, another tap below was used to empty the hot water—into a tin bath, or a bucket or bowl; whatever you needed hot water for. We didn't have a washing machine—that would come when I was fifteen—but in those early days my mother had an old and heavy iron wringer with wooden rollers and a long handle. It was set up in the garden; she would run the washed laundry through the rollers to squeeze out the water, usually to a refrain of "Mind your fingers!" if I was helping.

We moved into the house in November 1958, and it was freezing cold. My room was at the back of the house overlooking the garden and during that first winter I remember scraping ice from inside the window so I could see outside. The cistern overflowed as the water inside froze, so you had to be careful when you sat on the toilet because the seat became encrusted with ice and it was easy to slide off onto the cold stone floor. And there were often spiders on that floor.

The rent must have been a stretch, because my mother wore a furrowed brow more often than not, and became nervous when the landlady came every Friday to collect the rent money. Her name was Mrs. Drill, and she had grey permed hair and a circle of frosted glass on one side of her spectacles, plain glass on the other. I would watch while she counted the cash my mother handed her in a used envelope, and marked up our rent book with the date and amount paid. I was always aching to ask about her spectacles. I suppose it was around this time that my mother began warning me to "not say anything" when we went out, or to "mind what I said" in front of people. I was a curious child, always with lots of questions, and like many small children I didn't really have a filter. My mother maintained that one of her most embarrassing moments was when she was at the doctor's surgery for a pre-natal appointment, and having left me in the waiting room—I may have been only three and a half years old but I could be left alone and would simply get on with talking to other people—she heard me ask a particularly portly patient if he was expecting a baby, too. It must have been a relief when laughter followed my inquiry.

We lived two miles outside Cranbrook, the small town I think of as home. That town was like a metropolis to me. My American husband thought it was "quaint" and "charming" when I took him back there, proudly showing him the landmarks of my growing. This is where I went to primary school, and this is where I would catch the bus home. This is where a boy named Peter used to pull off my hair ribbons and throw them down the drain, and this is the grocery store where a shop assistant told my mother to go to the doctor to find out if she was pregnant again, because mum was buying onions and happened to say she had a real craving for them. I pointed out the pub where I was caught, drink in hand, by one of the teachers on the day before I left school, my place at college assured. The drinking part was legal—I was eighteen, after all—but it was probably the nonchalance with which I relaxed, sitting back in the chair while sipping my Dubonnet and lemonade as I responded, "Oh, it's all right, sir, we'll be leaving soon anyway." I wasn't what you'd call a drinker and I'd never been cheeky with teachers, but I liked the Dubonnet TV advertisement, and I so wanted to be that slender, confident French woman in a floaty dress who was languishing in a vineyard and sharing a Dubonnet with a gorgeous bloke. In truth I was in the George pub with three lads wearing school uniforms who were getting a bit tipsy on half pints of lager. But drinks with boys were long in the future when we moved to the house at the end of The Terrace.

Something else happened around the time of the move—I began to be very aware that I was happiest when I was out and close to the fields at the back of the house, or running in the woods, or on the farm where my mother went to work. That yearning to be out in the woods and fields, in the fresh air and on the land, began to grow as soon as my legs were strong enough to take me on long walks with my father, the dog at heel as we tramped across the countryside and through the forest, where he stopped to show me a rabbit burrow, a badger's sett, or a nest, or to break open the prickly shell of a chestnut, holding it out for me to inspect. We would collect wild strawberries in summer and Kentish cob nuts in autumn, and of course we'd bring home wood for the fire. The land had begun to define my young life as it had done for my parents; she had begun to wrap her arms around me. Arms I can feel to this day.

When the due date for my new sibling approached, Nanny and Grandad Winspear came to stay. Something I witnessed at that time piqued my curiosity about what had happened to Grandad in the war—his war, the one where he was so hurt he learned to scream. I could already distinguish that it was not the same as my mother's war. On the first night of their stay, I woke early, listening for my grandfather's footfall on the stairs, a signal that he, too, was up and about. I heard him go downstairs, so I slipped out of bed, put on my red dressing gown with Bambi embroidered on the pocket, and crept downstairs after him. Instead of running to him, I sat on the short staircase that led into the kitchen from the

dining room and peered through the bannister. Maybe I wanted
to surprise him, in the way that children do—planning to leap out
and shout as if playing hide and seek.

At night Dad would bank up the stove and close the dampers
to control the heat, before filling two large pans with water and
setting them on the stove so we would have hot water in the
morning. The first person downstairs would open up the fire's
dampers to bring the water to the boil. I watched as my grandfather decanted hot water into a bowl and then added copious
amounts of salt. He placed the bowl on the floor in front of a chair,
sat down and rolled up his pajama trousers. He lifted his feet into
the bowl and leaned over to rub hot salty water into his shins.
At that point Dad came downstairs and stopped to kiss me good
morning. He smiled and made a comment about spying again, and
then went to Grandad. I watched as my father put an arm around
Grandad's shoulders and asked, "All right, Dad?" My grandfather
nodded as Dad knelt at his feet and began massaging his legs, which
I could now see were lined with deep purple scars. Every now and
again he would tease out something from the flesh, and later my
heavily pregnant mother did her best to explain that Grandad had
splinters of metal from the war, shards that had remained in his
leg after a shell exploded nearby. Oh, I must have posed some difficult questions for my poor parents. I tried to take in the answers,
but it was a few more years before I came to understand what had
happened to Grandad in the Great War. My grandfather was still
removing tiny shards of shrapnel from his legs until the day he died
in 1966 at the age of seventy-seven. Those tiny painful splinters had
been inside him since 1916.

My father was at work when my mother went into labor. My
grandmother took me along to the shop to be looked after by

Phyllis Cooke until after the baby was born. In the meantime, Fred Cooke was phoning around the farms to try to find Dr. Wood, who was out on his rounds. The midwife was located, but for a home birth the doctor was supposed to be there. In the country, only the first child was born in hospital, with subsequent births taking place at home. Fortunately, my mother hadn't learned that this was only the second baby the doctor had delivered. It was said he'd come to the area following a career as a navy doctor, and there was a rumor that the first child he'd delivered had died at birth, though he was not at fault.

I remember Mrs. Cooke asking me what I would like for my lunch, and I remember replying that I'd like a soft-boiled egg with toast "fingers" and a cup of milky tea. She mentioned the exact nature of my lunch order to my mother later, because it had amused her no end, this little girl who knew what she wanted and communicated her requirements as if she were an adult in child's clothing. I can see how I must have appeared to Mrs. Cooke, and perhaps to other neighbors on our street—I recently told my husband that I felt more mature as a child than I do now. "You should write about that," he said.

The doctor was located in time for my brother's birth in the afternoon, while Fred Cooke had gone out once more in his big grey whale of a van to see if he could find out where my father was working and bring him back to the house. With the baby born, my grandmother came to the shop to take me home. And then my heart was broken.

Straightaway I went to my room to dress in my nurse's uniform and to grab the little black bag that held my stethoscope and various bits and pieces I would need to look after the new baby. This was of utmost importance, because from the moment I'd been told I would have a baby brother or sister, I was also informed that the new baby would be my job—that I had to look after him or her and I had to always make sure the baby was safe and protected. My mother had been serious when she gave me these instructions and it was clear that this was no joking matter. The expected little boy or girl would be my most important task, forever, and I had my marching orders. Now the job had finally entered the world. I ran along the landing and knocked on the door of my parents' bedroom—I was never allowed to just barge in. There was no answer, so I knocked again. Then the midwife came to the door. I can still see her as I write, with her cap perched on grey hair tightly curled. Her navy blue uniform was pressed, her white apron starched, and as if some of the starch had splashed against her mouth, her lips were tight across her teeth as she spoke down to me. "Go away. Go away now, little girl. Your mother has a new baby and she doesn't want you in here." Then she shut the door in my face. Tears smarted in my eyes and my nose began to itch, but hadn't Mum always told me that big girls don't cry? *Big girls don't cry. Big girls don't cry.* I walked toward the stairs trying not to let the tears come and began to go down to find my grandmother, but then my little legs gave way and I slumped down and sobbed.

I don't quite know what happened next, apart from the fact that once I'd started crying I could not stop. My grandmother must have found out that the crabby midwife had upset me, and I suspect that by the time Fred Cooke had located my father, who was working in a grand house miles away, she must have communicated the story to him. In time I heard Dad's footfall along the side of the house and voices downstairs as he spoke to my grandmother. I heard him make his way through the dining room and the sitting room, and I looked up expecting to see him at the foot of the staircase. Instead his hand holding a brown paper package with a very distinct shape appeared, as if it were a character entering stage left. Dad was standing in such a way that I could not see him, and could only see his arm, hand and the gift. Then he emerged, made his way up the staircase, sat and pulled me to him. He took a handkerchief from his pocket and dried my tears.

"Come on, let's go and give this a try."

Of course, I knew what it was—the shape was a giveaway. I ripped off the brown paper and gasped when I saw the bright red garden spade with a wooden handle. This was no plastic toy—this was a serious child's version of a well-known brand of professional-grade gardening tools. I loved working in the garden with my father and my new spade was perfect. Dad took me by the hand and led me out into the garden, showing me where I should begin to dig a furrow for us to put in the potatoes later. Only when I was hard at work, releasing the pent up hurt and pain of rejection, did my father leave me to greet his newborn son. Later he came to get me, helped me wash my hands and then took me to their bedroom, where my mother held out the tiny baby. The midwife had been dispatched—my mother let me know later that she had told her to leave the house. In fact, knowing my mother, upon hearing of the upset she might even have told her to sod off and never come back.

Now we were four. Our family complete. Years later, my mother told me that she thought I worried too much about my brother. "I saw it in your eyes the day he was born, my girl. You looked at him, your little brow furrowed—I knew then you'd always worry about that boy." I thought that was a bit rich seeing as she was the poster child of worriers and had reminded me that he was my job from the moment she held him out for me to look at, a strange little thing with jaundiced yellow skin. But I put everything into my job. Work was always a serious matter in our house, probably because we never had enough money—and not enough money was definitely a cause for worry. Not enough money ... worry ... not enough money ... worry. It was, as they say, a vicious cycle, one we chased around and around like a dog after its tail.

10

The Rhythm of Life

∽

My brother was a fractious baby, always crying—no, *wailing*—in his pram. He woke through the night, cried through the day and he would not sleep. I remember once two older boys from the neighborhood—the Pemble boy and the Saunders boy—came around with their bodge to see if they needed to rescue someone, because they'd heard screaming. Maybe my baby brother screamed because he felt he should be rescued, having intuited something untoward about this fey family he'd just been born into. It might have been a spiritual "I've made a grave error of choice" moment. The boys careened along the path with the bodge, a blanket for the victim/patient/deceased on board, and they were crestfallen when I said, "Oh, it's only my brother," their chance to be heroes thwarted. They left the house dragging the forlorn bodge behind them, as if it had lost some of its magic.

A bodge, by the way, is what kids called a sort of home-made go-cart in my part of the world. Boys were always scouring rubbish dumps for discarded old prams so they could tear off the wheels and suspension to make a bodge, tying planks of wood to the frame so they had something to sit on. One summer when my brother was about four or five years old and we were working in the blackcurrant fields, he lost control of his home-made bodge and went flying downhill along a tractor track, straight into a massive clump of stinging nettles. It was an easy enough accident and heaven knows he wasn't the first, because there was only a loop of string to control the front wheels on a bodge. I was standing at the end of my row, waiting for the trailer to come along and the farmer to weigh fruit from the morning's picking. Mum had walked to another part of the field to talk to a friend and I was left watching our trays—and I had a good few trays of my own ready for the farmer. Women had started to gather, chatting as they picked any stray leaves out of their trays of fruit, when John came hurtling down that hill, the sound of wheels clattering over bumps on the track drawing everyone's attention. Women and children looked up and there was a collective gasp as he landed in the nettles. The woman in the next row turned to me and said, "It's that brother of yours again. Better get him some dock leaves." But I was already on the job, pushing my tally card into the side of my top tray so the farmer could find it, before running to tear off leaves of broad-leaf dock to rub against the big white welts that were coming up all over my little brother's legs and arms and down the side of his face. He bit his lip and shed not one tear—and those nettles could really hurt.

But during John's babyhood, before she returned to work on the farm, on those rare days when he napped in the afternoon my mother would tell me her stories, or we'd do the housework together. I think I might have been the only four-year-old with her own set of dusters and child-size furniture polish. I wonder who had the bright idea of buying me that present. Can you imagine how such a gift would be received now, with its suggestion that a little girl should learn to look after the home? It's fair to say I also had a tool bag and train set, and could rewire a plug by the time I was eight, though there was that one incident when I managed to jettison myself across the room, so strong was the voltage that shot up my arm. "What the blimmin' hell do you think you're doing, my girl?" said my father, rushing into the room. I thought I knew exactly how to do the wiring, having leaned over his shoulder and watched carefully when he put a plug on the new wireless set. I'd stripped back the red and black rubber, and put each wire where it belonged, but I missed the bit about keeping the metal part of the red wire away from the metal part of the black wire. It was a lesson learned and it's possibly why I now approach all electrical work wearing rubber gloves—even changing a lightbulb.

Despite these non-girly experiences, there's that very vivid memory of Mum teaching me how to apply lavender wax to the dining room table and then polish it to a shine. The truth was that Mum hated housework, and would often stop what she was doing halfway through the job, perhaps for a cup of coffee and a cigarette, or a cup of tea, or just to have a "quick glance" at the paper. Sometimes we would settle in for *Watch with Mother* on the TV. It had all my favorite characters, though what I really liked was being allowed to watch television with Dad after we had our tea, because I would sit next to him on the settee, his arm around my shoulder as we paid attention to whatever was on the black-and-white screen.

I came to understand that what you called each meal revealed your station in life. Dinner was something my family had at lunchtime and tea was our evening meal. Posh people had supper in the evening, whereas "supper" in our house was that cup of cocoa and slice of toast before we went to bed. Out working in the fields, one of the women would shout out "lunch" at about half past ten in the morning, and we'd stop for a cup of tea and a biscuit. There would be another shout at half past twelve—"dinner!"—and we'd stop for our sandwiches. A cup of tea is only a cup of tea, and had nothing to do with our real tea, which was a cooked meal of meat and two veg with gravy.

After our tea, Dad would turn on the television to watch the news, and even as a child I really loved watching the news. A man named Tim Brinton was the newscaster—I remember Mum sitting down on her armchair and asking, "So what's old Brinton got to say for himself tonight?" My parents would talk about what was happening in the world as each news item was revealed, though it seemed that little would affect our tiny corner, and certainly not a man named Profumo, who was involved with a woman named Christine Keeler ("Little tart," said Mum). There was also that new president in America, whom my parents really liked. I can still see the look on Dad's face as the words "News Flash" came on the screen, and someone said that President John Kennedy of the United States had been shot. I also remember Dad saying "silly bugger" when that same man got himself into a pickle about a place called Cuba.

The seriousness of the news was always alleviated if it was followed by a Western. Dad loved Westerns, so I loved them too, snuggling in beside him to watch Jess Harper in *Laramie.* Jess Harper was my first crush, then there was Gil Favor in *Rawhide,* and even Mum said he was a heartthrob.

It's hard to believe now, when there are so many means of being entertained by a story on a screen, that there were only two channels available in Britain then, and following the afternoon children's programming and sometimes a bit of sport, there was nothing until the evening news, just a blurred image on the screen called the "test card." I still have a habit of asking "What's on the other side?" instead of "What's on another channel?" Our black-and-white Sobell TV was often temperamental. If the screen "went funny"—lots of squiggly lines where the picture should be—the solution was to whack it on the top with the flat of your hand. A good thump or two always brought the picture back, especially if it was Mum doing the thumping. If it didn't right itself, she would complain about needing a new "tube" and the television repair man would have to come out and fiddle with all the wires and bulbs in the back of the TV set to find which one had gone.

This was usually the point at which Dad would tell us it was a pity he'd lost touch with his mate George—"Georgie"—because Georgie was a genius with a television or a wireless. He'd have that thing working in no time and he wouldn't charge us either. According to Dad, the amazing Georgie could also turn an articulated lorry, what Americans might call an "eighteen-wheeler," around in a space the size of a matchbox, if he had to. I loved how my dad referred to Georgie's lorry as the "arctic" adding a middle "c" to the usual "artic" abbreviation for a lorry where the cab is hitched onto the load at the back. Dad's pronunciation made it sound as if it came from a very cold place.

Georgie and his arctic were elevated to god-like status in our house. I could see him in my mind's eye every time Dad mentioned his name—Georgie, god of the open road, waving at us from the cab as he drove past looking for a narrow street to turn that arctic around and show us what he was made of. Georgie was Dad's mate in Germany, when they were in the Royal Engineers, and Dad looked up to Georgie, so we knew he was one of those blokes who could do anything, when he wasn't walking on water. I remember him coming to the house once, with his German wife, Inga—"Auntie Inga"—whom he'd met when stationed there. They had two boys, and I remember the eldest, Luther, being so very kind to me. Perhaps those gentle boys had been taught kindness before anything else, because Mum told me that Auntie Inga had suffered in the war when Hamburg was bombed, and she had been scared when, as a little girl before the war, she had been chosen from all the children in Germany to present flowers to Adolf Hitler when he made a famous speech. The "honor" came as an order that her parents could not refuse, and as a child she had no say in the matter. The story about Auntie Inga fascinated me, because if I knew one thing, it was that Hitler had been a very dangerous bloke.

Almost as soon as my brother awoke from his afternoon nap—if he'd had one; even the neighbors would pray he'd have one—I was waiting for Dad to come home. I'd sit on the chair in the bay window and hold vigil, staring along the rough, pot-holed road that was The Terrace. I'd see the bus hove into view and slow down opposite Pete Eldridge's garage—which had once been stabling for the Duke of Kent pub—and then I'd be up and out the door, running along the street and into my father's arms. As soon as he'd had a cup of tea, we would be walking across the fields with the dog, come rain or shine, snow or hail, daylight or darkness. Walking across the fields at dusk in winter was my favorite time. There was something mystical about it, feeling the frost crunch under my feet. There was always something to see, always something he'd show me, kneeling at my side and raising his paint-stained hands—those knobby, flat-thumbed worker's hands—and pointing so I knew where to focus my gaze, perhaps to see a rabbit, or a fox. And there was also the long slide down the Burton Way to dread.

I'm always curious about how places come to have names, often linking people to something that happened long ago. We'd walk down the footpath at the side of the house, then along the track toward Five Acres, the big field before we reached Robin's Wood. We'd pass the stinky place where overflow sewage from septic systems came out—our community would not have a main sewer line until I was seventeen years of age. At the far end of the field was a stile and from the stile there were two paths—one to the left, a steep descent, and one to the right, which was more of a meander through the woods. My father always liked to take the path to the left; it was probably because hardly anyone ever went that way and my father liked to assert his independence by taking the path less traveled. I think choosing the trail with a challenging gradient was a variation on pitching his tent on the wrong side of the river in Germany—he did things his own way. But so steep was the path, I always fell down, often ending up caught in brambles. The first time I tumbled, my father said, "Oh, you've gone for a burton there, my girl!"

Going for a burton? If you search online, "Going for a burton" originated with the RAF and meant you were going to die, or you'd had an accident. *Interesting.* And here's why it's interesting—the locution was common in South East London, and there is a belief that it originated to describe the effects of Burton Ales. So, if you fall down, you've "Gone for a burton." My father would never have used any phrase that might link his child to a sad demise, and given that he'd used the term since boyhood I can only think that the internet is wrong in this case, though I can believe RAF pilots would co-opt the phrase "Going for a burton" to describe a fall from the skies following an altercation with a Luftwaffe Messerschmitt.

That aside, from the time of my first fall, I always asked Dad, "Are we going the burton way this time?" So that path became the Burton Way. Years later I was walking near the old house, long after my parents had moved away, and I heard some children shouting to each other, "Let's go down the Burton Way!" I smiled and watched as they ran off, gamboling down the track, past clean sweet-smelling woodland where the sewage used to come out, and on toward Five Acres and Robin's Wood.

I loved that walk, loved the wild daffodils that poked up through the undergrowth in spring; the rare wild magenta orchids and abundant custard-yellow primroses clustered under trees, delicate white wood anemones with their angel wing petals, and bluebells carpeting the ground underfoot. The blooms of pink mallow would dry as the weeks went on, becoming curly and webbed by summer's end, when they were known as "old man's beard" by the locals, though in America, "old man's beard" is a different plant altogether. Tall foxgloves grew wild and free, flanking the Burton Way—as I slid down the hill, I'd watch them rush past, poking up above brambles that, come September, I'd be reaching into for juicy blackberries. Every so often my father would call the dog to heel, and we'd stop. Both Lassie and I knew to be quiet, for my father was listening, sometimes cupping a hand to his ear. Then he'd point. *See that? See that bird?* or *See that butterfly?* or *See that field mouse? Wait—well, look at that . . . sshhh—see the fox? Over there—there goes a rabbit? And see that hawk—he's got his eye on the rabbit too, so he'd better get a move on. Look—watch him. He's hovering up there, and any second . . . there he goes—see him? See him swooping down?* And we would walk on, stopping to look, to watch, to see, to remember. *Come on, it's getting dark, your mum will be worried about us . . . stop . . . there he is, there's the badger. Sshhhh. Don't move. See him? Can you see him, love? Blimey, look at that!*

One morning, early, just before sunrise, my father came to our room and lifted my brother out of bed, telling me to get up and follow him to the attic. I rubbed sleep from my eyes as I stood by the open window that in daylight would command a view for miles across the countryside. He set my four-year-old brother next to me and pointed to the sky just above the horizon.

"There's a comet going over any minute now—you don't want to miss it, because you might not see another." My brother was leaning against me still half asleep, a thin line of saliva from his open mouth dribbling down my arm. We waited just a little while before Dad said, "There it goes! There it goes! See it now? Can you see it?" I gave my brother a big shove so he would look too, and there we were, just the three of us watching transfixed as a comet cleared the sky above the breaking dawn.

Dad loved the night sky, loved pointing out the constellations and showing us how to locate each one. "If you can find your North Star," he'd say, "you can find your whole universe."

Our evening walk after Dad came home from work was an hour of see this, and see that. Later he would tell us over dinner, "That was something, wasn't it, that hawk?" or "Some people never see a badger, unless it's dead at the side of the road. We're very lucky."

11

Community's Web

❧

O nce or twice each week we walked two miles into Cranbrook and I remember every step of the way, my mother pushing the pram with big wheels at the back and smaller wheels at the front. In summer she would fit a canopy of white broderie anglaise to shield John from the sun's rays, so the image of my tall mother pushing her son along in his carriage was for all the world like a ship in full sail. He slept for much of the journey. Despite being just four years of age, I walked all the way, only becoming tired as we made our way up the hill toward the war memorial on the journey home.

There was a predetermined route to be followed around the shops, based upon the logistics of filling the shopping bag. Though we grew most of our own vegetables, if we needed a top-up from the greengrocers, that would be our first stop, so potatoes could go into the bag before anything else. The greengrocer would shoot them straight into the bag, place a sheet of newspaper on top, and then add the other veg. Next we went to Ratcliffe's, the butcher, where I always tried not to look at the stuffed bull's head on the wall, a clutch of brown paper carrier bags with string handles hung over one horn. Even though that bull was dead and this was just his head, I was always prepared for him to come charging out of the wall to maim the butcher for diminishing his dignity by using him as a bag holder.

From Ratcliffe's we'd loop back up to the fishmonger to buy the Sunday tea. In true South and East London fashion, Sunday tea was always shellfish—not posh shellfish, but cheaper winkles and cockles and sometimes tiny prawns, all sold by the half-pint. Mum and Dad loved shellfish, but I hated even the thought of it. I would not taste any shellfish laid out on the table, limiting myself to a slice of brown bread and butter and perhaps some lettuce and cucumber with salad cream lavished on top. It was only when I was eleven years old and, having been persuaded by my mother to "please try some," that my life-threatening allergy to shellfish was discovered. I have always found that when I don't listen to my intuition, disaster ensues.

The last of the grocery shopping was a visit to the baker; bread went into the bag on top of everything else so it wouldn't get crushed. By this time the bag, which Mum pushed in at the end of the pram, had become fat, so John had to be scrunched up a bit, and that usually started him off crying. He definitely had to be rearranged, almost folded in two, by the time we came out of the library. Mum did the library run for the elderly people on The Terrace, choosing books for a couple of the ladies—the "Angélique" books by Anne and Serge Golon were a favorite—and Westerns for Mr. Kilby and Dad, especially Zane Grey's novels. Mum herself went through a Frank Yerby phase, though she always reread the classics.

I loved the library, a small room next to the Labour Exchange, the place where people went to find work or to sign on for assistance. It was also a place where families could get their free welfare orange juice and government issue formula for babies. The concentrated orange juice was a health-building drink issued to expectant mothers and children between the ages of one month and five years of age, and it was disgusting—sickly sweet yet bitter at the same time, though loaded with vitamin C. It boasted the juice of nine oranges and it had to be diluted, though I am sure Mum got the ratio wrong, or perhaps the stuff was supposed to taste like that. Ugh, it makes my saliva glands hurt just thinking about it. The juice was part of the government's efforts to boost well-being in the general population, though in truth it probably rotted teeth in a citizenry that wartime sugar rationing had protected.

The children's section of the library amounted to half a wall of books, and I always looked for the new ones. I loved a book that no one else had taken before, that had no stamps on the ticket and no folded corners or crumpled pages. I was allowed two books each week and devoured them as soon as I arrived home. A particular favorite were the Milly-Molly-Mandy stories by Joyce Lankester Brisley, and those wonderful picture books by author and illustrator Mabel Lucie Attwell. I loved her depiction of children with full rosy cheeks and dimpled legs and arms, often clutching puppies or sitting with fairies. I was fascinated by fairies, because I knew exactly where they lived.

There was one more stop on the High Street before the long, slow pilgrimage on foot back to Hartley, and that was to Sykes, the stationery shop. Sykes was also a toy shop and sold everything from newspapers and magazines, which were fanned out on the counter, to pens and pencils, erasers, writing paper, air mail envelopes, cartridges, inks, paints and sketchbooks. The oak floor creaked as we walked in; we left the pram loaded with John and the groceries outside. He was perfectly safe. Sykes was my stop on the High Street. It was my stop because it was where I was allowed a new notebook, a Silvine red memo book, which cost all of threepence. Or, as the lady behind the counter—was it Mrs. Sykes herself?—would say, "That will be thruppence, young lady." And I would reach up to hand over my twelve-sided, nickel and brass threepenny bit, and take my red notebook.

Before John was born, we'd stop for a cup of tea at the Corner Café on Stone Street, or even the café by the church steps. They were called "caffs" and served good strong tea from urns, and Bath buns, cream horns, Eccles cakes, scones and iced buns. The cream horns made with flaky pastry and filled with luscious cream always looked wonderful, but the pastry flaked everywhere the minute you bit into it, so even though we liked them, Mum and I would share an iced bun with our tea. The cream horns cost more too, which was another consideration. I remember on one occasion I had a new handbag with me—it had been a birthday present from my grandmother and I just loved it. I still have a thing about bags and purses. This bag was round, about six inches in diameter with a zipper and handle, not a strap, and was a child's version of the sort of portmanteau a world traveler might take on an ocean liner. Mine only held my handkerchief, notebook and a pencil. It was printed with colorful luggage tags bearing the names of different places and I remember asking my mother about each of those destinations— New York, Los Angeles, Nairobi, Paris, Berlin, Istanbul. Then I boldly announced that I would go to every one of those places on my bag when I was a grown-up. Funny, that, when I look back. It might have been when my wanderlust germinated, though I had felt my world expand simply by that walk into town, edging me out of the bubble of home and the farm. The town might as well have been the whole world, because on our way down the High Street, then round to Stone Street and back up the other side, there would be people to see, to wave to, to chat with and to ask about. There was conversation, laughter, commentary on how much I'd grown, whether the baby was sleeping through the night (fat chance), one person's "op" and another person's difficulties—all manner of subjects were brought out, jewels of local gossip to be held to the light, to be fingered and passed around; glue pulling together our web of community.

As we went from shop to shop, Mum always looked out for one other shopper in particular, a woman who was only occasionally seen in town. If Mum saw her coming out of a shop or getting off the bus, she immediately made a beeline for her, waving out and calling after her. "Ess—Ess, wait a minute. It's Joycie." Ess was a Romany woman Mum had known from her days in the caravan. She always seemed pregnant and always had a pack of children around her—Ess would hold out her arms to stop them in their tracks when she heard Mum's voice, reminding me of a hen gathering chicks under her wings. She had shiny jet-black hair pinned up in the sort of topknot that made it seem as if she had placed a lace mantilla on her head. Her skin was weathered and when she smiled her teeth were interspersed with gold. She wore a wide skirt under her jacket, and big gold hoops dangled from her earlobes. After talking about where Ess was living and working, Mum would always ask the same question: "Have you seen May?" Sometimes Ess knew the whereabouts of the woman who had helped my parents through their first winter living in the country, and sometimes she would shake her head and tell her that May had moved on to another "atchin tan"—another place to stay. Mum would be downcast if Ess hadn't seen May. "Well, when you see her, tell her that Joycie asked after her—remember me to her, Ess. Tell her you saw me. Don't forget." Ess would nod, smile her toothy gold smile and squeeze my mother's arm before they both went on their way.

It was on one of those journeys into town that my mother had a panic attack, though the term was not in vogue then and I wouldn't have known what it was anyway. The siren used to alert the volunteer firemen in the town was the same siren that had warned of air raids during the war. We were at the bottom end of the High Street when the siren began its long wail, rising from a slow, deep whine in an ear-splitting crescendo—ear-splitting because the siren was housed on top of the post office building and we were right next to it. At once my mother grabbed John from the pram, pulled me to her and cowered in the doorway, her eyes darting back and forth as she looked across the sky. I knew in an instant what was ailing her because I knew her stories, so I grabbed her sleeve and pulled it to gain her attention.

"It's all right, Mummy—don't worry, there aren't any bombs."

No one else saw what had happened at the moment the siren started screaming. It was over in seconds—all except the shaking. The shaking worried me. Worry had started to become my comfortable place; the place I knew where to be. My mother worried a lot; there was always something to worry about. But she was also a creature of highs and lows, given to dancing around the kitchen with John on her hip, or making people laugh, or shaking with fizzy energy, or shouting in a temper. The fizzy energy worried me, because it made her cough, and when she coughed she couldn't stop. She was getting thinner—I knew this because when she opened her arms to give me a cuddle, her sharp bones would stick into me.

By the time I started school, John was old enough for Mum to go out to work again. In fact, she'd started that spring at the nearby farm, working with other women to prepare the hop gardens for the coming season. Jobs for women with children were hard to find in the area and there was no provision for childcare. The best option was manual farming work, because children could accompany their mothers. Despite her professional skills in administration and bookkeeping, farm work was the only job for my mother—and remaining a stay-at-home housewife was not an option. It wasn't a matter of choice for many women in the area, so to have a mother who worked was not unusual among my peers at school. But there's a distinction between career and work—and no one chooses to work on a farm spreading cow dung around a hop garden with a pitchfork because it's a smart career move, any more than other occupational options in the area available for women who needed to work, which included washing sheets in the local laundry, or squeezing meat into tubes of sheep's bladder at the sausage factory. My mother worked on the farm because we needed the money and women could take their children to work, which you couldn't do if you worked in an office or a shop. Meanwhile my father was taking on night work in addition to his regular job.

At first, Mum pushed my old pushchair with my brother tucked up in it to the farm and work, but in time, when John was old enough, Dad found an old "sit up and beg" Raleigh bicycle for Mum: not fancy; one of those bikes that had front wheel brakes but no gears, and a metal skirt protector on the back wheel. He took it apart, restored it, found a child seat for the back of the bike and a basket for the front, and hey presto! My mother had her transport for the journey to the farm each day. Sadly, the basket didn't survive the first crash into a ditch when the handlebars came off. Around the same time, Dad found an old three-wheeler bike for me and, again at night when he came home from work, he restored it, painting it bright red as my big present from Santa that Christmas. The bicycle was a necessity as I would need my own wheels to keep up with Mum on her way to the farm during the school holidays. When I started school, Dad had a key cut for me which I kept on a string around my neck, in case I arrived home before Mum and John.

I loved going to the farm. I loved it whatever the weather, though winter could be a pain because even in winter there was work to be done and winter in England can last until late spring. My mother would wrap aluminium baking foil around our feet, which already had two pairs of socks on them. Then she'd secure a plastic bag around each foot because our rubber boots leaked and we couldn't afford new ones, though Dad tried to repair them with the sort of boot repair kit you could buy in those days. She'd decided that aluminium foil would help keep us warm after reading about the new "space blanket" material used by astronauts to keep the chill of outer space at bay. If that new material was basically silver stuff, then surely baking foil would do the same job. It didn't; when we took off our boots in the evening shredded silver foil would shower across the room like confetti, and our feet were still blue and damp.

Every morning, Mum would meet Auntie Glad at the top of the hill by Bishop's Lane and we'd set off to the farm, often with other women who were either pushing prams or riding bicycles with one or two children on board. Gladys Trower was my mother's friend whom she'd met on the farm. She wasn't a real auntie, like Auntie Sylvie or Auntie Dot, but she was loved enough to be elevated to "auntie" rather than the more formal "Mrs. Trower." As soon as we'd gathered at the hill, off we'd go, the women on bicycles flying along, crashing through puddles, bouncing in and out of potholes and across rubble on that rough track down to the farm. I felt strong, being part of this coterie of womanhood. I knew even then that they were tough, that they could do anything and that no one could push them around. I even had an idea that the farmers they worked for were just a little bit intimidated by them—and who could blame them? These were women who could hold their ground—they had muscle of body, mind and spirit.

Now I live in the place where mountain biking was invented—in fact, I have a mountain bike—and at weekends bikers going for the burn huff and puff their way into the hills. Road bikers cluster to whizz around the corners on our narrow highways, showing off their glutes in spandex as they terrify the drivers of cars. Well, they terrify me, that's for sure. Yet I know those hardy country women could pass every one of the gym-built city slickers, and they could do it while wearing heavy jeans or skirts with their Wellington boots, and sweaters and jackets in winter. Oh, and there would be a baby in the back seat and shopping bags on the handle bars, and they would do that ride on bikes with no gears and often no brakes, following a hard day's work on the farm. Sometimes when I see mountain bikers in their spandex and aviator sunglasses, I can't help thinking *wimps*.

12

School—Legally or Not

◈

At the house in Hartley, we only had to flick a switch in each room and the light came on—oh the wonders of electricity! Maybe that's why I had that strange fascination. Some years later there was a character on children's TV called *Catweazle*—a time traveler from the Middle Ages who referred to the "electrickery" that made the lights come on. I was a bit old for the show, but I loved the idea of electrickery. Trickery? I thought it was magic. There was no filling of oil lamps or the lighting of wicks and worrying that a blaze might start if the source of light tipped over.

The Victorian cast-iron stove, on the other hand, had to be made up every day, and every week it had to be cleaned out, brushed of ash on the inside, and polished on the outside. I can still smell the "blacking" that we used—a rich blueish-black polish the color of midnight, made especially for cast-iron stoves. I'd become good at polishing, so the stove and the hoods over fireplaces in the dining room and sitting room became my jobs.

While my father nurtured my love of the outdoors, Mum was the one to read to me and to have me read back to her. She would frown if she didn't think I was coming on fast enough and warned me that when I started school, I'd be the dunce if I didn't learn. I'd seen pictures of dunces in books. I dreaded being a dunce, of having to stand in the corner of the room wearing a pointed hat with a big D on the front so that everyone knew how thick I was. My mother had never been a dunce. So many times she told me how bright she was, how she'd won that scholarship, and how her hopes had all come crashing down when her parents said she couldn't go to the expensive girls' school, because her teacher had warned them about the cost of the uniform. Another teacher who my mum revered had broken down and wept when my mother told her she couldn't take up the scholarship. I knew that story down pat, even the bit where my mum seemed sad, remembering the teacher who'd cried at the unfairness of it all.

My mother was the teller of stories, the holder of family tales—and I heard every single one, the sad, the happy, the funny, the tragic. If I knew anything by the time I started school, it was that things could be very unfair for even the best people in this world.

Mum's stories and her obvious love of learning inspired me, so I could not wait to begin my education. However, due to the fact of my birthdate, I was too young to be enrolled for primary school that September, even though I was more than ready in my mind and in hers—but you had to be five years of age to be registered. Much to my mother's chagrin, I could not be registered to start the following Easter—I would turn five one week after the summer term started, so I had to wait until I was five and a half to begin my formal education in September 1960. But my curiosity about school became overpowering, and on the sly I'd been secretly attending primary school from soon after my brother's birth. All's well that ends well, but a few people were not best pleased with the modus operandi I employed to get into school.

By the time John was born, the National Health Service was fourteen years old. Health support systems had been put in place for the many babies born after the war, and on into the sixties—who knew we would be referred to as "Baby Boomers" one day? My mother had a weekly "new baby" appointment at the health clinic, a post-war prefabricated building where John was weighed, measured, inoculated against ills that had killed infants and children just a decade earlier—diphtheria, polio, smallpox, whooping cough—and he was generally examined to ensure he was progressing as a newborn should. He screamed from the moment he was taken into the examining room and put on the scales to the moment he was brought out, so there was never any doubt that the boy had lungs and fully operational vocal chords. I found the whole thing tedious and on one occasion, as my mother was called from the waiting room for her appointment, I decided I'd like to see what school was all about.

Conveniently it was right next door. I only had to slink out of the clinic, past the less than observant receptionist, and I was facing the back door of the school. On the day of my expedition into the world of formal education, I slipped into the nearest classroom—most of the doors were open to allow a breeze to flow through on a hot summer's day. I'd found a class where the teacher was reading a story, which was perfect. The children were listening, hanging onto the teacher's every word, so no one really noticed me, though Paul, the boy who lived up the road from me, frowned, and I experienced a frisson of jealousy when I saw him nudge the girl sitting next to him, causing her to look round at me. They were five, just, and I was still four, so they had a certain edge. In time that girl, Jenny, was to become one of my dearest friends; it broke my heart when her family emigrated to Canada.

There came a point where the teacher drew her attention away from the book and asked a question about the story. My hand shot up along with half a dozen others. The teacher scanned the room, ready to choose someone to give their answer. That's when she saw the interloper. It was at that very moment the headmaster entered the classroom along with the school secretary to let the teacher know he'd just heard that a child was missing from the clinic, and to look out for her. I'd been rumbled. The teacher pointed at me and I was led from the room like a common criminal, though I swear the adults were all laughing. My mother wasn't, though—she had been worried sick, and had imagined all manner of terrible things happening to me. It was only as we walked away from the school that she smiled, and began asking questions about the story the teacher had been reading. I absconded several more times during those weekly visits, but now the clinic staff knew where to find me, and generally the teachers just accepted that there was a little girl who might wander into their classroom once a week. I hadn't been fussy about which class I'd join—though the nearest rooms were for Infants 1 and 2, the five- and six-year-olds, and Junior 1, the seven-year-olds. I just wanted to be in school.

Eventually the headmaster allowed me to join Mrs. Bishop's class—she's the teacher who discovered me among her pupils on that first school adventure—so Mum would drop me at her classroom before taking John over to the clinic. Now I live in the United States, where many schools have their own police departments and even a four-year-old would be under suspicion and probably searched for weapons when found wandering around a school to which she had not been enrolled.

Here's what I remember about my first official day at school. I remember my uniform: a grey skirt, white blouse, green cardigan, green knee-high socks and new Clarks brown sensible shoes. My father had polished them with dubbin in anticipation of the wear and tear that school might inflict upon them, and followed the application by putting them in a warm oven so the oils soaked in to render the leather shoes waterproof, thus ensuring they lasted for as long as possible. Then he polished them to a shine you could see your face in. Every evening, when my dad polished his own shoes, he would polish my shoes for school. He might have been a house painter, but my father wore a clean, pressed white shirt every single day and walked up the road to the bus stop for all the world looking as if he were going to work at a bank, taking his overalls and painting apron, plus his own brushes—always the very best he could afford—in a small case.

I had new hair ribbons for my first day at school, and stood still while Mum braided my hair into two long plaits, each tied with a green bow. Though I could sometimes be fidgety when she braided my hair after buying me new ribbons, she would always sing "Scarlet Ribbons" as she brushed and braided, and I so loved the way she would brush in slow rhythm to the song.

Mum had taken a morning away from work on the farm to accompany me to school on the first day. She told me in later years that she had a lump in her throat as we boarded the bus at the end of the road and I said to her, "Don't sit with me—I don't want the other children to think I'm a new girl." At first I didn't know any other children who went to school on the Number 97 bus— we lived at the farthest end of the Cranbrook Primary School catchment area—but I wanted to be among them. I was wearing my green blazer with the school insignia on the pocket, and had a small wallet with a plastic window for my free bus season ticket and a cross-body shoulder strap to make sure the ticket wouldn't get lost. The school uniform had been bought from Don Baker's shop next to the Corner Café on Stone Street in Cranbrook, because Don Baker let his customers purchase "on tick" and came around to the house on a Friday evening to collect the weekly payment toward the bill. The shoes came from Freeman, Hardy and Willis, because they had the special measuring machine for children's feet, and my mum was adamant that we would always have shoes that fit, because she'd never had decent shoes as a child.

Mum accompanied me from the bus stop, along the street, past the church and into my first proper classroom, Infants 1. The teacher, Mrs. Willis, told me where to sit and to "Wave to Mummy." I gave a quick flap of my hand and began to talk to my neighbor, a girl named Wendy who would become my best friend. From the time we started school, people thought we were twins— we both had blonde hair, brown eyes, and were about the same height, though by the time she hit her teens, Wendy was a good inch or two taller than me. I thought she was just lovely, and I adored having a real best friend. My first ever friend and I wasn't related to her! Both Wendy and I were ahead with our reading and writing, and made it a point to keep neck and neck. I already knew how to spell my name and address, and could write sentences and short—yes, very short—stories, and I quickly learned how to spell Wendy's name. In time Wendy taught me how to spell her name in sign language. Both grandparents on one side of her family were deaf, so she was learning to sign by default.

One day, without meaning to, I managed to get Wendy into trouble with the teacher. I think I must have been bored, because I'd finished a writing task early, and in a moment of deep affection I wrote her name on her desk to let everyone know that it was her desk and no one else's. I never wanted another neighbor. As the teacher came around to check our work, she saw the name and reprimanded Wendy, threatening to send her into the corner with her face to the wall. I was stunned into silence. When Wendy said that she hadn't done it, the teacher said, "Don't be silly—no one else knows how to spell your name!" I should have confessed right there and then, but I was scared. Mrs. Willis could sting you, if she slapped you around the legs for an infraction. But Wendy didn't hold a grudge, and as soon as the bell went for playtime, we rushed outside to continue whatever game we'd been playing that morning before we'd had to file into the classroom in pairs to start our lessons.

Funny, I just stopped writing because I wanted to see if I could still sign Wendy's name with my fingers. And I can.

My mother only came to school with me on the first day. From then on I traveled on the bus alone, arriving home just after four in the afternoon. Sometimes I was home before Mum and John, though I had my instructions. Take off your school uniform, fold it and put it away, and change into your old clothes. Take off your school shoes. Peel the potatoes for dinner. And if it was still light and they weren't yet home, I'd run down to the woods with the dog, clutching a book as I sat in my favorite spot by the pond until Mum called from the attic window. You could hear her voice echoing across the fields for miles. *Jaaackeeee.* But I loved it if she was home before me. If it was raining, I *knew* she would be home. Those were the days when I would deliberately leave the hood down on my school raincoat during a storm, so my hair would get drenched as I walked slowly down The Terrace. I'd enter the warm kitchen, and as Mum turned to see me, she'd tut-tut-tut, grabbing a soft, warm towel from the rail above the stove, holding me to her so she could pull off the wet raincoat and rub my hair dry. I loved that. I loved the rubbing and warmth, the smell of the farm's fresh air on her skin, and her telling me that I'd catch my death if I wasn't careful, and I wasn't to be so silly again to get wet like that because it'll go straight to my chest and then what would we all do? Sometimes John was asleep, the day outdoors having lulled him. I always hoped he'd be asleep, because then I had Mum to myself and we'd talk over a cup of tea about what I'd done at school, and she'd usually have me read to her so she could make sure I was keeping up. Then she'd leap up. "Look at the time," she'd say, which was a bit pointless, because the black Bakelite clock on the mantelpiece above the stove, the one in the shape of a grand Grecian palace that came from Nanny, never kept good time, though she had the watch Dad had bought for her when they were engaged. That was the watch that, if it stopped working, she'd take it off and, grasping it by the strap would slap it across the table a couple of times, look at the dial, hold it to her ear and then say, "There, that did it." Slapping the TV, slapping the watch, slapping the radio—which we called a wireless—if something wasn't working properly, she would always sort it out with a sharp slap. It was a method she also employed when her children didn't seem to work properly.

There's so much I remember of those early days at school. As the warmth of early September gave way to autumn and then winter, almost every day I brought something new for the "nature table" in our classroom. There were leaves of crimson and gold collected as they fell from trees, a clutch of brown cob nuts, flowers, grasses, a snail shell, a feather, an abandoned bird's nest. Each morning the school caretaker, Mr. Chambers, would deliver a crate of thirty-two small bottles of milk to the classroom—one for each child, part of the post-war "free milk" initiative that was scrapped by Margaret Thatcher in the 1970s. In winter, Mrs. Willis would set the frozen bottles atop the tall coal-burning stove in the classroom. Columns of cream so cold they had poked through the foil tops slowly began to melt, so my memories of winter in Infants 1 are of acrid, cough-inducing coal fumes and milk burning brown as it oozed down the side of the stove. And I remember my freezing cold fingers and toes as I waited for the bus to and from school in wintertime.

I'd very quickly learned that arithmetic was something to be tolerated because there were other lessons I liked. I loved mixing up powder paints and I loved practicing my handwriting; light pressure on the upstroke, and harder on the down. At the end of my first year in primary school I won first prize for handwriting at the Hawkhurst Flower Show, and my best friend, Wendy, won second prize. I didn't even know the entire class had been entered along with other schools in the area, so I was thrilled—and even more thrilled at the five-bob prize money.

Mum made us save most of any money given to us, so I was sent along to the general store at the end of The Terrace to see Fred Cooke, who ran the sub post office inside his shop, and with my winnings I bought two half-crown savings stamps, the ones with a picture of Prince Charles on the front. The sixpenny stamps bore the image of Princess Anne, all blonde curls and a big smile. You could cash in your savings stamps for a premium bond when you had enough money—and if you had a premium bond, you might win a fortune in a drawing. Oh, how we wanted to win a fortune. All the ills of the world would go if we, the Winspears, could only win the football pools, or if one of Mum's premium bonds would come in for us. "I think my numbers will come up this week," said Mum every week as she filled out the football pools, a line of crosses against the teams she predicted would draw. She stuck to the same numbers every week because she hadn't a clue about football. I don't think anyone who did the football pools knew much about the actual teams, but they all had their favorite numbers. The pools man would collect her form on a Thursday night, along with the shilling it cost to play. I was six years old when a man called Keith Nicholson was the first person to win over one hundred and fifty thousand pounds on the football pools. To us, it might as well have been a million. I can see his wife, Viv, being interviewed on TV, holding out her arms wide and saying, "I'm going to spend, spend, spend." My mother rolled her eyes and said, "Silly cow, she should keep her mouth shut." Of course she was miffed that it wasn't her winning big, but she had a point—the couple went on a spending spree, and after her husband was killed in a car accident while driving his new flash car, poor old Viv ended up bankrupt. Her second husband was killed in another car crash, and her next husband was abusive. These stories made my mother bound and determined to remain anonymous when we won—though I thought people might catch on, because Mum said the first thing we'd do was put in a proper bathroom. Funny, that, considering the house wasn't even ours, and if we had a great influx of winnings, we would probably spend, spend, spend on a new place to live. Not a flash car, though, because we know what my dad was like with cars. It would be a few years before he passed his test, and the Morris Traveller, registration number PJG 876, was to come into our lives.

13

Dear Octopus

❧

I'm not sure when I realized I had a big family, that I was a small cog in a much larger wheel. Perhaps I'd always been aware of what author Dodie Smith called, "The family—that dear octopus from whose tentacles we never quite escape nor, in our inmost hearts, ever quite wish to."

The first cousin I remember is Celia, who is three years older than me. I remember her coming to Nan and Grandad's house when we lived in London. She had lovely soft dark hair, almost black, styled in ringlets that spiraled down to her shoulders. As soon as I saw those ringlets, I wanted some exactly the same. And I was fascinated by a dark red stain on her face, something to do with an illness. Last year, as we sat drinking tea in the conservatory of her home in Hastings, East Sussex, I asked her about that red mark. At first she seemed perplexed, because she could not recall the mark, and then remembered she'd had some sort of fever that caused her to have nasty red blotches all over her face and neck. Was it rheumatic fever? Or scarlet fever? Or one of those other childhood illnesses? It might have been something I could have caught, because that was a time when if a mother heard of the children in a family going down with mumps, chicken pox, whooping cough or measles, she'd send you round there to play, so you could catch whatever it was and get it over with—and I never caught what Celia had.

But I certainly caught her love of fashion, probably due to the fact that I was given her hand-me-downs. She had two older sisters, Pat and Rita, so I had the castoffs from all three—but it was Celia's discarded clothing that I loved the most, because by the time she hit her teens, Celia was a dedicated follower of fashion and she moved onto the next thing very quickly. The "Twiggy" dress with an empire line and three little bows meeting at a Peter Pan collar—thank you, Celia, for those two dresses! The air-force blue wide-wale corduroy suit with a matching miniskirt and long thigh-length jacket from Clobber, the range launched by then hip designer Jeff Banks, who was married to singer Sandie Shaw—thank you, Celia! The black miniskirt . . . the Old English oversized red watch . . . those burgundy velvet jeans—thank you, Celia! And then I grew taller than Celia, but the die was cast. Now when I see her we'll often admire each other's clothing. We dress in a similar fashion—tunics with mandarin collars, long jackets, nice soft cardigans, white blouses, and the same kind of leather boots. Our hair is very different, though when I was six, as soon as my hair had grown long enough, I asked my mother to put my hair in ringlets just like Celia's for the school photo. She did—though I hadn't grasped that before I went to bed my hair would have to be twisted into rags my mother had ripped from an old table cloth. Having slept with those green and white check dreadlocks pulling at my roots, I woke with a bad headache that stayed with me all day, so I was hard-pushed to make even my toothless gummy smile. I had lovely blonde ringlets, though.

But time marches on. When I saw Celia earlier this year, she commented that she really liked the way I was letting my grey hair come in. Hers is still almost jet black.

☙

My cousin Tony was living with Nan and Grandad when we went back to London. He was a teenager then, and thought that teaching me to swear when no one else was around—telling me to say "F**k you" instead of "Thank you"—was just hilarious. He still laughs about it, though my mother heard me say that dreaded word just once before she dragged me off and slapped me so hard, my legs stung for a day. For a long time I just nodded when I should have been saying, "Thank you" just in case the wrong word came out.

Cousin John came to stay with us at The Terrace when his dad had tuberculosis and was in hospital having half a lung removed. This was the second time John had stayed with us because his dad was ill and my parents loved having him around, especially Mum, because he was the son of the sister closest to her, and she adored young Johnny as if he were her own. I wasn't at all keen, because I had to sleep in my brother's cot in the room we shared, while Johnny slept in my bed. Of course the side rails of the cot were not raised, as they would be for my baby brother, so I felt as if I were in a bed—I didn't want to be considered a baby anymore. One morning cousin John pulled up the rails, locking me in the cot, and proceeded to poke a stick at me as if I were an animal in a cage. When my mother ran in to find out why I was screaming, John looked saint-like and innocent, shrugging as if he had no idea. My mother would have let him get away with murder, yet she would never tolerate her children crying for nothing—her favorite line was, "If you don't stop crying, I'll give you something to cry for." On that day, I was the one who was told off. Like an elephant, I remember that.

What I really loved was the mass onslaught of family, the caravan of cars that would come rolling down the road to our house at the end of The Terrace: cars full of aunts, uncles and cousins from London—here was my mother's side of the family turning up en masse on a Sunday morning, or sometimes on a Saturday afternoon to stay overnight. Dad would bring out his pasting tables, the long trestles he used for work to lay out wallpaper for pasting, and those would be set up in the dining room for the kids, covered not with tablecloths but with old scraps of wallpaper, because you know what kids are like with food. The "grown-ups" would sit in the kitchen. Packed around those tables like sardines, we'd all be gabbing away, my cousins excited about being in the country and us just happy to have company. None of the families had much money, really, but everyone brought something to add to the feast. It was noisy, colorful and suddenly not so calm any more—The Terrace was a quiet place, as a rule, mainly elderly folk, and we were that young family at the end of the street.

When we first moved to The Terrace, only one car was ever parked there, and that belonged to the Martin family, who'd take me to Sunday school in their big woody wagon, until they moved away to a place called Birchington when I was five. After they left I was taken to Sunday school by Miss Jenner, who lived along the main road—she would let me sit next to her in her maroon car with the big steering wheel. But on a Sunday afternoon the entire Terrace knew when we had company because you could hear the cars as they turned into the street. A couple of my uncles didn't have cars, so everyone would be piled in with those who had. The neighbors probably dreaded hearing our tribe turn up—a veritable battalion of kids screaming and yelling in the garden, then running down to the woods to create all manner of worlds, from the Wild West, to the jungle and even outer space, cousins making the most of being in the country before time and the fast approach of Monday called them back to London.

I have a photograph on my mantelpiece, taken when I was about six and John two. Auntie Sylvie and Uncle John had come down from London for the day and we'd all gone for a walk along Bishop's Lane, toward Furnace Farm—one of the farms where Mum and Dad had lived and worked during those earlier years. We stopped at a row of deserted hopper huts that were fast becoming derelict. You could still go into the individual huts and you could walk over to the old brick cook house where everyone gathered to make an evening meal during the days of hop-picking, before the farmer invested in a machine to do the work. But the wooden weatherboards on the outside of the huts were deteriorating and planks had been taken away for other purposes, or stolen.

I love this photo, which my dad took, because I can remember that day and that walk down the lane on a summer's afternoon, the midges buzzing above our heads. I remember my brother getting tired and Dad carrying him, and I remember Mum seeming to frown, but she wasn't, it was only her way—and her eyes were getting bigger, because that's what can happen with Graves' Disease. Uncle John's in the background, and there's Auntie Sylvie and Mum, who's holding onto my brother—because there were three Johns in the house when they visited, my cousin was known as "Little John" and my brother became "John-John." I am sitting next to Martine. My beloved Martine, whom I adored. She was just six months younger than me, and her mother, Auntie Sylvie, was my mother's closest sister. In almost every photo of us together I have my arm around her, or I've taken her hand, or we're linked at our elbows. Martine was so witty. Even as a child she would have everyone laughing with a joke or an observation; her comic timing was a rare talent—and she always had interesting toys with her, the sort of playthings you couldn't get in the country and that only London kids seemed to have.

Martine died in 2012, the same year as my dad—and from a blood disorder. That was too much like a bad coincidence, though in her case it was leukemia, exacerbated by the Addison's Disease she'd endured for years. I always thought it a strange turn of events, that a girl who had more energy than she knew what to do with—effervescent energy, always up for laugh-out-loud fun, always there with a joke, a fast quip, a nudge in the ribs as she teased you—was felled by a disease hallmarked by extreme fatigue and often an inability to even lift a hand.

Sue and Jane, Rosehannah and Janice, Linda, Stephanie and Gillian, Martine, Jackie, Barbara and Karen, Josie and Sharon . . . we were a tribe of girls in what seemed like a family ruled by women, and we knew there were more because Auntie Ruby had another Janice and a Christine in Canada. Of course there were the boys, too. My childhood seems framed by this big, boisterous family. By aunts who laughed a lot and had good gossip to eavesdrop on, and uncles who entertained us until our sides hurt with the giggling; Uncle Joe who would strip off his shirt and pin clothes pegs to the skin across his torso, then chase us as the Peg Monster, and Uncle John who would show us the scar where they took his lung, and could make it move as if it were about to talk. On one of our trips to the coast, as the cars caravanned along, Uncle Jim stopped his car in the middle of the street, which caused drivers behind to pull to a halt. He leaped from his car, and ran back to have a mock fight with Charlie, who jumped out of his car, fists raised and shouting back at him. Uncle Pete emerged from his car and was roped into the act, calling out to my dad for help. We cousins squealed with laughter and the aunts tut-tutted as we watched the four of them pretending to have a punch-up in the sleepy town where Jim had decided we kids needed some entertainment. A crowd had gathered to watch, but soon the uncles and Dad jumped back in the cars and we were off again, ready for anything.

There's a day that will remain in my memory forever. We were in Charmouth, in the county of Dorset on a cold blustery day. I think our company totaled about sixteen cousins and the uncles and aunts, so we were once again a tribe at play, wrapped up warm against the elements and not letting anything get in the way of a good time—which in Charmouth includes the collecting of fossils. But as we each stashed our hoard of ammonites and belemnites to take to our respective schools, Uncle John found an old tin water tank washed up by the tide, perfect to shield the camping stove, upon which the aunts made tea and fried sausages, which we ate with fresh, crusty bread. Then all the kids, uncles and aunts started playing football, which turned into any old game with a ball because it's hard to kick a ball along a pebble beach. Injuries began to mount, so with rain pouring down, Uncle Charlie shouted, "Let's start a band!" Pebbles in Tupperware, sticks of driftwood, spoons, forks and knives, the tin water tank—everything we could think of was drafted in for use by our family band of jesters. Despite the rain and a biting coastal wind, we sang our hearts out that day, and the cousins still talk about it.

My mother was always in her element when her family came down to see us, even though she'd pretend to complain, saying, "Here they all come for their Sunday dinner." But we didn't mind, even though the roast that should have lasted us through Tuesday, at least, would be gone by Sunday afternoon. Then there were the parties, big London parties with all the family dancing to old songs and new. Sometimes there was a reason for the celebration, but more often it was because we happened to be in London— everyone came together and there was a party. It would be late, often in the small hours, when someone would call out for Mum to end the evening, and you'd hear another voice yell, "Belt it out, girl." She'd clear her throat, take a sip of her gin and tonic, and then the room would go quiet and she'd start to sing "The Party's Over."

I loved the way she drew out the word *masquerade*, lingering on every syllable—*it's time to wind up, this mass-cure-ayd*—with a wobble in her voice before leaving a breathy second in the air and continuing on. She sounded a bit like Shirley Bassey, who had recorded a version of the song in 1959. My favorite song in her repertoire was "Moon River"—she would put her heart and soul into it, smiling when she came to the part about "two drifters, off to see the world." After my dad died, she told the hospice chaplain how much she loved the song, and that it was a reminder of her and Dad, when they were young, because they were two drifters off to see the world.

Mum was a good singer, and according to the stories, during the war she had a chance to go for the big time when a well-known London music promoter heard her singing in a pub that was more of a club. That was the pub Uncle Jim came into one night when he was home on leave from the Royal Marines, a coincidence that ended with him grabbing my seventeen-year-old mother by her collar as she came off the stage, and telling her to go home and never let him see her in a place like that again. That's big brothers for you. Mum told me that she knew how it was going to end as she was singing. She had been looking around the room, at the audience watching her, and then in the wide mirror behind the bar she saw her brother's reflection as he walked in with some of his mates. Apparently she tried to turn so he wouldn't see her face, which was futile because he would have known that voice anywhere. But on VJ Day, as street parties erupted across London and the rest of the country and then went on all night, people in

Mum's neighborhood carried an upright piano from one street to the next so she could really get the celebrations going. Mum could play piano by ear, but the only piano she ever owned was left at Black Bush Cottage on the night they left following Dad's row with the farmer.

A couple of years ago, I was visiting my cousin Larry when we began talking about those good times of family and parties and everyone coming down to see us; days when he and his brother would run around the corner to play with the Saunders' boys as soon as Uncle John had parked the pale blue Austin Cambridge motor car. I reminded him about the time he and his brother had tied Martine and me to a tree because we were supposed to be Indians in the Wild West, and they ran off on some expedition only to forget all about us. It was later, when Martine and I failed to turn up for tea and were not responding to calls from the attic window, that Mum and Auntie Sylvie had come looking for us and found us still tied to the tree, happily chatting to each other as if we'd only just been abandoned. We'd been sitting on the damp ground down by the stream, bound by an old rope for hours.

"You know, we used to visit you a lot because of your mum," said Larry. "Her brothers and sisters knew she was lonely, living in the country."

I sat back in my chair—we were having lunch at a pub in Whitchurch, Hampshire, where Larry lives—and I let his words settle in my mind. *She was lonely*. Was she? It had never occurred to me that my mother could have been lonely, but of course she must have been. She had been raised in a big family, amid the noise and energy of a city, in a tight neighborhood, and my father—who had always lived in a quiet house, and who was essentially a quiet man—was completely happy in the country. Now I wonder if she felt as I often feel living here in California, miles away from my roots—*neither here nor there*. She didn't want to live in London any more, yet she missed so much of what she'd left behind.

My mother was a gregarious woman, a woman of sharp intellect and a killer wit. In just a few years she had gone from having a good government job and spending time with her family or friends—where she was often the center of attention—to doing back-breaking work on the farm. Now her only social life was with the clutch of other women she worked with on the farm and an hour or so of community interaction in the town on a Saturday morning. Was it any wonder that she loved to entertain people with her yarns, recounting her own past, warts and all, or making up tales for the kids on the long journey back from the farm, or retelling stories she'd heard from the other farm worker women as we sat down for our tea in the evening? I knew all about Gladys's life as a Land Girl, how she was conscripted in the war to join the women who kept farms running when men left for the services, and how she and the other girls were out on the farm where they'd been billeted and had been dying for a pee, so had rushed into the bushes to squat down— only to find they'd chosen a place with a massive nest of red ants, so they all ended up with sore bums. I loved that one. And I knew a lot about Shirl, who'd been "on the stage" at thirteen, and would have gone home with a man just to get a decent meal. It was a while before I knew what the bit about "going home with a man" meant, but I knew it wasn't a good thing for Shirl to have done that at thirteen.

Everything was grist to Mum's story mill. Indeed, it has only been since I began to write this memoir that I have reconsidered the power of storytelling on so many levels. Of course, we know a story can change even a nation—the stories told by politicians, especially tyrants, dictators and despots, have sent young men and women to perish on battlefields for millennia. Countries and peoples have been brought to their knees by stories, and equally they have been given the strength to rise up, to endure and to show strength beyond measure. But as much as stories bring warmth to our days, help us find our voices or work things out, stories—even the ones considered entertaining—can also damage, create doubt, cause an aching distress or a wounding humiliation. Words have the potential to cause such pain, it's a wonder the dictionary doesn't come with a government health warning.

"Sticks and stones may break my bones, but words will never hurt me." So said my father when I came home upset after being called names at school. It was a good mantra to offer a child who had no choice but to return to school the next day, and at a time when parents would never pay a visit to the teacher to complain about bullying—if you had a problem, you had to sort it out yourself. Yes, the verse was temporary balm, even though it was wrong. Words have always hurt me. When I was young and alone, I wished my cousins were just around the corner, so I could take the whole gang from London to school with me so other kids— one or two in particular—knew I had an army at my back.

14

This Time Next Year
We'll Be Laughing

ᘓᕈ

While Dad was in Germany, blowing up those bridges and enemy communication lines, he managed to get rust remover into a cut on his hand and a severe infection developed. He was sent home to recover for a couple of weeks, stepping off the boat wearing a "medical blue" uniform—the colors that let the civilian population know that a man was not a shirker, not a conchie—a conscientious objector—but a soldier wounded in the course of his duty. The special uniform was an attempt to avoid what had happened in the 1914–1918 war, when women gave white feathers to men not in uniform. The trouble was that many of those men not wearing uniforms had in fact been to war and come home with wounds that were not visible, or were only apparent when a man turned to the woman with the feather and the sharp tongue, to reveal half a face, a jaw torn away or sockets with no eyes inside them.

I first heard that story when I was ten, in Mr. Leech's class at primary school. He was telling us about the White Feather Movement. It was in that same lesson he told us that when he was a boy, he was on a bus in London and it was only when the young man sitting next to him turned to ask if he could squeeze past to get off at the next stop that he saw the devastating wounds the man had suffered in the 1914–1918 war. Half the man's face had been obliterated. I never forgot that lesson, never forgot the image conjured up by my teacher, and added it to my cache of things about war to be sad about. Perhaps even then I was collecting other people's memories in the way that some children collect shells, to look at, to remove from the jar and turn over time and again. I sometimes reflect and wonder, was it ever a surprise that such terrible facial wounds were at the heart of my first novel?

My father was grateful for the respite, because he hated the noise and the hell of working with explosives. With the war edging toward a close and the London he came home to bomb-scarred beyond belief, I wonder if that might have been the first time he uttered the words, "Never mind—this time next year, we'll be laughing." It was one of his favorite phrases, and it sums up not only his own attitude to life, but an attitude of a whole generation who lived through the darkest of times.

I remember the very moment those words were spoken by my dad as he put an arm around my mother's shoulders, followed by an all-knowing wink—it would seem as if I were in a movie, with shafts of light pouring through the window onto our table of plenty. I could see it in my mind's eye. All would be well in our world, and there we would be, the Winspears, clutching our sides with mirth, joyous at our good fortune, at the abundance raining down upon the house at the end of The Terrace. And it would all happen by this time next year. Not so long to wait, though it seemed that as I approached my sixth year, freedom from worry couldn't come fast enough.

I sometimes wonder at what point my mother decided to go to the doctor about the weight loss and coughing fits. Mum was shaking so much she could barely get a cup of tea to the table without dropping it. The sound of china hitting the thick Victorian terracotta tiles on the kitchen floor had become a regular refrain, and as this was before you could buy unbreakable crockery, Dad had started to buy our cups and saucers from a bloke who could get wholesale prices. Yet upon reflection, I think I know the exact moment the tipping point came. It was toward the end of the year I started school—the first term had just ended, and the women were out in the hop gardens clearing old bines and burning them, ready for the men to start stringing, come spring. Using a long pole with a hook to guide the heavy string, each man would work part of the hop garden, weaving a geometric pattern for the young hop bines to grow up and around. Each cluster of shoots, known as a "hill," had a loop of sturdy metal secured in the ground, and with the pole, the man would guide the string through that metal loop and up so that it was attached to the wires that criss-crossed the hop garden some fifteen feet above the ground. The movement was rhythmic—up and down, up and down, stringing each hill with four long lines before moving onto the next hill a few feet away. When that job was done, the women would follow with the banding in, pulling the four strings together at shoulder height with another shorter string to form a square, before tying off and moving to the next hill. The banding-in was required to maintain tension in the stringing and to bear the increasing weight of the growing hop bine.

But for now we were gathering the piles of spent bines from the previous season and burning them. It was another cold day and the women had started a wood fire down near the tractor shed so the children could be kept warm. At dinner time—midday—Mum half-opened a tin of Ambrosia Creamed Rice Pudding and pushed it in between the glowing embers; a warm pudding for my brother and me to share following a toasted sandwich. I'd found a good thick hazel branch to use as a toasting fork and broken off the ends, leaving a Y shape for Mum to stick through a cheese sandwich. She would hand the fork back to me and I'd start to toast our sandwiches on the open fire, watching as melted cheese dropped into the flames. The other women began handing out sandwiches to their children and settling in for their own repast and a cup of tea from a thermos flask, the kind with a glass insert to keep the beverage warm. Mum dropped our flasks at least once a week, so Fred Cooke had ordered in more stock of the replacement glass linings at a cheaper price for us.

The gathered women started talking about the work, how long it might take to finish Hawkhurst field before they moved onto Mullpits field and then the Upper Eight and Bedgebury Field. I don't even know if that's how you spell the name "Mullpits"—it might have been "Molepits" or perhaps "Mowpits." If you'd asked each of those women to spell the name, you'd have received five different versions.

Then during a lull in the conversation while everyone was eating, Joan looked across at my mother and said, "You know, Joyce, you've got really expressive eyes."

My mother gave her a look I knew only too well and I swear the birds stopped singing. I held my breath, because I knew what was coming. "What you mean is that my eyes are popping out of my sodding head!" said Mum, and she threw our flask at the wall of the tractor shed, the sound of the glass liner shattering as she walked off into the woods.

I stood up to run after her, but Auntie Glad caught me by the arm and told me to let my mother be. Then she turned to Joan and said, "That was a blimmin' stupid thing to say—can't you see she's not well?"

Because Dad had taken on night work as well as his job with Abnett's Painting and Decorating, John and I went on the bus with Mum to the doctor's surgery the following evening. I watched as "Woodie"—that's what everyone called Dr. Wood, who had delivered John—felt around Mum's throat and said "Hmmmm." Then he looked into her eyes and said the same thing.

"Stand up, please, Joyce."

Mum stood up.

"Hold out your arms, hands flat, like this, and see if you can keep them still." He demonstrated, looking like a cartoon ghost I'd seen on the television. I knew for a fact that real ghosts looked nothing like that.

My mum held out her arms, hands flat. Only she couldn't keep them still. They moved up and down, shaking.

"Hmmm," said Dr. Wood.

He told her to sit down, and as he took his own seat, he told her that he was referring her to a specialist at the Kent and Sussex Hospital and that she probably had an overactive thyroid. He asked if there was any in the family, and she told him that several of her sisters were having thyroid trouble and it seemed to appear after the birth of their second child.

"Hmmm," he said, again.

He wrote notes on a card and pushed it back into the buff envelope that was her medical record, but Mum wasn't quite ready to leave. The bus fare was money and money was usually in short supply, so going to the doctor was a bit like shopping as far as my mother was concerned—you made sure to get a few things sorted out at the same time.

"And could you look at Jackie's eyes. I think she has a lazy eye, but I'm not sure which, because they can both cast out to the side, but not all the time. And she's seeing double."

Dr. Wood looked at me. "Seeing double! Seeing double!" His eyebrows rose and I knew he was about to become the children's doctor, with a ready smile and a joke. "Comes in handy when you're looking at shillings! Now then, let's have a look at those nails first, young lady." He reached for my hand and I knew he was taking my pulse, something he always did before anything else. Then he gave the back of my hand a gentle slap. "No biting the nails. I want proper fingernails by the time I see you again, otherwise it's bitter apple for you!"

I giggled, though I had no idea what bitter apple was and I didn't like the sound of the word "bitter."

"Right, let's have a look at those eyes." Everything was "let's" and "we" with Dr. Wood. A few years later, he asked my then six-year-old brother, "How are we today?" and John replied, "I don't know about you, mate, but I'm all right."

My mother realized I had an eye problem one evening before Dad came home from work. I was sitting at the kitchen table with my *Janet and John* book from school, reading aloud for Mum while she sliced carrots into soup. Soup was always made in the pressure cooker, but because we'd lost the valve that controlled pressure inside the pan, she used an old knitting needle in its place, sticking it in the hole where the valve should be placed, so the pointed end of the needle faced upward out of the lid. It never quite held the increased steam inside. Under pressure that knitting needle was known to shoot up with a loud bang and stick into the ceiling. I was reading to her because although I had started school ahead of the other children, I was now falling behind with my reading, and falling behind at school was not acceptable to my mother.

"Jackie, why are you reading with your head sideways, as if you're only looking out of one eye?"

I raised my head from my book. "So I can see the words properly."

She rubbed her hands on a tea towel and came to stand behind me. She placed one hand on either side of my head and directed my gaze to the mantelpiece above the stove.

"How many pepper pots can you see?

"Um . . . two."

"How many clocks?"

"There's only one clock, Mum."

"I know—but how many can you see?"

Tears welled up.

"Tell me how many, Jackie—come on, love. Everything will be all right."

"Two."

She let go of my head, and pointed to the page.

"What happens when you look at the page with both eyes?"

I pointed to a line. "That word gets mixed up with that word."

"But you can see the words. Are they blurry?"

"No. Just mixed up."

She sat down and put her arm around me.

"Everything'll be all right, love," she said again. I could feel her ribs sticking into my shoulder as she held me close.

"My head hurts," I said. I'd been getting headaches lately too.

"I'll get you a junior aspirin."

She stood up, pulled out a chair and reached up to the top of the kitchen cabinet where medicines were kept well out of the way of little children. Well, sort of well out of the way. A few weeks earlier Mum had come into the kitchen to find my eighteen-month-old brother had pushed a chair next to the freestanding cabinet, which was of 1930s vintage, and using the doors as if they were steps, he was hanging on by one hand and reaching for the bright crimson lorry-shaped bottle of junior aspirin. Mum wrote to the company to tell them they shouldn't put dangerous medicines in bottles that would tempt children to reach for them. She was sent a box containing samples of all the company's products, with enough junior aspirin in plain bottles to last me through many headaches, which was just as well. Mum would become expert at getting free stuff through the technique of a well-written letter of complaint.

"And she's getting headaches," Mum continued.

The doctor picked up a pen that was also a little flashlight, and with a finger under my chin to keep my head still, he asked me to follow the tiny beam of light with my eyes. As I looked from left to right, up and down, he asked more questions.

"How often do you get these headaches, Jackie?"

"I don't know. Sometimes."

"When do they start—do you know?"

"Sometimes in the sunshine." I paused, trying to remember. "Sometimes when I'm reading, and sometimes on a Monday, when the school's clean?"

"Isn't the school always clean? I'll have to send someone in there with a mop!" said Dr. Wood.

I giggled. "No. On Mondays there's more smell."

"More smell?"

"More disinfectanty smell."

"Ah, I see."

"Do you hurt anywhere else when you get a headache?"

"I feel sick. And I get lights."

"Lights?" He released my chin, switched off the flashlight pen and put it on the desk. "What lights?"

"Squiggly. Like the telly when the tube's gone."

I looked over at my mother, then back at Dr. Wood.

"Jackie, I think you're getting something called a migraine. It's not usual for little children to get them, and when you're older, they'll probably go away. But when you get one, you've got to tell

Mummy so she can give you an aspirin, and then she's going to take you to your bedroom to lay down for a while, and she's going to close the curtains and put a nice cold cloth on your forrid until it's gone." He said "forehead" just like the verse.

There once was a girl
Who had a little curl
Right in the middle of her forrid
When she was good
She was very, very good
And when she was bad
She was horrid.

Looking back, I think it was his way of settling children, not speaking over them with instructions to the parent, instead telling a child what was the best remedy for something while at the same time letting the parent know what they must do. Perhaps he said "forrid" because he knew my headaches were horrid.

So began our regular visits to the Kent and Sussex Hospital in Tunbridge Wells, my mother having written to the two departments—endocrinology for her overactive thyroid, and opthalmology for my wandering eyes—so that our appointments could be coordinated because the bus fare was expensive.

The journey by bus was an ordeal, because motion sickness rendered me tired and weary, even if I clutched Mum's magic penny. I wasn't allowed to take Kwells, the tablets for motion sickness, because they made me too sleepy for my appointment. As soon as the bus stopped in Tunbridge Wells, our entourage of three—Mum, me and John—would go straight to Woolworths so Mum could use the big red weighing machine with its giant dial. Mum would look around to see if anyone was watching, then give me her bag to hold before placing my brother's hand in mine. She would step on the scale, put a penny in the slot and watch the needle. After registering her weight she would step off with tears in her eyes.

"Right, then, we've got to hurry now." And she would rush us up to the hospital for my appointment, which always came first.

On my first visit, after my initial examination by Mr. Coogan, a large man with half-moon glasses and a light that seemed to come right out of his forehead, I was sent to Miss Trew. Mr. Coogan was an important man; we knew this because he was a "mister" and not just a "doctor." In Britain, when a doctor climbs the ladder to become a specialist of high enough standing to be a surgeon, then they are known as "mister" again. I still don't get it. For her part, Miss Trew was the orthoptist, a highly skilled practitioner of non-surgical conditions involving eye movement. I had to get some of that information from Wikipedia, because at the time I only knew that the lovely Miss Trew was the woman who guided me through a series of exercises with a pen light just like Dr. Wood's. Then came the special machine. It was black, and reminded me of a crouching reptile, a frog perhaps. I was instructed to put my chin on a chin-shaped little ledge and look into a viewer, then I was to follow her instructions using handles on the left and right of the machine, while she slotted slides into a viewer at each side. A dog and a kennel. A rabbit and a hutch. A man and a house. Miss Trew would ask me to put the dog in the kennel, and then she'd fiddle with her dials and the dog would be out of his kennel, so I had to put it in there again. And again, and again. Same with the rabbit and the hutch and the man with his house—oh, that rabbit, especially, could be a frisky little fellow, getting out of that darn hutch as soon as I'd managed to get him in there.

While I was in with Miss Trew, Mum took John with her to the man she called the "thyroid bloke."

That first day at the Kent and Sussex Hospital sticks in my mind, as does recounting it to Dad, when he came home from work. I was in the dining room—we called it the "middle room" because it was the middle of the three downstairs rooms, situated between the kitchen and sitting room—curled up in an old armchair that my mother used to sit in while nursing my brother when he was a baby. It was a soft chair, one you could sink into and that seemed to envelop you with comfort if you were ill—or if your head hurt. When we arrived home, Mum had covered me with a blanket and placed a cold compress on my eyes in a half-darkness, because the curtains had been drawn and the junior aspirin was doing its best to work magic with my migraine. I liked using this new word to describe the pounding in my head. I heard Mum tell Dad that they were trying to correct my vision with exercises and I had to do them at home, too. I was to wear an eye patch at school for a while—and if that wasn't an open invitation to my bullies, I don't know what was. She explained that when I'd reached a certain point, Mr. Coogan would operate. That sounded bad. Then she said something about herself and radioactive iodine, followed by, "They said they'd probably have to take it out, and I told them I wasn't having that done. Not on your life!" I heard the pressure cooker begin to hiss. "They're not taking my effing thyroid out so I've got a sodding great scar on my neck." Then the needle torpedoed from the pressure cooker and hit the ceiling.

I think it was "radioactive iodine" that really scared me. I knew what radiation was because I'd watched a science program on the telly. It was all about nuclear bombs, so I'd asked Mum if she knew about these bombs and she said they were made from radioactivity, and then told me all about a very brave woman called Marie Curie. My mum always went the whole hog when you asked her about something, so I ended up thinking that Marie

Curie could help my mum with her thyroid, a word that from the start I'd never really heard properly. I called it her "rawhide" because that was a word I could say, given that *Rawhide* was Dad's favorite TV show and we watched it with him every Saturday evening. Well, on Saturdays when the tube hadn't gone.

After months of fortnightly appointments, Mum was still thin, but not losing more weight, and it soon became time for Mr. Coogan to operate on my eyes. Dad gave me a long cuddle on the Monday morning Mum, John and I set off on the early bus, with my change of clothes, pajamas, face cloth and toothbrush in a carrier bag. The night before, Mum had pulled out the tin bath and filled it with hot water from the copper at the side of the stove, so I would be "nice and clean" for the hospital. That bath came out every evening, so I was already nice and clean, as far as I was concerned. She'd even bought me a new dress, navy blue with little kick pleats just above the hem, and a white Peter Pan collar set off by a bow of thin red ribbon. I had new white socks and wore my school shoes—the only good shoes I had, because if I wasn't at school, I only needed plimsolls, my jelly sandals or my rubber boots. I would be in the hospital until Saturday morning, and Mum had already explained that she'd see me again when she came to collect me—the fare was a lot of money to come visiting. I understood. I was an independent child so I wasn't scared. Not really. Well, perhaps a little.

Here's what I remember about that stay in hospital. I wasn't put into a children's ward, because children having eye surgery were not allowed to run about and play, and had to remain still. Despite being subject to early 1960s hospital discipline, the children's ward could be a bit boisterous, because it was understood that play and fun could help children get better. I was put into a room with an elderly lady who was having something done to her eyelashes, which were growing into her eyes. Now that scared me—perhaps more than the radioactive iodine my mum was taking, courtesy of a woman named Marie Curie. "Never mind, love," my dad had said to Mum. "You might save us money on the electric bill when you start to glow." The eyelash lady would only be in the bed next to me for twenty-four hours after her operation. I had to stay for all sorts of reasons—my age, the fact that I had to keep quiet and still after they'd done whatever they were going to do to sort out my vision, and I had to ease back slowly into using my eyes after surgery. In short, they wanted to keep an eye on me.

The room had Beatrix Potter characters on the walls, which I thought was a bit babyish, though it was a little more welcoming for children coming in for eye surgery and who couldn't be placed in the ward with other children. Across the corridor was a large ward with a sign for "Men's Surgical" and at the far end of a long hallway was "Women's Surgical." I had no idea what those things meant. In between was the sterilizing room with something called an "autoclave" and there was also "Sister's Office" as well as a kitchen and a break room for the nurses.

The morning after the operation my eyes were stuck together underneath big pads and I couldn't make them open no matter how hard I tried. Then my favorite nurse came in—I recognized her by her soft voice. She was tall and blonde and wore her hair in a French twist under her cap. I knew from *Emergency Ward 10* on TV, which I watched every week, that her ornate belt meant she was the Staff Nurse, just one promotion away from being a Sister—who had responsibility for that whole floor of wards. It was a matriarchal system, and you never saw nurses move so fast as when word went around that Matron was on her way to inspect the ward. Even doctors could get shaky when Matron was on her rounds—especially the younger ones, who Matron always saw fit to put in their place. The following year, I wrote to Matron asking her if I could be a nurse at the hospital when I left school, and she kindly replied, encouraging me to study hard for my O levels first. Some years later, when I was a live-in volunteer at a residential school for disabled children, most of whom had spent a good deal of their childhood in hospital, I understood why almost all the girls wanted to become nurses at Great Ormond Street Hospital for Children when they grew up. Nurses were the source of comfort at the scariest of times.

I liked the caps the nurses wore and the navy blue capes with a red lining they'd put on when they came on duty, or left at the end of a shift. I also liked the idea of living away from The Terrace in a nurses' home with other girls. From *Emergency Ward 10*, I knew nurses had lots of fun when they weren't running with bedpans back and forth to that thing called an autoclave.

Staff Nurse lifted away the pads and with soft cotton cloths she bathed my eyes until all the sticky stuff was gone. I'd never felt such smooth hands against my skin—it was a luxurious sensation. I hated the eye drops that followed, but I loved the way she helped me out of bed and took me by the hand to the bathroom, where she ran a bath for me and made me feel so cocooned with caring. Every day Staff Nurse came to my room in the morning, switched on the hospital radio and bathed the sticky stuff from my crusty eyes so I could open them. I loved her. And so did Mike, the male nurse. I knew Nurse Mike loved her because of the way he looked at her and made her blush, which made him blush too. He was tall and young and good looking, and as he walked down the corridor toward Men's Surgical he'd spot Staff Nurse in the corridor and start singing "Be-bop-a-lula, She's My Baby," glancing in to see me, as if he meant the song for me, but I knew it was for my Staff Nurse.

On the third day Staff Nurse let me help with taking round the Guinness to the patients in Men's Surgical, only I didn't touch the bottles of Guinness. Instead I helped with filling the water glasses. It was common for hospitals to give patients—especially the men—one bottle of Guinness each day if the doctor decreed it could be tolerated, because it's filled with vitamins and it lifted the spirits, in the same way that a bit of play helped the children. Years later, when my mother was admitted to the local hospice, the doctor came in to see her and the first thing she asked was, "Would you like a drink, Mrs. Winspear?" My mother smiled at the doctor, a coy smile. "Do you mean, a *drink* drink?" The doctor nodded. "Well, then," said my mother, "I wouldn't mind a nice cream sherry." So the doctor left the room and came back with a nice cream sherry for a dying woman.

One day I got Nurse Mike into trouble. I wasn't allowed to read and I wasn't supposed to run, but by day four I was getting a bit fizzy. I loved the hospital radio, and I loved it when Nurse Mike passed and heard a song he liked, because he'd come in and we'd sing together, especially if it was my favorite, "Little White Bull," by Tommy Steele, which seemed to be playing all the time. And of course, we liked Tommy Steele in our house, because he was a Bermondsey boy—local boy made good from my parents' part of London. Nurse Mike would sing along with Tommy, and I'd join in to shout the refrain: *Little White Bull!*

The singing was all very well until the day I decided to run to find Staff Nurse. Was I about to try matchmaking? Probably not deliberately, but I loved to watch him sing when she walked by. I ran from the room and Nurse Mike came after me, calling out for me to stop. I thought he was chasing me in fun, so I giggled and ran a bit faster, but came tumbling down to the floor with a great whack that brought Staff Nurse from the kitchen just as Nurse Mike bent down to pick me up.

"What do you think you're doing?" she asked, hands on hips.

"It wasn't Nurse Mike," I confessed. "I ran."

"Well, now you've got to lie down on your bed."

Poor Nurse Mike was told to sort out Mr. So-and-so in Men's Surgical, and Staff Nurse took me to my room, where I had to rest on my bed with the curtains drawn and the radio off. I woke up when I heard voices in the corridor outside my room. Auntie Iris, Dad's cousin, had come with Uncle Reg, her husband. They were my godparents, and had come down from London on their motorbike to see me, bringing me a gift. A gift! A gift for having an eye operation! It was a small overnight case with a rounded top of the type fashionable with women at the time. Auntie Iris used one for her knitting and I'd admired it weeks ago when they'd visited us—that bag fetish meant I was very observant when it came to women's bags and purses. At that point they didn't have children, so they often came to see me, their only godchild. I don't remember much about the visit, except they were both wearing leather jackets and trousers, and carried crash helmets. Uncle Reg was a policeman and was apparently an expert police driver, so they always had crash helmets, which at that time were not required under the law. But I loved that case and was thrilled to have something better than a carrier bag to take my clothes home in. And going home was getting closer.

My mother held me to her when she walked into the room on the day of my discharge, and I discovered later it was because looking at my blood-filled eyes and the large bruises that extended down to my cheeks had almost caused her to faint, though she wasn't the fainting sort. I didn't know how my eyes looked, because there were no mirrors in the bathrooms. My parents had been warned to remove all mirrors in the house until my eyes had healed. I was given a pair of special sunglasses to wear as I left the hospital, and was instructed to keep them on whenever I went outside in the sunshine, just for a few weeks. Mum let me wear my new navy blue dress home, and Staff Nurse had braided my hair. I knew I would miss her soft hands around my eyes in the morning because my mother's were rough and worn from the farm.

Though I had no idea what my eyes looked like, I knew something was wrong when we stopped outside a shop on the way to the bus stop. I was in the shade, so I thought it was okay for me to take off the dark glasses. A woman passing gasped and frowned at my mother.

"If you think that girl wearing those glasses is going to stop people knowing you've beaten your child, you've got another think coming."

I know my mother was about to give the woman "a piece of her mind" and it might have even been "a mouthful," which was a much bigger piece of her mind altogether. But instead she turned to me,

"Put your glasses on, Jackie—you know what the doctor said. And tell the lady why you're wearing them."

I looked at the woman through a foggy dark veil. "I had my eyes operated on so I could see properly."

The woman put her hand to her mouth and rushed away.

"Silly cow," said my mother. Then added. "But I'm glad she noticed. Next time it could be another child, and she could be right." Mum looked at her watch, and slapped it to make sure the time was right. "Come on, let's go to British Home Stores for a cup of tea before we get the bus."

Dad was anxious to see me so he came home early—he always worked on Saturdays—and he didn't go out to work at his second job after tea that night. He was hardly able to talk when I ran into his arms, because seeing my poor black and blue eyes and cheeks had startled him.

"Come on, let's have a look at these new eyes," he said when he'd caught his breath. Having pulled me away to inspect the doctor's handiwork, he told me they were smashing eyes, that old Coogan had done me proud. He looked up at Mum and held me close again. "Never mind, love," he assured me. "It's over now, and anyway, you watch—this time next year, we'll be laughing."

Dad had thrown out that mystical line into the future once again, the grappling hook landing in the rock of tomorrow, ready for us to pull ourselves in toward better times. At once the kitchen seemed to light up and the table was filled with plenty. All would be well. We just had to wait another year.

Then the knitting needle exploded out of the pressure cooker and hit the ceiling.

15

The Fledgling Writer

◈

I decided I wanted to be a writer on one of those long journeys to and from the ophthalmology department at the Kent and Sussex Hospital in Tunbridge Wells. Mum hated being on the top deck of the bus, but on our return journey, she always gave in to my brother's desire to sit upstairs right at the front so he could pretend to be the driver. By the time we clambered aboard, I was so tired, I just wanted to fall asleep with my head resting on my mother's lap as she ran her hand across my hair.

As the bus rumbled along following my first day as an ophthalmology department patient, I had almost drifted off, my eyes weary from putting the rabbit in the hutch, the dog in the kennel and the horse in the stable, time and time again. I was nursing a migraine from following the tiny light and Miss Trew's pointed finger—up and down, side to side, here to there. Soon the bus pulled up to a halt for Pembury passengers to get off and new passengers to get on. I glanced down into the bay window of the Edwardian villa situated alongside the bus stop, then sat up to take account of what I saw before me. A desk was situated in the bay window to the right of the door, probably to take advantage of the light, even though there was a tall hedge between the villa's small front garden and the street—I could only see in because I was on the top deck of the bus. There was a typewriter on the desk, a pile of books to one side and sheaf of papers on the other. There was a sheet of paper in the typewriter. A cup and saucer had been set just in front of the books and a cardigan had been draped over the back of the chair. Every wall in the room beyond was covered with bookcases. I didn't think ordinary people could own so many books. I could just about see coals burning in the fireplace. Whoever lived in the house had probably just left that room. I wanted very much to see the person who owned all the books—but the bus moved off.

A fortnight later, I was ready at the bus window when we reached Pembury. Some of the books had been moved from the desk and a clutch of papers had been laid across the top of the type-writer. There was a cup and saucer as before, and a fire alight in the grate.

"Mum—Mum, come here." I was sitting farther back in the bus than my mother and brother, who were right at the front, my brother's hands stretched out, gripping that imaginary steering wheel.

My mother turned around. "What is it? Do you feel sick? I've got a magic penny for you."

I shook my head and beckoned to my mother. "Come here, quick . . . quick, before the bus leaves again."

Mum left her seat and leaned across me to look in the direction I was pointing.

"Who do you think lives in that house?"

She stared, squinting her eyes. "I reckon that's a writer's study—yes, I would imagine a writer lives there."

I nodded, staring at the typewriter, the desk, the pile of books, the sheaf of papers, and the cup and saucer. Then I looked at the library beyond, and the fireplace with hot coals in the grate. I loved this room.

"I'm going to be a writer when I grow up," I declared.

My mother didn't miss a beat. "Well, you'll need another string to your bow, my girl. Something to fall back on, if you want to be a writer. Be a teacher, or something like that. You can't just be a starving writer in a garret."

Then she sat down beside me. I rested my head on her lap, tired and starting to feel sick again, so she pressed a magic penny into my palm. As my brother made engine sounds at the front of the bus, turning a steering wheel only he could see, I closed my eyes and fell asleep wondering what a second string to your bow meant. I'd have to find out, because I was determined to become a writer one day, even if I had to starve in a garret, whatever that was.

I began to collect the things I'd need for my writer's room. Fred Cooke gave me the old ledger style desk that his daughter, Lyn, had outgrown, and I snagged a chair from the dining room, which was fine because the only time we sat down at the table was at Christmas or when all the family came to visit and the kids were sequestered in there to eat their Sunday dinner with the door closed so the adults could talk in peace. Mrs. Croft gave me an ancient anglepoise lamp with an ornate copper shade that sent a shock through my arm the first time I plugged it in. Soon I was lobbying for a typewriter, and by the Christmas of my ninth year, Mum had saved enough of her Kensitas cigarette coupons to get me the blue-and-white Petite Junior Typewriter, designed especially for children. I would sit at that desk, set a cup of tea to my right, casually drape a cardigan across the back of the chair—just like the writer who lived by the bus stop in Pembury had done. I'd slip a sheet of paper into the platen, zing it back to the paragraph stop, and begin to tap away. Mum had been teaching me to touch-type.

I didn't say anything more about my plans to become a writer—I knew I'd just get a lot of talk about second strings to my bow—though it was clear I loved composition at school, where we wrote our essays about what we'd done over the weekend, or were tasked with making up a story. I could get lost in books to the extent that I would hide so my mother couldn't find me when I was deep into a novel—if she saw me, she would have a job for me. I had three favorite places to hide. One was in the big lilac tree outside the back door of the house, though that only worked in summer when the tree was in full leaf and blossom. My memory of *Little Women*, in particular, is laced with the sweet fragrance of lilac. I remember my mother coming to the back door to call me in, and watching her become more frustrated at my non-appearance.

"Jackie! Jackie! I've got a job for you." Pause. "Jackie—I know you're somewhere with your nose in a book. Where are you? If you don't come in, I'm going to find you, and then you'll know all about it."

But I was already a Jo March and on that day I just kept very still and did not turn another page until she'd gone indoors, complaining to herself.

Another place was a space at the top of the stairs that led from the kitchen to the dining room. There was one shelf in that space, which was visible if the door to the dining room—to the left of the staircase—was closed. But if that door was open, you wouldn't know the space was even there. I could snuggle into the cavern under the shelf, draw the door that led into the dining room back on itself and no one would guess I was tucked away in the small secret place. Not only could I read in peace, leaning to take advantage of light coming through the bannister from the kitchen, but I could listen to all manner of conversations, especially if someone had dropped by, a neighbor or someone my dad worked for.

Perhaps the darkest of my secret places was the hole in the wide privet hedge at the bottom of the garden. I could literally crawl inside the hedge and no one would see me there. Except the spiders, so I dragged in an old sack to sit on, leaning to one side to catch the shaft of sunlight illuminating the pages. That's how I met the girl who was visiting her grandmother, who lived in the large house on the other side of the hedge. The girl's name was Clarissa and we became great friends, playing together every time she came to stay with her grandmother—Clarissa's father was in the army overseas, so she and her brother were at boarding school in England. They would come home to the grandmother's house during school holidays and sometimes at weekends. Her grandfather lived in Ceylon—now Sri Lanka—managing the family's tea plantation. I loved visiting Clarissa's grandmother's house, not least because she had a library—or at least shelves and shelves of books. One day I was leafing through the collection, waiting for Clarissa to come downstairs—she'd been sent to change into her old clothes as we were going down to the woods to play. Her grandmother allowed me to look at the books because she knew I handled them with care. When I picked up a book by Vita Sackville-West I read the inscription inside, which was in a firm hand and clearly indicated that this book was a personal gift from "Vita" to Clarissa's grandmother. I already knew the famous writer had lived in Sissinghurst, on the other side of Cranbrook, so I was intrigued enough to ask about it.

"I was once her secretary," said Clarissa's grandmother.

I felt a shiver of excitement as I held the book in my hands. I was just a hair closer to my dream—I knew someone who knew someone who was a really famous author. If I'd known about "degrees of separation" in those days, I would have been jettisoned to the moon on the excitement building inside me.

One of the most intriguing elements about going to play at Clarissa's grandmother's house was her great aunt, or perhaps she was even a great-great-great aunt, a woman I'll call Raven. She had that sort of name—one word, which wasn't her real name, but the name she had been known by her entire life. And she was birdlike—very thin, with purple wrist bones that seemed as if they would detach from her liver-spotted hands if she so much as sneezed. Raven dressed in clothes more suited to Victorian times, in long skirts, high neck blouses with a shawl around her shoulders, and sometimes she wore a little cap on slate-grey hair pulled back into a bun. She was very old, or so it appeared to both Clarissa and me. She moved quietly through the house. The first time I was aware of her immediate presence, I was walking with Clarissa from the drawing room through the dining room and saw the hem of her long skirt as she closed the door that led from the kitchen into the part of the house that was her private domain. She fascinated me. I didn't know anyone like her and I wanted to know more.

One day, Clarissa came round to ask if I could go out to play, and as we walked down the footpath toward Five Acres, she told me that, "Raven wants us to have tea with her this afternoon." I felt a ripple of curiosity spiral into my chest and could not wait until three o'clock, the allotted hour when we would knock on the door alongside the dining room to be admitted to the small attached cottage that was Raven's home.

That afternoon, dead on three o'clock, Clarissa knocked on Raven's door. I was at her shoulder, taller than Clarissa and leaning in to listen.

"Come," the voice instructed.

Clarissa pushed against the door and we stepped into a hallway that opened to a dark sitting room. Raven was seated on a sofa next to a cold fireplace. She was covered in newspapers and had just sat up from a sleeping position as we entered. A teapot, milk jug and three cups and saucers had been placed on a small table in front of the sofa by the housekeeper, who had probably returned to the main house by another door. There seemed to be nooks and crannies and doors everywhere.

"Sit down, Clarissa. And you, Jacqueline."

The room was dark, a window at the far end offering little light—hardly surprising as the curtains were almost closed. Another window to the right provided a shaft of illumination, lighting up dust motes that seemed to dance as we took our seats. A staircase led upstairs, but apparently Raven did not sleep there— another ground floor room I could not see was her bedroom and somewhere there was a bathroom—at least I think there was; it was very dark in Raven's domain.

I have no recollection of the conversation, apart from being asked about school, about what I liked to read and the sort of questions elders ask children. Then Clarissa asked if we could play in the attic and Raven, now becoming tired, said we could. I looked back as we made our way up a rickety staircase that narrowed as we reached the door to the attic, a large room in the eaves of the house. As soon as she'd dismissed us, Raven had pulled the newspapers up and around her, as if she were snuggling under a blanket. As I cast my eyes around the room, I realized that every single piece of furniture had a label on it bearing the name of the family member to whom the piece would be given when she died, which at that particular moment didn't seem so far into the future. I ran up the stairs to catch up with Clarissa.

The attic was fascinating, and as time went on Clarissa and I would venture up those stairs many times, often sneaking in while Raven was asleep and creeping out again before she realized we'd been there. Every single time I went into that attic, I felt as if I were walking back in history, almost as if I'd landed in another country. There were trunks of old clothes that a young woman might have worn decades earlier, at the turn of the century. We tried on calf-length lace-up boots in fine cream leather, silk blouses and taffeta skirts. There were hats with feathers, gloves with little buttons at the wrist, and wonderful dresses. And there were the letters tied with red ribbon, written to a young woman from her love—and all bearing South African stamps. I knew enough history to conclude that the love of Raven's life had been lost in the Boer War, when she was probably in her late teens or early twenties. Clarissa wanted to undo the red ribbon and read each of the letters, but something stopped my growing curiosity in its tracks. Perhaps it was the single dried rose slipped underneath the crimson bow that secured the ribbon, but I felt that the letters were incredibly private, as a declaration of love between two people should be. A photograph of a young man in uniform was slipped under the bow of another clutch of letters, all bearing that same post mark. It was a studio photograph typical of the day, with the soldier standing alongside a large leafy plant on one side, and on the other a curtain draped behind him. I imagined he must have been a cavalry officer, given his uniform, tall boots and the crop he carried under his arm.

I loved going to Clarissa's house. Everything seemed so genteel. The children had their tea in the late afternoon—it was called a "nursery tea." I have vivid memories of one occasion when John and I were invited to join them—by now my brother had struck up a friendship with Clarissa's younger brother, Adam. It was summer and we were seated outside at a wicker table on Lloyd Loom chairs. Then we were given cold baked beans in bowls with brown bread and butter, and orange squash to drink. Both John and I were a little surprised, but whereas I wouldn't have said a word, my brother piped up.

"These beans are cold—they haven't even been cooked. And where's the proper tea?"

"What do you have for tea, John?" asked Clarissa's grandmother, setting a glass of orange squash in front of him.

"We have it cooked—meat and potatoes. Not cold beans."

She smiled and, I think, suppressed a giggle.

"I daresay you'll get some hot food when you get home."

I was mortified, so I kicked my brother under the table to keep quiet, but he yelped and said, "You kicked me!" I was only nine years old, but I knew that our tea was not their tea. We might all have been friends, yet I understood Clarissa and Adam were different. For a start they went to boarding schools. At that time I would have given anything to go to a boarding school, to live in a dormitory with other girls even if it meant cold showers in the morning—I'd never seen a shower anyway, so how bad could it be?

Whatever school held for me in the future, I was becoming more sure that one day I wanted to be a writer, and I knew the direction I would take. At school one day, when I was about nine years of age, the teacher began a lesson by asking each child what they wanted to be when they grew up. There were the usual firemen and policemen, soldiers and teachers, and secretaries, doctors and nurses, and one or two odd ones—a boy called Ronald wanted to race motorbikes and another boy wanted to be a Formula One mechanic at Brands Hatch. I think a few boys changed their minds when they heard those ambitions voiced, because we all knew who Jim Clark was, and if that boy became his mechanic, it would be something to talk about. Then the teacher pointed at me.

"Journalist," I said. "I want to be a reporter."

Jenny nudged me and giggled. She'd claimed "air hostess" and I was beginning to wish I had, too. Everyone was staring at me.

"Well I never," said the teacher. "A journalist, eh?"

I nodded. "I want to write about important things in the news."

She laughed. "You'll never get that with the *Kent Messenger!*"

And I remember thinking, *Kent Messenger*? I had my eye on Fleet Street. I knew my grandfather had worked for the *Daily Express*. However, some five years later, by the time I'd reached the age of fourteen, I would have given anything to get a job at the *Kent Messenger*, if I could. My ambition did not waver, though my future seemed set in stone when I reached sixteen, and a compulsory vocation test taken at school, designed to guide you in the direction of your ideal career path, indicated that I would be best suited to teaching.

Clarissa's grandmother moved away when I was about twelve and I never saw my friend again. However, it's probably true to say that those hours spent in Raven's attic—the immersion into an age gone by—gave me a mound of material for the writing that came later in my life. The hamlet seemed to be mainly old people in those days. An odd smattering of children moved into the neighborhood when I was in my early teens, though I didn't really know them because they were closer to my brother in age. I became friendly with the daughter of the pub's new landlord, but they moved after a couple of years and we lost touch, and then a boy a year older than me came to live in the house with orchards and paddocks that was situated on the other side of the footpath next to our end of terrace home, so we became friends, even an "item" for a while, before going our separate ways.

But the language and history of those old people remained

with me. There were the women of a certain age who were still "Miss" because a young man they might have married had been lost in the 1914–18 war. Following the war, in 1921, a government survey revealed that there were two million "surplus women" in Britain. They were women of marriageable age for whom there would never be a husband and children, because so many young men had perished on the battlefields. There were newspaper articles written about the "problem of the surplus women" who would become mad without the calming hand of a man upon them. Hartley House, the home for old people where my friend Jenny's dad had been the superintendent, was called the "old ladies' home" by the locals, because many of the residents were elderly women who had never married due to that terrible war. There were only a few men. The home itself was housed in the former workhouse for the area, a forbidding building with a big chimney in the center. Jenny and I used to hang out in an old air raid shelter in the grounds—I'm not sure that many people even knew it was there. Much of the old Hartley House has been demolished now and that which remains is a more upscale home for seniors, its history as a former workhouse now a selling point.

Of all the elderly people in the area, it's two brothers who come to mind so often, old men who had both lost their sight in the Great War. It wasn't just that they could not see—they had no eyes in their sockets, which wasn't an uncommon wound in that terrible conflict. They walked to the shop several times each week, one with his hand on the shoulder of the other, who tapped a white cane from side to side in front of him as he led them down the hill toward the shop. Years later, while visiting the Imperial War Museum in London, I stood before the painting *Gassed* by John Singer Sargent, studying his depiction of a line of men blinded by gas in the Great War as they were led away from the bodies of wounded and dying—and I thought of the two old men making their way along to the shop. When I was a little girl, if I was in the shop they'd ask my mother if I could sing and dance for them, so I did—I'd dance and belt out a song, twirling around until I was dizzy, making sure two elderly men enchanted by a child in a most innocent way could hear my feet tapping the floor. Now the memory of it breaks my heart, though those wounded men and lonely elderly women gave me images I would come back to time and again in later years.

16

Saturday's Child

ॐ

O ne of the first things I remember my mother telling me about myself was that I was Saturday's Child, and she pointed out that according to the rhyme, "Saturday's Child works hard for her living." I think I must have been preordained for the role, because photographs taken when I was young reveal not childish, soft hands, but large hands, with no dimples, and long fingers where clumsily endearing digits should be. And in a few of those photographs what I am doing is significant, because I am working. No, not pretend working, with a child's typewriter or even miniature garden implements—although I already had the latter, along with the necessary size-appropriate tools to clean a house from top to bottom. In one I am standing with my own personal basket into which I am picking hops, alongside the wood and sackcloth bin that my mother and grandmother are using for the same task. You can't see all this, but we are collectively trying to pick as many hops as we can, because hop-picking is paid on piece work, which means not by the hour, but by the amount picked. Children often worked alongside their parents out in the hop gardens, sometimes picking into an old laundry basket, or a shopping bag—when full, those hops would be thrown into the bin, ready for the farmer when he came round for the counting. It was like a game, and kept the children close at hand. The peppery, spicy hops stained my hands for weeks to come, and the bines cut my skin. Later, as my mother rubbed a flannel with soap and hot water up and down my arms before I could sit at the table for my tea, I squealed with the stinging, so she rubbed Nivea into the welts left by my endeavors.

I was six years old when I learned something about work that would remain with me my entire life. I learned that you could get something you wanted if you were only prepared to work for it. And I so wanted a Cinderella watch.

The Cinderella watch was linked to the Disney *Cinderella* movie, though I wouldn't have known about that because we didn't go to the pictures, as a rule. Though the animated film came out in 1950, the watch was probably still doing well because it was for sale in the jeweler's shop in Cranbrook. Or perhaps it had been sitting there for ten years. I'd seen the watch as we walked past one Saturday, and I thought it was the loveliest thing I'd ever laid eyes on. I would rush around to the jeweler's every day after school just to look at it in the shop window. In the process I almost missed the bus home on several occasions, running after it along Stone Street as it rumbled toward the bus stop outside the Congregational church on the High Street. The Cinderella watch had the heroine of the tale on the dial, which was white and mother-of-pearl. The band was pale blue, and the watch came presented in a crystal shoe. Really, it must have been glass, but to me it was crystal. I wanted that watch and I really, really wanted that shoe.

One day I was brave enough to go into the shop to inquire about the price, and discovered that it cost two pounds, eighteen shillings and sixpence. I said, "Thank you very much," and left doing my very best to appear as if I didn't care after all. I didn't have that kind of money and an entreaty to my mother was met with an almost humiliating peal of laughter followed by, "Do you think money grows on trees?" Or she would open her purse to show me the meagre contents. Or, even worse, she would say, "So, now you know what it is to want—call it an experience."

School ended in late July, and on the final day before the summer break I took one more look at the Cinderella watch and then sloped away toward the bus stop. I must have seemed crestfallen by the time I walked into the kitchen that afternoon, my forehead worn into a frown, because as we finished our tea that evening, Mum laid out a plan. She had probably been trying to work out what to do about my dark demeanor ever since I came home.

"Blackcurranting starts on Monday. If you like, you can work mornings and we'll keep a tally book for you. You might be able to earn enough money for your watch."

I liked that idea very much, and I was ready to put my back into the job.

On Monday morning we walked down to the farm, the sun already warm on my tanned arms and legs, the day starting out humid. As soon as we arrived, we walked over to collect a few fresh wooden trays from a pile at the bottom of the field, and sheets of the fine waxed paper provided to line them. Mum demonstrated lining the tray and then showed me how to pick, using my forefinger and thumb to pinch away each sprig of blackcurrants from the bush. Then she showed me how to do it even faster. She warned me to be careful, that I'd be docked for damaged fruit, and that I'd also be pulled up short for an underweight tray. Mum started me off picking the first bush before she set to work on the second. When I finished one bush—and she said she'd check to make sure I was a clean picker and that only green fruit was left behind—I was to move onto the next bush beyond her, and so on until we'd finished that row. I tried hard not to squash fruit, and was doing my best to coordinate my thumb and forefinger and therefore execute a perfect tearing of the sprig from the branch.

I finished my first tray and set it beside my mother's already picked tower of trays. I was not intimidated by her speed, but lined a fresh tray and went back to work. My mind wandered as I increased my pace, filling the next tray faster, my fingers now weaving through the bush until I'd picked it clean. Then came a shout across the rows of blackcurrants, one of the workers letting the pickers know that the tractor and trailer with the weighing machine was on its way. It stopped every few rows for the farmer to weigh the picked fruit, which would then be taken to the storage shed to be collected by lorry that night. These blackcurrants were bound for the Ribena cordial factory.

As she made her way back down the row with her full tray, my mother stopped to check every single bush I'd worked on, and then she pointed to my trays. "You need to pick cleaner—hurry, you've got enough time to get those leaves out of your trays before Mr. David comes for the weighing." David was the farmer's first name, and because his brother had the neighboring farm, they were known to workers as "Mr. David and Mr. John." I cleaned my trays, and began to worry. When the trailer reached us, Mum lifted up her trays one by one to be placed on the scales. Mr. David weighed each tray, marked her tally book and handed it back to her. Then she lifted my trays, and handed him my tally book. He looked at Mum, then at me, and smiled before weighing the trays and marking up my book. Children weren't officially supposed to work—there were laws against it—but I knew many who did, their picking recorded on their mother's tally book, a boost to the family income. My mother made it easier by creating my book using drawing paper and marking up columns on the pages, so I wasn't using an official farm document for keeping track of my earnings—and those earnings would be all mine, for my Cinderella watch.

"You've worked enough this morning, love," said Mum. "You can go and play now—but wash your hands in the stream first."

I was hot and sticky, so I ran into the woods, took off my sandals and stepped into the cool stream, bending down to reach through the water until I could touch the stones and sand at the bottom, and rubbed my hands together. Then I stepped back and sat down on the sun-dappled bank amid the pungent wild garlic and deep yellow celandines that grew alongside the water. I grinned. I'd just earned some money. I didn't know how much, but I'd earned some money.

Some days were more productive than others. If it rained hard, we couldn't go to work, but we had to get the picking done soon, otherwise the fruit would spoil under the heat of summer sun. The stain on my hands from one day merged into the juice from the next, and during that season's work, I never managed to rid myself of the purple taint on my fingers, even though I slathered them with the special gel Dad used to clean paint from his hands. Blackcurrant picking continued for two or three weeks. It was the last of the season's soft fruits; strawberries had been picked in June and early July, and loganberries on another farm. All too soon, picking ended and the seasonal workers left. Mum and Auntie Glad, and the other regulars, Joan and Flo, moved into the oast house for the next job—mending hop pokes for the coming hop-picking season. Then apple picking would begin, our lives and income dictated by the rhythm of the agricultural year.

I loved the oast house. I felt comfort in the heady aroma of last year's hops, musty and pungent, and the clammy warmth the ancient building generated. I would watch the way the women wielded long needles, blanket-stitching torn seams of thick hessian sacking with heavy string, and all the while chatting, telling stories, gossiping. I wanted to mend hop sacks and earn some more money, but Mum said it was too difficult for little hands, and to go out into the fresh air with the other kids or read my book. My brother was only two so he played with his toys, or slept. Finally, he was getting the hang of sleeping.

Then one day, as I returned from playing with the farmer's children, clambering up the wooden steps onto the cooling floor—the part of the oast house next to the roundel, where mounds of hops would be shoveled in after drying—Mum looked up from her stitching. "Mr. David came up with the blackcurrant picking money. He said you could take round a wheelbarrow to collect your earnings." The women laughed. I could hear them as I jumped down the stairs and ran to the farmhouse side door where Mr. David had his office. He was waiting with the small brown paper envelope—I later learned that Mum had asked him to make up a wage packet for me instead of just slipping the money into hers. She wanted my accomplishment to be special. "Well done," he said, but hardly had time to finish before I ran off around the back of the oast house, whereupon I studied the figures on the front before opening the envelope and counting my earnings three times. One pound, eighteen shillings and elevenpence. Not enough for the Cinderella watch. That evening, Mum and Dad agreed it might be cheaper in Maidstone, the market town an hour away on the bus.

Tuesday was market day in Maidstone, and I don't know why Auntie Sylvie and Uncle John came down with John, Larry and Martine, but I think it must have been some sort of holiday, because both my parents were off work and so were my aunt and uncle. It was decided we'd all go into Maidstone on the bus. Here's what I remember about the bus. It was raining that day and the bus seemed to be slower than usual, which was a special sort of hell for both Larry and me because we suffered from travel sickness, despite being given Kwells and my mother pressing a penny into each of our hands, promising, as always, that they were special magic pennies that stopped you being sick. We all went straight to the top of the double-decker bus, where Larry sat in front of me with Uncle John. Dad sat next to me, with Mum across the aisle with my brother. Larry lost his breakfast about halfway to Maidstone, and I remember Uncle John holding him to the window and whatever it was he was throwing up splattered sideways and ran down the window next to me. I closed my eyes, clutched harder at my magic penny and thought about the Cinderella watch.

In Maidstone, my brother was left in Auntie Sylvie's care, while Mum and Dad led me away from the market and toward the shops. We found a jeweler's on Week Street with the Cinderella watch in the window. We all stared at it, then I looked up at my parents.

"Come on then," said Dad. "Let's go in."

We entered the shop, and as the bell over the door summoned the owner, I stared at the glass cases on either side of the wall. Rings, brooches, watches, necklaces, bracelets. It was so sparkly.

"And how may I help you, sir, madam?" The jeweler looked at Mum and Dad in turn.

"The young lady is your customer," said my dad, his hand on my shoulder. He gave me a gentle prod, encouraging me to step forward.

The jeweler looked down at me as I blurted out, "May I look at the Cinderella watch, please?"

I half-felt my parents move away. This was my wanting, my money, my purchase. They were leaving me to it.

The man unlocked the velvet-clad doors that opened onto the window, reached in and picked up the Cinderella watch. I swallowed a mouthful of saliva, and tried to swallow my desire along with it. He put the watch in front of me, slipped the blue strap away from the shoe, and set it on a velvet pad. I stood on tiptoe to look. He held out his hand for my wrist and I gave it willingly, pulling up my sleeve. I felt the weight of the watch as he secured it, and I held my breath.

"It's beautiful," I said, half relieved when he took it from my wrist and set it back in the shoe. "How much is it?

"Two pounds, ten shillings and sixpence."

I tried not to appear downhearted, but I knew my parents could not afford the difference and I imagine it showed on my face.

"How much money do you have, young lady?" he said.

I pulled my little coin purse from my pocket, unzipped it and poured my hard-earned cash onto the counter. He counted the money.

"Ah," he said. "Very good. I have something special to show you, and it's only just come in." Again he went to the window, this time he turned holding a watch with a round face, plain numerals and a thin black leather band. "This is a very fine, elegant watch for a young lady such as yourself." He removed the watch from the open box, releasing it from a royal blue satin pillow, then reached for my wrist again, securing the strap. He picked up a pen and pointed to the face. "Strong stainless steel." He hovered the tip of the pen in a circle above the dial. "Clear numbers." Then he drew attention to the strap. "Genuine leather. You will get what you pay for at one pound, eighteen shillings and sixpence." He allowed a pause before pointing to my first choice, which was still on the counter. "The Cinderella watch will be out of fashion in a few months—we only stocked it because the film is doing the rounds again. It has a nylon strap and a plastic dial. What you're really paying for is a glass shoe." He tapped the pen against the shoe. "If I were you, I'd go for quality. Not that shoe."

I turned to my parents.

"Gentleman's right, Jackie—go for quality."

So I went for the quality and said I'd like to buy the watch with the leather strap. I was asked if I would like to wear my new watch and I said I would keep it on. Much was made of wrapping the box with the royal blue pillow and handing me the receipt to put into my coin purse along with the remaining five pennies. We thanked the man and left the shop, though I lingered on the street to stare at the window as the Cinderella watch was replaced on the display shelf in its glass shoe. That lovely glass shoe. The man waved, and we went on our way.

The leather watch lasted a good few years, and was still on my wrist in my early teens, when Celia became bored with her big flashy red watch and it was handed down to me.

I continued working on farms throughout my schooldays. Though it might seem harsh now, where I was from it was common to see children working—after all, that's what those long summer breaks away from school were originally designed for; children were needed to bring in the harvest. By fourteen I'd picked every kind of fruit grown in Kent; I drove a tractor before a car. I'd fed lambs abandoned by their mothers, moved cattle from one field to another, whitewashed farm outbuildings for the summer and done many of the usual jobs that kids do—babysitting and house-cleaning, shop work, waitressing, washing up at a restaurant, Saturday girl at a hairdresser's when I was thirteen—which I hated, because the very nature of being a Saturday girl involved all the dirty dogsbody jobs: scrubbing the floors, sweeping up hair, washing mirrors, filling up the small bottles of shampoo from the gallon can, so customers thought they were getting some fancy shampoo, but really it was cheap stuff that even my mother wouldn't put on her hair. I had to use that shampoo on the floor and to wash the cups and saucers we used to give the ladies a cup of tea. I also had to shampoo hair when the older ladies came in, which was always a bit tricky because some of them had hardly any hair, so it was basically a bald scalp I was looking at while trying not to worry about the hair that was coming out in my hands and wondering if it was all my fault. One of the hairdressers, Cathy, had a terrible temper and was always shouting at me. I told my parents about it, and was surprised when Dad said, "Next time that happens, you down tools and you walk out of there." I loved that phrase, "down tools"—and imagined myself throwing some combs and a mop on the floor and walking out, though I thought I wouldn't have had the courage to do such a thing. However, the next time Cathy shouted her head off at me in front of a whole salon of ladies, I rested the broom against the wall, took off my overall and walked out—but not before I'd held out my hand for the ten bob she owed me.

I didn't like strawberry plugging either. That was a job I did with a friend when I was ten. We'd walk to the farm a couple of miles away—not the farm where my mother worked, but another near my friend's house—and go straight into one of the barns where a long line of buckets filled with imperfect strawberries was waiting for us. The perfect fruit had already been sent to market for distribution and retail sale. There were two upturned wooden crates for us to sit on at the end of the barn, and a stack of empty buckets to one side for us to use as we worked. Our instructions amounted to taking one full bucket after the other from the line and then working as quickly as we could, we had to pull out the plug and any mold in each strawberry. We would throw the plugs and moldy bits into one empty bucket and the good part into another. That long line of buckets filled with imperfect fruit had to be finished before we went home, and those strawberries stained our hands and soon made them so sore the skin on our fingertips broke open. Our backs would ache after several hours of sitting on wooden crates and leaning forward to do our work. The buckets with the good parts were bound for the jam-making factories, and the rest would either go into pig swill or chicken feed. I have noticed that American strawberries don't seem to have that plug that goes down into the fruit from the stem, something I rather like about American strawberries, though they don't taste as good as strawberries grown in Kent. Needless to say, I also prefer homemade jam.

The job I detested most, though, was a summer packing eggs at a place where the manager couldn't keep his hands to himself. I always had two or more jobs on the go. From age sixteen until I went away to college, I would sneak out of school early three days a week for my job as the evening receptionist for two local doctors. At twenty-one, when I presented my resume for my first real job, I was exactly what the photographs predicted I would be: an old hand when it came to work, a Saturday's child. But I'd learned a valuable lesson at an early age—that if you wanted something, you had to take care of business yourself.

17

The Railway Child

✦

Sometimes, when I look back at those early years as John and
I grew up in the house at the end of The Terrace, the word
"rhythm" seems to echo time and again, and I find myself repeat-
ing it—the sort of repetition a copyeditor flags when she goes
through a manuscript. When your days revolve around the land
and the seasons, there's more of a sense of life's backbeat, from
turning the soil in winter, to spring seeding, to the harvests of
summer and autumn.

Though to outsiders our lives might have seemed as soft
and undulating as the countryside around us, my mother's stories, told each day as we sat down for our tea, seemed to catch
us on a wave and propel us through a series of highs and lows.
"I told him straight" or "I put her in her place!" were common
refrains, because if there was one thing my Mum could do, it was
put people in their place. Then she would tell a joke, something
about what she saw and how she quipped, and we would laugh
because my mother was a very witty woman. With a certain pride
she'd told us that her father had admonished her with that well-
worn phrase, "Sarcasm is the lowest form of wit." To which Mum
would respond, "But it takes a witty woman to be sarcastic." Oh,
she could be sarcastic!

But if Mum rendered us co-stars in her story simply by making us the audience, then Dad grounded us. He always grounded us; with a comment he could calm the air following the out-of-key bang, crash, boom rhythm of one of Mum's stories, bringing us down to earth safely again.

My father's solid nature was rooted in his love of the land— and even then he would often voice a warning that the earth was something we should cherish. "If we're not careful, that'll be a Tesco's over there," he said, pointing to a bank of bluebells as we tumbled after him through the woods one Sunday afternoon, meandering off the path because the path represented someone telling him exactly where to go. We stopped and stared at the woodland before us, imagining it sullied by a Tesco's supermarket.

"And a garage over there, with a car park," John added.

"And a block of flats right there," I chipped in.

We did this a lot on walks with Dad; we glimpsed into the future to see the worst that might happen to our country idyll, if we weren't careful. Perhaps that's why he pointed out every movement of wildlife, every badger, hawk and fox, and the changes that came with the seasons.

Dad hated seeing countryside developed and his fears were prescient, as if he knew the earth was at risk even then. But he was sadder than most when the railway closed—it was as if part of his childhood had been snatched up and away from him, his escape route from London gone, even though he'd already found freedom. Perhaps he felt bereft because, as a boy, he'd traveled on the branch line from Paddock Wood down to Goudhurst for the hop-picking, and it was the same line that linked us to Paddock Wood and then Tonbridge and London, and of course home again. Always home again.

Cranbrook Station, two miles out of the town, was inconveniently situated for everyone who actually lived in Cranbrook, but was a boon for us because it was a twenty-minute walk from the house, up to the top of The Terrace and then down Station Road. The train was our nearby link to a bigger world. My swing had been delivered by train to the station. I'd seen it even before it was brought to the house on the back of the coal lorry—I knew it had been ordered because Mum could not keep a secret, and on our way down to the farm one day, I looked across to the station as we walked over the railway bridge and saw the swing-shaped brown paper package leaning against the station house. I knew it was mine, because who else would be expecting a swing to be brought to Hartley in the goods wagon of the train?

We traveled to London on the train a couple of times each year. A "push and pull" locomotive was used on the line, so if a passenger was a bit late getting to the station, the station master was known to blow his whistle and wave to the guard in the signal box, and the train would stop and come back again for the tardy passenger. That happened to us a few times. I enjoyed the train because I didn't get sick and the rhythm lulled me. And I loved the way Mum dressed to go to London, in her New Look coat from before she was married and her one pair of leather shoes. She would buy a new pair of nylons for the journey if her old ones were laddered. In winter she'd wear her black woolen scarf with silver thread woven into the pattern, wrapping it around her head and shoulders as if she were a film star, and in truth, she still had something of the Rita Hayworth look about her that everyone had commented upon when she was seventeen. We'd clamber onto the train, with me wearing my flannel pajama bottoms underneath the woolen plaid trews that Mum made us put on for travel to London to keep us warm. I was allergic to wool and would come up in red welts if it touched my skin, and I had to be careful with the seats, too, because they were covered in old red woolen fabric in a paisley pattern fashionable in Victorian times when the railway was built. Once we were settled, Mum would look into the mirror set on the wooden carriage bulkhead between two lamps in the shape of shells, and apply her red lipstick from its case of twisted golden metal. She'd press her lips together and then take her seat, checking and rechecking that she hadn't lost the tickets.

I think the first time I was aware of my mother's claustrophobia was on a train. It was just the three of us, going up to London—Mum, John and me. John wasn't walking, but we didn't have a pushchair with us because it would have been too much to take on the train. Perhaps we were going to see Auntie Sylvie, and she would have one somewhere. When the train stopped at Paddock Wood, we were the only passengers in the carriage and Mum could not get the door open to step out onto the platform. She tried to pull down the window in the door, but it wouldn't move, so she told me to quickly turn and run along the carriage to the other door, and that one wouldn't open either. Then she started to cough, and I remember thinking that we had to get off the train very quickly. It was probably only a few minutes that we were stuck, but I was scared because I could see the fear in my mother's eyes, and if she was scared I knew we were in trouble. Then the guard on the platform saw Mum struggling with the window, and came to open the door.

"Turned it the wrong way, love," said the guard, pointing to the door handle before touching his cap as if in salute after he'd helped us from the train. "No need to rush, the up train hasn't come in yet." The up train, the down train—I was fascinated by the language of the railway.

The locomotives were old and the carriages ancient. Dad came home from London one winter's night—he'd been sent up to

town on a special job with another man from the painting firm—
and told us about the carriage he'd been sitting in for the journey
from Paddock Wood.

"Should've seen it—it was like a posh hotel, with seats
arranged around an open fire, right there in the carriage. I asked
the conductor about it, and he said they had to bring it out of
storage on account of repairs on another carriage. I felt like a
king in there."

We marveled at the story, because we liked a bit of elevation in
life, us Winspears. I'm like that myself when I get upgraded to first
class on a flight. Jackie Winspear, queen of the red-eye.

But there would be no elevation to another class of rail travel
after the branch line closed in 1961, which meant we had to take
the motor coach up to London. Losing the trains saddened our
small community. Dad always blamed the station's demise on
Dr. Beeching, the Chairman of the British Railways Board, who
was responsible for closure of branch line stations up and down
the country, along with thousands of miles of railway tracks,
when he published his report that led to what became known as
the "Beeching Axe." Increased road passenger travel and freight
movement were blamed for the closures, which were designed
to reduce government railway subsidies and the number of loss-
making stations. Dad always said the people who closed the
station "couldn't see any further than the ends of their noses," but
he said that about all politicians. Sometimes, if they really irked
him, he said they all ought to be "put up against a wall and shot."
The truth was the station had never made money because it had
been built in the wrong place, a place chosen to save on restitu-
tion payments.

In the great industrial age of Victorian Britain, landowners
had to be paid when a new railway line was constructed across

their land, especially if it was agricultural land. The landowners closer to Cranbrook were asking a pretty penny for the railway to go through in the mid-1800s, so instead the station was built in the hamlet of Hartley two miles outside the town. And there it lost money hand over fist, because not enough people wanted to come from Cranbrook to the station. Yet there's many who would agree with my dad about the shortsighted Beeching and his axe, as Britain's roads became choked with traffic—perhaps in time many of those railway lines and stations could have become profitable. Certainly old Beeching might have had a change of heart if he'd ever been in a car stuck on the M25 outer London orbital motorway at any time of day.

Railway economics probably went over the heads of most locals, but they knew they would miss their railway. On the June day in 1961 when the station closed and the last push-pull train rumbled on its way, more people came to buy tickets and sit on that train than had journeyed by rail for years. The station was resplendent with hanging baskets filled with blooms and window boxes spilling over with color. As always, the station master walked ahead of the train to open the level crossing gate where the rail met Bishop's Lane—the very place where my mother would race us across even if a train was nowhere to be seen or heard, and where I was always scared I'd get my foot caught between the rails and be run over, just like heroines in those old silent films sometimes shown on Sunday morning television. I wonder how our station manager felt, closing that gate for the last time and walking back to the station to close the ticket office forever.

The Hawkhurst Line was often said to be the most beautiful railway line in the county, if not the whole of England, as it meandered through the Weald of Kent countryside, past fields of barley, past apple orchards where our Russets, Cox's Orange Pippins, Bramleys and Worcesters grew. And past our cherry orchards, boasting those tallest cherry trees in the world, and our precious hop gardens and farms; past forests and small cottages, past the Marguerite daisies that grew on verges along with wild lupins, pink mallow, foxgloves, primroses and bluebells. I loved hearing the train in the distance if we were working in the fields and I'd always look up as it came closer. Sometimes I ran to the fence that separated the land from the railway line just to see the train come along, steam punching up through the trees as it took people, produce, milk, parcels and letters to the bigger world beyond, and brought that bigger world to us, even when it was a new red swing. If the driver saw me, he'd wave.

There were times after the line closed when I would be helping Mum as she worked in a field, and I'd hear the distinctive whistle of the train as it reached Bishop's Lane. I'd hear the clackety-clack, clackety-clack, clackety-clack rhythm of the wheels on the tracks and I'd look up, ready to see steam coming through the trees. But there was nothing, for the trains had long gone. Then I'd look around and see someone else staring toward the old railway line, as if they'd heard it too, and it made me wonder if trains could become ghosts.

Many years later, as I rode my bike from my home in Ojai, California, down to the beach in Ventura, I stopped at a crossing to wait for the Coast Starlight train to pass, en route to its next stop in Santa Barbara before making its way onward to northern California and Washington state. On a whim I waved to the driver and he waved back and sounded the horn. It warmed my heart, and I thought about those trains of my childhood and realized that some ghosts reside in the heart. Perhaps that's why I've always loved trains.

18

The Horse, of Course

~~

It seemed that so much happened during the year I turned six. Mum's thyroid trouble appeared to stabilize, though she didn't gain weight and would sometimes still drop cups and saucers or have coughing fits. Her weight loss was such that the skin on her neck seemed to have been sucked into her chest—I would run my fingers along her collar bones and refer to the deep recesses at the base of her throat as "Mummy's buckets." Whenever she pulled me in for a cuddle, I could feel her bones sticking into me.

My eyes improved, so I started to catch up with my schoolwork, and was relieved because I wouldn't have to wear the dunce's cap after all. And I had two friends I loved: Wendy in Cranbrook, who was my best friend at school, and Jennifer who lived about half a mile away in Hartley and was my best friend at home—at weekends I could walk to Jenny's house, whereas Wendy lived on the other side of Cranbrook. At school, Jenny tended to pal around with a girl named Janet, who lived in the town. Their joint birthday party in Cranbrook was the first party I had ever been invited to, and after that I was only ever allowed to go to a party at Jenny's house, because Dad could walk along the road to bring me home. In fact, if it wasn't for Jenny's dad having a car and me being friends with Jenny, there's a lot of things I wouldn't have been able to do. If her Dad was taking the family to Hastings for the day, or Jenny to another party, I was allowed to go.

I was sometimes allowed to stay at Wendy's house for the odd overnight sleepover on a Friday evening after school. Wendy and her brothers would walk me to the bus stop the following morning. I loved Wendy's house because she had three brothers and a sister, and they had bunk beds—and they seemed to have so much boisterous fun. Wendy's mum always had chocolate spread on the table to have with bread, and that was something my mum would never buy, because it was too expensive. Oh what fun it was at Wendy's house. Wendy sometimes came home with me after school on a Friday. I remember one Saturday two of her brothers rode out to the house on their bikes during a warm summer storm because they missed her so much. Mum sent us up to the shop to buy Mivvi bars, a sort of ice cream bar coated with strawberry flavor sorbet. A Mivvi bar was a rare treat. Years later, during the Falklands War, I wept when my mother telephoned to let me know that Wendy's younger brother, Anthony, had been killed on HMS *Sheffield* when it was hit by an Exocet missile. The image that came to me was of a gaggle of kids standing by the back door, giggling and eating Mivvis on a hot, sticky day while watching summer rain pour down outside.

Jenny was the friend who came around on her bicycle to see me on the day I was discharged from the hospital. I later discovered that as she waited for me to come to the door, my mother told her that she wasn't to say anything about my eyes, and that they wouldn't look like that forever. I can still see Jenny standing by the kitchen door, backlit by sunshine as I came running when Mum called out to say she was there to see me. Jenny looked at me and said, "Oh Jackie . . . your eyes are . . . your eyes are so beautiful." And then she collapsed into my mother's arms in a flood of tears. That's when it occurred to me that it was a funny kind of beautiful that made people cry.

Jenny was enrolled at the Audrey Hill Ballet School in Hawkhurst on Tuesday evenings after school, and on that day she would stay on the bus to get to her class. Her dad would collect her afterward in their creamy yellow Vauxhall car. My parents couldn't afford ballet lessons, but I really wanted to dance and to wear that same white dress with the pleated skirt and the "AH" insignia embroidered on the pocket in red silk that Jenny wore to school on her ballet days. So I sometimes stayed on the bus with her, and was allowed to watch, and every now and again Miss Hill felt sorry for me and let me join in, just for one dance, usually tap, because then I could keep my shoes on. Jenny had pink ballet shoes and red tap shoes and I thought they were beautiful. I was not perturbed by the fact that I was a spectator—it was quite enough just to be there with other girls I didn't know who came to the ballet classes from different villages. Jenny's dad would drop me off at the top of The Terrace later.

It was all very nice, watching Jenny dance, but what I really wanted was a horse, though I knew that was a wanting all the blackcurrant picking, apple picking, hop picking and loganberry picking in the world wouldn't get for me. I had fallen in love with horses soon after we moved to The Terrace. Well, to be accurate, I fell in love with one particular horse. Mum and I had walked up to the cottage near Tubs Lake, where a woman ran a small grocery shop. Perhaps it was a Wednesday afternoon, early closing for Cooke's, the general store at the end of our row of terrace houses. The woman's cottage had a very large egg-shaped dent in the roof where a bomb had dropped on it and then bounced off in the war. In fact, that small area was already legendary, given that Tubs Lake was so named because, apparently, when the notorious Hawkhurst Gang of smugglers rode through in the mid-1700s, chased by the excise men, they would throw their tubs of contraband into the lake for collection later. There was always talk that there were still tubs from those days at the bottom of the lake, which over the centuries had become a pungent pond, full of decomposing vegetation. By the time my brother was ten years old, he had waded into the muddy swamp many times to see if he could find sunken treasure, and then received a clip around the ear for his trouble when he got home on account of the smell he brought into the house.

But on this day our only treasure was a quarter pound of tea and a bottle of milk carried home from the little shop in a string bag. When we reached the crest of the hill I could feel my eyes widen as a magnificent black horse came galloping up to the fence to greet us. I pulled away from my mother and ran to the fence, looking straight up at the massive head above me. He leaned down and I reached up to rest my hand on his soft nose.

"Come away from that horse now!" said my mother, running to catch up with me. I disobeyed her and knelt down to clutch at clumps of the sweeter grass and clover on my side of the fence, then held it up to the horse. My mother intercepted and snatched the grass from my fingers.

"That thing'll have your hand off."

I shook my head. I'd been around big animals since we lived at Black Bush Cottage. Cows and sheep held no more threat than dogs, though I treated approaching a cat as something of a risk. I'd heard stories of me as a two-year-old marching through a herd of cattle, elbowing them aside in my quest to get through to the far end of the field where my father was mending a fence, or spreading out feed. But this wasn't a cow, this was a horse, and I had lost my heart to him.

I loved it when we walked along the road to see the black horse, who would trot from his place on the top of the hill down to the fence. Soon we were bringing carrots, though I was never allowed to offer him food in case he'd have my hand off, so we threw treats over the fence. Then one day he was gone, yet each time we came to the top of the hill, I continued to stand there, waiting, just in case he would come to find me. When he didn't we'd continue on, either to the farm or the little shop with the bomb-shaped dent in the roof. But I'd made up my mind—I was going to have a horse, come what may.

I was eight years old and walking back from Five Acres, the field at the back of the house, when I saw a chestnut thorough-bred in the paddock next to the imposing manor house. In our part of Hartley—the older part; newer houses had sprung up on the way to Cranbrook over the years—the hamlet seemed almost medieval and would have looked so to someone peering down from an aircraft. There was a manor house, an old oast house now converted to a home, and a farmhouse next to it. Further on there was a series of older cottages where workers at the manor house must have lived very far back in the day. Other farms were located nearby with the occasional ancient manor house in between, along with more cottages tied to the job and the land, which was marked by a patchwork quilt of fields, some laying fallow and some with crops or used for grazing. Farming then was not far removed from the field rotation system first employed in the Middle Ages.

The thoroughbred mare belonged to the daughter of the manor house—I knew the horse was a thoroughbred because I'd saved up to buy the *Observer's Book of Horses and Ponies*. I'd imme-diately written my name and address inside, adding Great Britain, World, Universe, just to make sure it came back to me if I lost it.

I still have that book—it's on my desk, and there's still a check mark where I'd identified the horse's breed following the walk back from Five Acres.

I'd only needed one long look across the paddock toward the horse and I was in love again. Every day after school, I'd finish my chores and run down to the paddock, usually with a carrot taken from the larder. The mare would nicker and amble over as soon as she saw me, leaning her head over the gate to take the treat. Then I'd pull sweet grass from the verge for her to nibble and I'd just sit on the gate, stroking her neck, dreaming. I dreamed a lot about having a horse. Some days I'd run to Five Acres and pretend I was riding a horse. I'd slap my hip and clutch invisible reins, then leap over jumps only I could see, giving myself faults for a pole knocked down and of course congratulating myself on a clear round. I'd seen jumps of red and white set up in the field opposite the paddock, so I knew the thoroughbred was a jumper.

I was sitting on the fence stroking the horse's head one day, when a girl—she must have been in her late teens or perhaps early twenties—entered the paddock at the far end and began walking toward me. She was wearing a white blouse and a pair of beige "elephant ear" jodhpurs, the sort people wore then—well, the people who were lucky enough to ride horses. Her tall black leather boots were polished to a shine, and she tap-tapped a riding crop against them. I didn't know whether to run or stay. I slipped down from the gate, but did not leave.

"Hello," she said. "Who are you?"

I told her my name and pointed to where I lived. And I showed off a bit—I didn't want her to think I was a complete neophyte when it came to horses.

"What's your thoroughbred's name?"

She seemed surprised I knew the breed. "Her name's Honey," she replied, adding, "Do you ride?"

I shook my head. "No, but I want to, and I'm going to have a horse one day." The words seemed to tumble out of my mouth before I could stop them. "And I'd love a horse just like Honey. She's wonderful."

We chatted a bit more about horses, about Honey, and then she said, "So you want to ride. Well, we'll have to see what we can do for you."

I ran home that day filled with hope, bursting with fizzy excitement. That girl was going to let me ride Honey, and she was going to teach me to ride. Wasn't that what "We'll have to see what we can do for you" meant? Someone with a horse had seen my wanting and would help make my dream come true.

I blurted everything out to Mum, who was home by the time I rushed into the kitchen.

"Just don't get your hopes up, love. You know what people can be like, especially those sort of people."

Those sort of people. I'd heard that phrase before, so I knew exactly who those sort of people were—they were rich people, people who weren't like us, and they looked down their noses at ordinary people, apparently. We had a well-developed sense of those sort of people when they looked down their noses at us—as my parents would have us believe, those rich people didn't like it when you got above your station.

"But she wasn't like that—she was nice," I whined. I know I probably whined.

"All the same, don't get your hopes up."

But I did. Of course I did.

Every day for weeks on end, when I came home from school I'd put on a pair of Celia's castoff beige cotton trousers. I'd keep on my white school blouse, though I rolled up the sleeves to below the elbow, just like the girl who owned Honey. I'd put on my black Wellington boots—they would have to do until I'd saved up for a leather pair—and then I'd run down to Honey's paddock clutching a couple of carrots, and I'd wait. I would wait and wait. Sometimes I would see the girl in the field, jumping over the red and white poles, soaring through the air on Honey. Then she'd dismount and lead her horse into the barn. She'd never even look up to acknowledge me.

One day I ran down to the paddock, and Honey was gone. She wasn't there the next day or the next.

"Come here, love," said Mum, as I walked back into the kitchen, as downhearted as a horse-mad girl without a horse could be. "There you are, down in the dumps again." She rubbed her hands on a tea towel and pulled me to her for a long time. "Now then," she said, releasing me from her grasp. "Take off that school blouse and put on an old shirt. And take off your boots. I've got a job for you." A job was always thought to be balm for any distress to the soul in our house. A job calmed anger, sadness, too much energy, not enough energy and any malaise you could think of.

That night I did my best not to shed tears for Honey and for the fact that I wasn't one of those sort of people who could afford a horse. But I wasn't giving up so easily.

I entered a competition to win a Palomino pony, convinced that mine would be the best entry, the most compelling sentence in fifteen words or less describing why I wanted the Palomino pony. "When I bring home my Palomino pony, he will be the best pal o' mine!" I wrote.

I didn't win.

Another competition run by KP Peanuts promised the winner thousands of pounds, but involved a bit more creative work. On the entry form there was a template image—the outline of two peanuts. You had to make it into a cartoon and come up with a comic line. I drew a face on each peanut and gave them both a soldier's helmet. I gave the peanut soldier on the left a monocle. A speech bubble coming from the peanut on the right said, "We're being shelled, kernel!" I thought it was hilarious and was convinced I'd win enough money to buy my horse.

I didn't win.

I begged Dad to buy me a horse and pony magazine during the month it came with a free hoof pick. I believed that if I started gathering various items I'd need for my tack box, my horse would materialize. It was not a cheap magazine, but he bought it for me—that hoof pick was a sign of the coming horse as vivid as the olive branch the dove brought to Noah to mark the end of the flood. I needed a safe place for the hoof pick in the bedroom I shared with my brother, and it would have to be a very safe place indeed, because to my brother, the hoof pick would be a tool. John liked tools. He liked them for breaking things apart to find out how they worked. I hid it in the drawer underneath my school knickers. There is no way in the world that those ugly, baggy green uniform thick cotton briefs could be known as anything other than knickers. The hoof pick would be safe there.

As my tenth birthday approached, I began lobbying for a horse. "Don't be ridiculous," said my mother, opening her purse to let me see the emptiness inside. I asked again, this time as she swapped over the flat irons, placing one back on the stove's hotplate to heat up while wielding the other, then continuing to press the sheets and pillowcases. We didn't have an electric iron until I was eleven, when a Morphy Richards iron came as a free gift with our first refrigerator.

"Oh *sure* you can," she replied.

I heard, "Oh sure you can," as in, "I've changed my mind and you can have a horse."

What she really meant was, "Don't you understand? It's still ridiculous. We can't afford a horse and never will."

I ran downstairs on my birthday, expecting to see a horse like Honey standing outside, his head poking through the kitchen window as he waited for me with a big red bow around his neck. But there was no horse and no gift, just my cards on the kitchen table.

Things looked up when I found out that Wendy's sister had a Saturday job at Benenden riding stables, part of the private boarding school for girls in a local village. It was several miles away via the twists and turns of Swattenden Lane, but I thought I could easily walk to the stables, work all day, then walk home again, so I began asking her if she could get me a job there, because after a day of mucking out stables, you'd earned either ten bob or a free riding lesson. Margaret reported back that a Saturday job was available, I only had to go round and see the person in charge. This was a job I knew I could do easily. I was strong and I was used to hard work—and I would get to ride! What could go wrong?

Dad stared at me across the dinner table, pointing at me with his fork. "I'm not having you shoveling shit for those sort of people."

"And you're not walking all that way on a Saturday morning all on your own," added Mum. "Anything could happen."

Mum was always hyper-vigilant, and often threatened us with "anything could happen" when she felt an element of control slipping from her grasp.

"But they're not *those sort of people*—lots of girls work there," I maintained.

I wasn't going to win the argument—after all, this was the

stables where Princess Anne rode her horse because she was a pupil at Benenden School. Not only were the prices high, but it was the only riding school for miles around.

"Please let me do it—please," I tried again. "The lessons normally cost ten shillings, and I'd get one just for working a day."

"No. And let that be the end of it," said Dad.

It was the end of it for some time, until one day after our tea. John had gone out to play, but Dad and Mum asked me to remain at the table.

"Your Dad and I have decided that if you want riding lessons, we'll pay for you to have riding lessons, and you can go on the bus to Benenden on a Saturday."

I looked at my parents, in my heart knowing that they couldn't afford ten shillings, because really ten shillings would become a pound—if I had ten shillings' worth of something, then John would have to be given the same amount, plus the bus fare. It was a rule—what one had, the other had, too. When it came to allocating money to be spent on anything, Mum always made the point that "It all adds up." And I didn't want to even think about the cost of a "riding habit": jodhpurs, jacket, boots and hat. They were strict at the riding school, so I'd need the correct clothing. The girls who boarded there even had their own special short red duffel coats for winter riding. Even if I managed to get a pair of hand-me-down jodhpurs somewhere, the rest would cost a fortune.

I shrugged. "It's all right," I said. "I've changed my mind anyway. I don't want riding lessons. I'll get a job somewhere else."

Dad looked at me. He knew I was lying, and that it wasn't really all right, because he loved horses and he knew they were my passion. But he was only too glad to let it go—it would have been a stretch, and he was already working two jobs. I would lie awake at night, feeling heartsore to the point of weeping, I was so upset that my father had to work harder than anyone I knew, and I would not settle until I heard his footfall on the path alongside the house. Sometimes he would work so late he would miss the last bus, and walk home over ten miles in the snow on a winter's night.

"I told you she'd grow out of it," said Mum, getting up from the table.

I never grew out of it, though, and was always one to leap at the chance to ride, if it came along. I'd linger if there were horses in a field on the way home from school; I'd forget the time and have to run all the way to get the tea going.

I was finally earning enough money to learn to ride properly when I was twenty-four. Every Saturday morning and Sunday afternoon at the local riding stables near my home in Surrey, I would have a private lesson before going out on a long hack across the countryside. On the first Christmas after I started my lessons, as a gift Mum and Dad gave me the money to buy my breeches, tall boots, a helmet and the coveted Harry Hall hacking jacket. The boots wore out long ago, but I still have that jacket, and though the breeches are a bit threadbare, I kept them—my first riding breeches.

Several years after that lesson, I earned a trophy and a rosette when I came first in a local showjumping competition, though I still didn't have my own horse. When I called to tell Dad about the trophy, his voice cracked as he congratulated me and he began to weep. Mum took the phone, so excited you would have thought I'd just won an Olympic medal. I could not stop smiling for days.

When I was twenty-six and ready to buy my first house, I was in two minds about the decision. A horse I loved to ride was coming up for sale, and I had more than enough to buy her because I'd saved the down payment on the house, plus extra to give me a cushion during the first year of ownership. Dora was a slate-grey ex-racehorse with a lot of attitude, but I loved her. On Saturdays my friend Debbie would ride a horse named Cherie, another former racehorse, and I'd be on Dora, and off we would go for a couple of hours, across the countryside until we reached the gallops at Epsom Racecourse, where the Derby was held every year. The racecourse is private property with access restricted to resident horses in training, but those long gallops were way too tempting. We'd trot along a bridle path through the woods, bringing the horses to a halt at the spot where we could see across the racecourse. We'd watch and wait to make sure no one else was on the gallops—the racehorses usually came out really early, and it would have been dangerous to ride ex-racehorses anywhere near the gallops when the pack was being put through its paces—during races, even the mounted police have to move their horses as the pack comes around because they get too excited. As soon as we were satisfied that there were no racehorses and no rangers patrolling, we'd take off, galloping round at speed. As soon as we heard the ranger warning us through a loudhailer, we'd turn into the woods again, pop over a few logs on the way, and then back to the bridle path. It was wonderful. Every time I went out on Dora it was a thrill, and I felt so lucky.

"The trouble is, you want a hose, but you can't decide if you want it with a U or an R in the middle," observed Mum, as ever enjoying a play on words.

Good financial sense got the better of me and I chose the house—the hose with a U—though I continued to ride Dora for several years.

I was forty-five years of age and living in California when my husband bought me my first horse. That horse had to be sold following a serious riding accident, and afterward I thought I would never be able to ride again. Yet I was back in the saddle within six months and subsequently had three more horses—one I had to sell as I began spending months on end in England when my dad and later mum became ill, and two who sadly had to be laid to rest, one due to age, and one illness. Oliver was the jet-black Friesian who reminded me of my first equine love, the horse on the hill. Doesn't every horse-mad young girl who read *Black Beauty*, by Anna Sewell, want her own black beauty? Oliver died less than three months after Mum passed away, and as grief's dark shadow settled into me, I thought I would never have another horse, so deep was the ache in my heart. But now I have Calvin, a beloved big bay Dutch Warmblood who nickers and comes to the gate as soon as he hears my call, and rubs his soft nose against my cheek. I still feel so very fortunate, so privileged whenever I see him, and even more so as I slip on his saddle and bridle, ready to ride.

"We'll see what we can do," said the girl with elephant ear jodhpurs who owned Honey, the chestnut thoroughbred. I learned never to trust anyone who said they could do something for me—after that, I took promises with a pinch of salt; people could be so fickle. Yet I also learned that in claiming responsibility for making my dream come true, so much sweeter was the accomplishment. And in the grand scheme of things, the wait at the gate wasn't so long, really.

19

The Rule of Three

֍

I wonder if events in life come in clusters. Certainly my mother thought so. If she read about a plane crash, she would wait for the next one, and if it came quickly, she would say with great authority, "There'll be another." It's amazing how many times she was right. I began to think of the "rule of three" whenever disaster struck—though sometimes one was enough.

My brother hated school. He hated it from the moment his uniform was on and he had to spend just one day inside in a classroom instead of on the farm with my mother. He had become used to following old Bill Wickham, one of the farm hands, around on his three-wheeler bicycle, the same one my father had refurbished for me when I was four. Bill would be up ahead on the tractor turning the land and my brother would follow, pretending to be in charge of his own tractor plowing right behind Bill. I'm amazed that when Bill was spraying crops with fertilizer, probably with some nasty chemicals in the mix, no one stopped my brother following in his wake.

Without doubt, being in *my* wake at Cranbrook Primary school was a fate worse than death for John. He screamed and cried every single day. Mum had to accompany him to school because he would not set foot on the bus without her, and when he did, he would hang onto me until one of the teachers came to extricate me from his grasp and I would run to my classroom, weeping—it was clear I was failing at my job because my brother was so unhappy. One day I broke down in the cloakroom just before going into Mr. Croft's class for morning register. Wendy found Mr. Leech—the deputy headmaster, who was also one of our neighbors in Hartley and someone I revered, and told him I was upset, and when Mr. Leech came into the cloakroom to talk to me I collapsed into his arms, blurting out that I didn't know what to do because John hated school and I couldn't make it right for him. That evening, Mum and Dad told John he had to be good and get down to work, because he was making poor Jackie ill. It took a long time for John to settle down, though by the time he was seven years of age he had some friends. Yet the end of term could never come fast enough for my brother.

That year, 1966, was also the year that the Drills decided to sell a few of the houses in The Terrace, and ours was one. Getting "chucked out"—that was my mother's term—had become a real possibility, so my parents decided to try to buy the house. Thus 1966 became the year we took on a mortgage. It was fortuitous that a new government initiative was launched, offering mortgages at low interest rates for qualifying families seeking home ownership. Only it was not just a mortgage. As far as my mother was concerned, it was THE MORTGAGE, in capital letters and neon lights, and the way she uttered those words, they might as well have formed the title of a scary thriller. I could imagine the book's cover, with my mother in a noirish pose, her hands clutching the sides of her head, eyes wide, screaming, "Remember, we've all got to pull together, because of . . . THE MORTGAGE." She'd worked her way through a lot of paper "reckoning up" the household finances, and the new mortgage meant she would have to leave the farm—something she was quite looking forward to because another season requiring her to go dung spreading was just one season too many.

The trouble was that, as my mother soon discovered, even with her qualifications in administration and her experience in the Civil Service, landing a new job wasn't going to be easy. But she prevailed. When she heard that our dentist needed a new assistant—training on the job offered—she jumped at the chance and was hired. She started the new job just before the end of the school summer holidays, so we'd at least have the summer on the farm, followed by our first family holiday in Devon with all the uncles and aunts and cousins. Dad had passed his driving test at last and we had the Morris Traveller. We also had a dog—Rex—who joined our family a year earlier. Our lives were showing such promise—a house that was ours, a car, a new dog—and a real holiday!

For my part, I knew that more responsibility was now on my shoulders. Both Mum and Dad would not be home until after six in the evening, so I had to make sure John changed out of his new school uniform so he wouldn't tear it up when he went down the woods with the boys from up the street. I also had to give him something to eat to keep him going until we all had our evening meal together—we Winspears tend to get cranky when our blood sugar is low—and then I was to start work on our proper tea. Easy, as far as I was concerned, though I had a long slog home from school with Jenny.

The thing Mum most feared now was losing her job, or Dad losing his job, because the shadow over our heads of The Mortgage, and if we weren't able to pay the bills it would mean The Bailiff—picture my mother on the front of another book, screaming, "The bailiff's coming!" Though I had no real idea who the bailiff was, she had been threatening his appearance for years. Mum knew all about bailiffs from her childhood, and it was a fear with deep roots in her psyche. If my brother and I had a fight, you can bet we stopped as soon as the bailiff was mentioned—according to my mother, he would chuck us out on the street if the neighbors complained. My brother was threatened with the bailiff on the day he decided to unravel a whole roll of toilet paper in the outside WC, and I was told in no uncertain terms that if I didn't get my chores done in the house, then Mum would in turn lose her job, and we would be homeless. I didn't doubt that it could happen.

We'd been back at school about a month when John came home with a bad stomachache. I can still see him rushing past the side window in the kitchen, straight into the outside WC. It was to be a few more years before we received a government grant to put in an indoor bathroom. My brother was quite poorly, so Mum called Dr. Wood as soon as she was home and he came to the house. After examining my brother, he said it was a bug. He prescribed plenty of water and predicted that John would soon be as right as rain. I stayed away from school the following day to look after my brother because Mum could not take any time off from her new job. I didn't mind because it was Miss Chapman's cookery class on a Friday afternoon, and not only did I hate the class, but Miss Chapman picked on me relentlessly. It wasn't any easier at home, because when I gave Mum the list of ingredients we were required to take to school for the lesson each week, she always said, "What do they think we are—made of bloody money?" To be honest, we were making silly things like cakes and pies; probably half the girls not only already knew how to make cakes and pies, but had to cook an entire dinner as soon as they got home from school. They could certainly make a hot cocoa, which was the first ever lesson in Miss Chapman's domestic science class.

John was still not well all day Friday. Mum called the doctor again that evening and was assured the bug would work its way through—apparently there was something "going round" and lots of children were coming down with it. It was the new school year, after all, and these things happen—in fact, they happened every year.

Both Mum and Dad left for work on Saturday morning and I remained at home to look after my brother at the start of what was to become one of the scariest days of my eleven-year-old life. Mum had said I should run to the shop to buy some ginger beer as soon as it opened—after all, her mother had always sworn by ginger beer for a bad stomach. I was at the shop with my list, and though I bought the ginger beer, something stopped me giving it to my brother—which is just as well, considering how the day unfolded. Instead I thought he needed something to give him some energy, to build him up a bit to fight the bug, so I mixed a teaspoonful of glucose with water and took it to him.

I knew glucose was helpful to give you energy if you had a stomach upset—I had them all the time so Mum would give me glucose water if I looked "peaky." At age fifty, and having had no help from any doctor regarding lifelong stomach problems that had escalated during a book tour, I took the advice of a friend and traveled to Provo, Utah, to see an ordinary family doctor who had a worldwide reputation as someone who could help with intestinal issues. It was well worth the trip, because he drew a direct line from those massive doses of penicillin I'd been given following my scalding at fifteen months—a time when a child's gut flora is at a crucial stage of development—and the digestive problems I'd had my whole life. I suspect my parents accepted the doctor's diagnosis of my brother's illness because they were so used to me having stomach upsets, and believed it would pass. I understood exactly how my brother felt—or I thought I did.

John was in Mum and Dad's room, tucked up in their bed. I

sat with him and drew pictures of Father Christmas and a sleigh filled with toys for him as he snuggled into me holding his side. Fred Cooke at the shop along the road had already put up his Christmas display; it always went up on October 1st, and we were very excited. I drew pictures of a car John had his eye on, and I showed him what a whirlpool looked like, spinning the spoon around in the glass of glucose water, then lifting his head so he could drink it as it spiraled in the glass. By afternoon, I was sitting with my arms around my brother and worrying, counting the hours until Mum came home. I ran to the telephone box at the end of the road once to call the dental surgery, but Mum said not to worry, it's just a bug, and she wouldn't be long, reminding me that I shouldn't really call her on the dentist's telephone line. But I knew she *would* be long.

Toward the end of the afternoon, John started screaming in pain and I didn't know what to do. At some point, I knew I had to do something, but I was so scared I'd do the wrong thing— and perhaps my fear at the time has played a part in the fact that this is where my memory fails me. Did I call the doctor or the ambulance? Did the doctor come and then call the ambulance from the shop? I just know that by the time the ambulance came, my brother was in critical condition. John was rushed to Pembury Hospital, my mother by his side, while Dad and I followed in the Morris, and in torrential rain. The windscreen wipers had packed in, so for most of the journey, Dad had one hand out of the window on his side wiping water off the windscreen, while I kept the inside free of condensation.

John was taken straight into what we used to call the "Casualty Department." By the time Dad and I arrived, he had already been seen by the surgeon on duty, who had needed only seconds to diagnose the problem. Dad and I lurked at the door, watching as the junior doctor with a broad West Indian accent leaned over my brother, asking questions.

"When did you last urinate?" asked the young doctor.

John strained to understand the question.

"Don't be bloody stupid," said my mother, her tension showing in her manner. "He's a little boy." She held my brother's hand. "When did you last have a wee, love?"

I chimed in. "I got him to go at about four o'clock."

Then we heard another voice—a loud, pounding, American voice—as a stocky man with a bald head came striding along the corridor. A nurse ran behind holding a clipboard. He reminded me of that politician I'd seen on the news, the Russian one they called Khrushchev.

"That boy should have been in surgery two days ago," he yelled at another nurse. "I'm taking him into that operating room alive and I don't know if I can bring him out of there alive, he's so far gone."

John's appendix had already burst, probably that morning, and he had raging peritonitis.

Dad was in shock and my mother silenced. I knew this was a man who took no prisoners—I'd heard that phrase on an American TV show.

"I think he means the operating *theater*," I whispered to my father.

The surgeon—whose name I cannot remember—introduced himself to my parents, then waved to the orderlies, who wheeled my brother away. As he set off after my brother toward a sign indicating "Operating Theater," he was already taking off his jacket, throwing it to a nurse and holding out his arms so she could slip on the overall as she trotted alongside. Another nurse, already clad in green scrubs, touched my mother on the arm, looking from one parent to the other. "He's here on a fact-finding tour and is one of America's best surgeons. He's very good—if anyone can save your John, it's him." Then she ran down the corridor to join the famous American surgeon who was going to try to bring my brother out of there alive.

When the operation was over, Khrushchev walked into the waiting room, his green scrubs stained, sweaty and damp. He told my parents that the next forty-eight hours would be crucial and we should all go home and get some rest—there was nothing to be done by sitting there, waiting. If my cousin who thought us fey had been with me that night, she would have thought I'd completely lost my mind.

It was past midnight when I slipped into my narrow bed in the room I shared with my brother and closed my eyes. Though I was exhausted, I could not sleep. John was always a noisy sleeper, snuffling and snoring, and I would often ask him to try to be quiet. Now, on that night, with my brother far away in Pembury Hospital, I could hear him breathing, and it scared me because the breathing I heard was faltering, was becoming fainter and fainter and fainter. I was now too tall to sleep under the bed if I was scared. Instead I said aloud, "John, just breathe with me, listen to me breathing and breathe with me." I accentuated the sound of my breath and I heard him begin to follow me, shallow at first and then gaining strength. I fell asleep as I heard his breathing fall into a rhythm. I remembered everything the following morning, and upon seeing the empty bed, I shivered with fear of what the day might bring. I was sure of one thing, though—that my brother was still alive.

We were halfway to the hospital that Sunday morning when I told my parents what I'd heard in the room. To their credit, they didn't make any comment, though I remember them exchanging looks. Those looks were nothing like those they exchanged later when the surgeon who reminded me of a Russian politician told them that at one point, around midnight, he thought they'd lost my brother, that he despaired of saving him, but then John's breathing picked up and soon he was out of trouble. Not quite out of the woods, but perhaps out of that particular tree. My brother and I might have had our fights—and we could really get into it—but I had once been told he was my job. I think it was a responsibility that was very much alive in my soul.

My mother's employer, Mr. English, told her she was not to come back to work until John was safe and sound and out of the hospital, so she remained by his side, sleeping in a bed in his room. The American doctor, who called John "my miracle boy," came to his bedside every day. There was a beautiful Dutch nurse, Nurse Van Klonk, who had to give John his antibiotics each day, injecting the infection-fighting liquid into an IV, before embarking upon her next task, which was to syringe out the septic matter that came from a tube that went from his nose into his stomach. We all adored Nurse Van Klonk, and though the American doctor was hard to adore, we loved him all the same. He had saved my brother's life and he had done it with all the bluster of a sheriff in one of the Westerns Dad favored.

The daytime ward sister was a short, round Irish woman with a laugh that echoed along the hallway and signaled her imminent arrival as soon as she embarked upon her rounds—and my brother was always her first stop, not only because he was the most serious case on the whole floor, but because she had a soft spot for him. On one occasion, she was taking John's blood pressure when my father walked into the room and greeted John with, "'Allo Mush—how're you feeling?" before leaning across the bed to kiss his son and run his fingers through my brother's blonde hair. The word was spoken to rhyme with "push" and means "man" in Romany, though it is one of those words that had also become part of London's working class lexicon. Dad often called John by that name when he'd been up to some mischief. Sister loved the nickname, and thereafter would enter the room and say, "How's my Mush today?" in her Irish brogue, before checking the tubes attached to his little body. Then Nurse Van Klonk picked it up, and we all thought it was hilarious, a Romany word spoken with a Dutch accent.

While John was in the hospital, I broke my finger playing netball at school, and slipped away from my brother's bedside to ask a nurse if I should do something about it—she sent me up to casualty, where another nurse confirmed the break and bound the injured finger to the next. It didn't get me any special treatment, though, not like all the new toys, cards and balloons that were now adorning my brother's room.

It was as John made a slow recovery in hospital that a terrible disaster was visited upon the people of Aberfan in Wales, when a colliery slag heap collapsed and in a matter of seconds had enveloped a school. One hundred and sixteen children and twenty-eight adults were killed. I remember my mother weeping as she read the newspaper, sitting beside my brother's bed as he slept. An IV drip-dripped antibiotics and fluids into his arm, while tubes in his nose and at the site of the surgery all worked together to bring him back to health. "At least I still have my boy," she cried. "Those poor, poor people have lost their kids—but I still have my boy."

Two weeks after John came out of the hospital he found an old meat skewer in the garden that Dad had used to secure string when he was marking off a row of potatoes. Having discovered this new tool, my brother managed to poke it in his eye while using it to take a toy car apart. There was no serious injury, though Dr. Wood commented, "That boy will be the death of me." As far as Mum was concerned though, that was it—John's burst appendix, my broken finger and then John almost poking his eye out—the three things had come to pass, so she could rest, bring down her guard.

Then Abnett's closed and Dad lost his job. And we had The Mortgage, only now, as my mother said, it was "around our necks." I imagined a series of four nooses, just like I'd seen in Dad's Westerns, only they were underneath a banner proclaiming the cause of our collective demise. *"THE MORTGAGE."*

20

Fat Arse

જી

I still have the rubber stamp with "Albert Winspear, Painter & Decorator" above the address of our house at the end of The Terrace and our telephone number. Dad starting up on his own meant a telephone had to be installed—eventually. We still didn't have a phone when Jennifer emigrated to Canada when I was thirteen. My recollection is that I was sixteen when we finally had our own telephone line, because I remember at around that age running to the telephone box at the end of the road when the house next door caught fire, and they yelled out for someone to call the fire brigade. It was only as I walked back down the street in my pajamas and with no shoes on my feet that I wondered why they hadn't called themselves—after all, they had a telephone and we didn't.

In the meantime, anyone seeing Dad's advertisement in the *Weald Events*, a local weekly free booklet filled with community announcements and classified ads, would have had to write or call at the house if they were interested. There were two postal deliveries then, so a postcard or letter mailed in the morning could arrive by the afternoon, and one from farther afield would be delivered the following day. I didn't realize exactly how good the British postal service was until I came to live in the United States and was told that my letter to an address just seventy miles away would be delivered in about four days, and two if I chose to pay for Priority Mail.

Dad was able to get work almost as soon he was laid off, but even though Mr. Abnett sent clients his way, our luck had yet to swing round in the right direction. And my Jenny was leaving for Canada—I was shocked for weeks when she told me the news. Each day we would talk about Canada on the way home from school, often with both of us close to tears. Soon her parents were selling everything they owned; every single item in their house had a sticker on it with a price, so if you visited and you fancied a coffee table, you could walk out with it for ten bob. Or the kettle, or the chair in the corner, the one Jenny's dad would sit on when he conducted the name game at her birthday parties. For the name game, he had a list of about twenty place names and everyday items, and had drawn pictures of their constituent parts—as he held up two pictures at random, we had to guess the word. So, if he held up one picture of a weight with "One Ton" written on it, and another with a bridge, someone would yell out "Tonbridge!"—the name of a town in Kent. An old maid in one hand and a stone in another yielded another town, "Maidstone!" And so it went on.

And so it went on. The selling, the packing, the ending. As we walked home on the final day before Jenny and her family were due to fly to Toronto, we held onto each other and wept as we said goodbye. She promised to write every week and I promised to write back. I cried myself to sleep and never felt lonelier than when the bus pulled in at her stop the following Monday and she wasn't there. I even forgave her brother for stealing my bike every time I called at their house.

On the following Monday at school, as I sat outside during morning break, my friend Anne-Marie came over and sat down next to me. We had got on like a house on fire since meeting during our first week in the same class.

"You all right, Jacs?" She'd always called me Jacs, and spoke my name with a little Welsh lilt. Anne-Marie's family came from Brecon, in South Wales.

I shrugged.

"Would you like to come over to my house after school this Friday?"

I rubbed the back of my hand across my eyes and nodded. There and then, Anne-Marie became my new best friend—a most precious lifelong best friend.

Jennifer kept her promise and wrote often, but soon her news seemed far removed from my life in the country. She was in a softball team, and I had no idea what softball was. She lost a tooth playing ice hockey, and I could only imagine how terrible a game that was. We had to play field hockey at school, and because I didn't have shin pads, I was always returning home with massive bruises. I still have dents on my shins from field hockey. Jenny sent me a small ornament made by Indians—no one called them "First Nations" people then—it was a baby in a thing that looked like a snowshoe and contained a message: *To My Best Friend Ever.* I still have it.

Teen years are never the easiest of times, but during the year Mum left the farm tensions seemed to rise in the house and life became—for me, at least—like being on a seesaw, or a roller-coaster. Both my parents were working hard, but the highs and lows of my mother's moods became troubling for me in a way I think my brother avoided, and not only because he was a boy and younger, but because Mum looked upon him differently. Since his brush with death it seemed there was nothing he could do wrong, and though he wasn't mollycoddled, without doubt he avoided Mum's temper. On the other hand, even when I tried to lie low, I seemed to become the lightning rod for it. One reason for her moods was the financial pressure. I was growing fast, and she hated having to buy new school uniform items, complaining bitterly about the cost. Fortunately, a grey school skirt had been passed down to me from a cousin, and though it was too long when I started at the Mary Sheafe School for Girls, Mum made me turn it over at the waist and pin it, not only so it fitted around my middle, but wouldn't drag around my ankles. That was to be my school skirt until I left at sixteen—by which time I was turning it over at the waist again so I had a miniskirt. My blouses were bought large to last me, as was my school sweater. My gym kit was brand new—the red shorts and yellow Aertex shirt—and we had to have our summer dresses made in a specific fabric to an approved design because the dresses could not be bought off the peg. I heard the refrain time and again, about the school thinking we were all made of money, until Mum was put in touch with a friend of a friend who would make the dresses for me.

I was thirteen when Celia came to stay during the summer. I was so excited, though I can't think why she came to stay because she was a teenager with a great social life in London, and there wasn't anything for a city sixteen-year-old to do in our neck of the woods. She was training to be a hairdresser at Vidal Sassoon's salon in London's West End, and had a lovely short haircut, and of course we know about her clothes. I was so excited because she had come to stay for a whole week and I would have her to myself. She was a big fan of Paul and Barry Ryan, the singing twins who had a hit that year with a song called "Eloise," although Celia would sing their earlier hit, "Don't Bring Me Your Heartaches" time and again. I think she found it frustrating that we didn't have a record player.

I had so much fun trying to copy Celia, and she helped me out with her Mary Quant Paintbox. That was the name of the box of makeup produced by Mary Quant, the hippest fashion designer in London and Celia had one. While Mum and Dad were out at work, Celia would apply makeup to my eyes and I was thrilled to look so different. I felt really grown up and not like a gangly kid—in fact, I looked at least eighteen and I knew it. On one occasion, Mum came home from work and stared at me, taking in the eye liner and eye shadow; the heavy mascara, the hint of blusher across my cheeks and the fact that I was wearing one of Celia's Twiggy dresses. She'd styled my hair in a low bun at the nape of my neck, so it looked as if I had short hair, and for a brief moment I kidded myself that I looked like the famous model. I wasn't sure about the way Mum looked me up and down and for a second a silence seemed to fill the air, so I had a sense that something was shifting, and she wasn't at all happy with what she saw before her. Then she told me I'd better wash that stuff off my face before Dad came home because he'd go mad if he saw me looking like that, and to change into my own clothes.

One day Celia wanted to buy a plain white T-shirt and some colored tape, as it was "all the rage" to wear a T-shirt with your initial on the front. We walked into town, found the requisite T-shirt and iron-on tape in navy blue and came home, whereupon Celia put together the fashion statement for all to see, the giant "C" on the front of a white T-shirt. Mum and Dad commented that it was all very nice. After Celia left to return to London, I took out some of my savings and on the following Saturday morning I walked into Cranbrook to buy a white T-shirt and some red tape. I planned to copy Celia and put my initial on the T-shirt. Dad came home from work that afternoon just as I was pinning the large "J" onto the T-shirt.

"What're you doing, Jack?" he asked.

I explained that I was going to iron my initial onto the T-shirt, because it was the fashion and "everyone is doing it."

Any reasoning that included reference to what "everyone" was doing was always like a red rag to a bull to my father. It was one of the few things that would make him mad.

"Why would you want to be like everyone else?' he would ask.

I never found the right answer, but on that day Dad gave me a piece of advice that seems to have underpinned not only my life, but my brother's. Dad knelt down beside me, picked up the tape and said, "Jack, you've got to think different. Let's you and me find another design, do something else with the tape—let's go and buy some more colors. Think different, love—always think different."

Yes, my dad got there with the "Think Different" slogan before Steve Jobs, except that with Dad's Cockney accent, it was "Fink Different."

Soon after school began again following the summer hiatus, there came a day that I will never forget, because it marked a turning point in my relationship with my mother that was perhaps seeded when she came home and saw me wearing Celia's makeup and a very fashionable minidress—which she left for me when she returned to London. I realized Mum saw me as some sort of competitor, that I was no longer just a daughter, but someone she didn't quite know how to deal with, living in the same house.

We had the Ford Cortina estate car then, a beige vehicle that followed a terrible green Morris 1100 that looked like a squatting frog and was always breaking down—that in turn had come after the trusty grey Morris Traveller. My father had complained bitterly about the newer Morris, wishing he hadn't sold the old one, though the Cortina was decreed "a nice little runner." Perhaps it was Mum's day off, but whatever the reason, she picked me up from school, a rare event. I was surprised when I saw her waiting outside the school for me, with John in the back seat. After doing some shopping in Cranbrook, we set off for a house in Benenden where Dad was working with one of his former colleagues from Abnett's. Most of the laid-off painters had set up on their own and would get in touch with each other if a big job came up needing more hands. On this day Dad was working with Bill—a lovely man who should probably have retired, but was still working because he and his wife liked to take their caravan over to Europe, and the extra money helped pay for their wanderlust.

I can still see Dad and Bill packing up their overalls and brushes as we came along the driveway of the big house. We all got out of the car and as I walked toward Dad to give him a kiss, Bill said, "Albert, that girl of yours is growing into a beauty." It's the sort of thing adults always say about their friends' daughters and was in the same vein as how tall they've grown, and was it only yesterday they were running around in nappies. I blushed, but my mother hadn't missed a beat.

"She may be growing up, Bill, but she'll never be as good looking as her mother."

I wanted the ground to eat me up and never spit me out again, and I blushed even more. Mum's words seemed to hang in the air for a second that seemed like a minute, then Bill winked at me and said, "She's getting there, Joyce—she's getting there."

I walked back to the car feeling as if even the roots of my hair would combust into flames. While my mother could be my greatest supporter, one who I know loved me very much, it was as if a line had been drawn in the sand that day and I became an enemy, the daughter who had to be shown who was boss, or who had to be taken down a peg or two. In truth, I was so lacking in confidence, I don't think I was up even half a peg in the first place.

There was sometimes little warning of an incoming verbal missile, or a lie told about me in company, or an opportunity to make a joke at my expense. I would sometimes hear her talking about me to her sisters, when they were exchanging stories about their teenage daughters. I'd hear her say, "You'll never guess what *it* had the cheek to say to me the other day . . ." And there would be a made up story of something I was supposed to have said, or done—or more accurately, what *it* had done. There were times when she just needed a sparring partner, probably because my dad was one to seek the easygoing quiet life, as was my brother, who kept his head down most of the time.

Sunday mornings could be the worst. I would always get up early, often to go with Dad when he took the dog for a walk across the fields. Or I would walk by myself, increasingly seeking the quiet balm that the woods offered—I'd sit alone for hours, afraid to come home to the fusillade. Sometimes I'd sit for so long at the base of a favorite tree that I thought I could feel it growing along my spine, or I would lie on my back in the middle of the five-acre field to watch the clouds scudding along, convinced I could see the sky moving past as the earth turned in space. I'd often place my hands against the base of a tree to feel the warmth, in the same way that I rest my hands just above my horse's hoof to feel his pulse. I would never have said as much, but in my solitude I had a deep sense that every tree was connected to every other tree, and was even linked to the blades of grass and the flowers in the woodland around me. I could feel the aliveness, and liked the company.

Mum slept late on Sundays—and who could blame her? She worked hard all week. But if I was in the kitchen, I could tell from the way her feet hit the floorboards three floors above, how her approaching footfall echoed down the stairs, whether she would appear singing, "Oh what a beautiful morning," or if she would be yelling, "Where's that girl—where's that lazy little cow, I've got a job for her." Then the nagging would start, and go on, and on, and on. I might have been a lot of things, but I wasn't lazy. And then there was the mirror.

We had a mirror in the kitchen, useful if someone else was in the bathroom and you needed to make sure your school tie was straight before you left the house. It was an old art deco mirror, rectangular with beveled edges and a broken chain on the back. Although there was a place for it to be shoved away underneath the counter next to the stove, so you could whip it out if you needed it, we tended to leave it on top of the counter for much of the time because it was heavy.

My mother would often stand in front of the mirror when she was shouting at me, staring at her reflection as if she had been drawn in by the furrowed brow and the flared nostrils, a hallmark of her temper. This fascinated me, the urge to watch herself losing her temper. One day when I was about fifteen—and, let's be fair, sometimes answering back—I watched her looking at the mirror as she nagged, and I said aloud, "Mirror, mirror on the wall, who's the—" And I ran to my room and didn't come out again for a while until she'd calmed down. I thought she would kill me. I think it was not long afterward that I dropped the mirror and it broke into hundreds of pieces. An accident. Just slipped through my fingers. Really.

Yet amid all those verbal attacks, I adored her. I thought she was the most wonderful woman—witty and intelligent and I knew she had a capacity for deep compassion. My friend Anne-Marie loved her and said she thought my mum was really funny. And she was. It was just that I was often the subject of her jokes. But even then I realized that my mother's disappointment at leaving school when she was fourteen must have been so much more difficult to bear as I reached the age at which she had been sent to work in a laundry. As I approached that same marker, the minimum school-leaving age in England was raised to sixteen, so I worked even harder to buy any clothes or other essentials needed so there was no family burden, and of course I looked forward to that regular big plastic bag of hand-me-downs from Celia and her sisters—though they were fast becoming too small as I had grown taller than the girls on that side of the family.

My despair became even darker when Mum decided I was putting on weight. It started when she noticed I had "puppy fat" and escalated the day she told me I had legs like a footballer. I dropped my hems and I walked two miles on roads without pavements (sidewalks) to buy a pair of baggy jeans from a shop in Hawkhurst that sold clothing for men in the building trade. The torment escalated with my new nickname: Fat Arse. My family thought it was just hilarious when she called me Fat Arse the first time. John then started calling me Fat Arse, and Dad laughed—and the fact that Dad laughed crushed me. I thought he would be the last person to add to my humiliation. They all laughed a lot about me being Fat Arse, then when I became upset I was admonished for not being able to "take it." You had to be able to take it in our family, whatever the *it* was. To this day, I hate hearing people teased or on the end of unwanted attention and then hearing someone say, "Oh, they can't take it." Even worse is when the person doing the teasing—and teasing is never as innocent as it sounds—says, "Oh, she's all right—she can take it." I've never worked out why people have to "take" verbal abuse dished up as humor and then be accused of not being able to "take a joke" if they fail to laugh at themselves.

My mother stopped calling me "Fat Arse" when I'd lost so much weight she didn't quite know what to do—she thought I had an overactive thyroid and sent me to the doctor, who in any case had been feeling around my neck every time I'd seen him since I hit puberty, on the lookout for the family thyroid problem. He also continued to slap my hand because I couldn't stop biting my nails. Having noticed the weight loss, Mum had no idea that I wasn't eating much for two reasons. Not only did I want to put a stop to being called Fat Arse—and in truth, I was never fat at all—but I also felt guilty about the fuss she'd made about the cost of school meals when I was sixteen and transferred to Cranbrook "Grammar" School to do my A levels. After my first year there, I withdrew my name from the meals list and instead ran around to the grocery shop to get a yoghurt and apple for lunch. By that time Mum had left the dentist and was working for the government. I don't think she noticed because she only noticed things that were on the school bill, not things that were missing.

Jenny noticed, though. It was a late summer evening in the year I turned seventeen, when Jenny arrived at the house out of the blue. I was aware of movement outside the window and saw her run past toward the front door—a taller version of the friend who had left four years earlier. I could not believe my eyes, but I had the door open even before she had a chance to knock, and we just held onto each other, crying. I had no idea she was coming over from Canada—she'd wanted it to be a surprise for me. Her accent had hardly changed, but she seemed so international, so different, in a way. Yet the same. The same Jennifer. She wanted to go to a pub and drink a pint of Newcastle Brown Ale, her favorite (When had that become a favorite drink? Could you even get Newcastle Brown in Toronto?), and she wanted to see her old boyfriend, Steve. She blurted out that she wanted to do this, and wanted to do that, and wanted to hear all my news. But as she stood back to look at me, she said, "Jack, you're even thinner than me, and I'm shorter than you!"

Mum and Dad came from the kitchen when they heard me call out to say that Jenny was right there, in the house, all the way from Canada. Mum had heard what Jenny said about my weight, and added, "You're right, Jen—I've been telling her for ages to put some meat on those bones."

I looked at Dad. He looked at Mum, then John interrupted, "What sort of car have you got in Canada?" He's still what they call a "petrolhead."

I can't remember the answer and the question of my weight was forgotten—but not by me. I knew Fat Arse could come back to torment me again.

21

Ch-ch-ch-ch-changes . . .

◆

A friend who is the same age as me, born in the mid-1950s, recently asked me if I consider myself to be a child of the 1950s or 1960s. I shook my head and laughed. "Neither," I said. "My childhood was more Edwardian until I was about fourteen." Then I became a child of the '60s. Sort of.

The year I turned fourteen was a year when so much changed for us, though perhaps I was the only one to notice the shift, to join the dots of meaning in this year we weren't laughing, despite last year's promises. Jenny had left. I was becoming even more unhappy at home. And then our small community seemed to lose the final tenuous threads that still attached it to the Edwardian age. The petrol station and car repair shop at the end of the road changed hands—it was housed in what had once been the stables for the old inn that had preceded construction of The Railway Arms, which in turn was built at the same time as the railway. The pub had been renamed The Duke of Kent years earlier, but there was still something old and ancient about the way "the Duke" was part of the community. The local hunt still met at the pub for a "stirrup cup" on foggy autumn mornings, before galloping off in search of the elusive fox. Although I hated the idea of hunting foxes, I loved the tradition because I would walk up to the top of the road on hunting days to watch the ladies, especially, as some still rode side-saddle and wore little bowler hats with a veil to shield their eyes. Now the hunt met somewhere else—perhaps the hunt protesters had moved them on. In time I would be a vocal opponent of fox hunting, but I also knew that most foxes managed to avoid the hunt. They're clever, canny creatures.

Pete Eldridge sold the garage when he and his wife, Kay, moved to Tenterden. We visited them once, and Mr. Eldridge gave John and me little "Esso" key rings and other trinkets he'd received as giveaways from the petrol companies. Now the new garage owner was demolishing the old stables and was building a big, modern petrol station and garage, and was parking cars for sale over the back, near the duck pond. Then we heard someone had bought land behind the pub and wanted to develop it, but old Mrs. Oyler put a stop to that, as she had before when a former publican tried to do the same thing. She'd lived in the area from girlhood and knew many of the ancient land laws. She pointed out that, according to a particular centuries-old law, the land could not be developed. So it wasn't—at least not then.

We were shocked again when Fred Cooke sold the general store at the end of the street. The Cookes had owned that store for years, before my parents came from London to live in Kent, and they had been there through so many of our trials and tribulations. In his big bulbous grey Standard Vanguard van, Fred Cooke had searched high and low, driving to farms and out-of-the-way villages, to find the doctor on his rounds on the day my mother went into labor with John. And it was the Cookes who had waited up for us when John was rushed to the hospital with a burst appendix. I can still see their daughter, Lyn, holding out her hand to me as we clambered out of the car late at night—Fred had flagged Dad down as soon as he heard our car turn into The Terrace. "Don't worry about that boy," he'd said. "He's not finished causing me trouble, not by a long chalk—he'll be out of that hospital and right as rain, just you see." My brother was already known as something of a "Dennis the Menace" in the hamlet.

Now the Cookes were moving on, to take over a shop in Frittenden.

To add to the misery, Dad managed to rupture himself that spring and by summer was scheduled for a hernia operation. He tried to work at the same clip, but couldn't, so some jobs had to be passed onto Bill and Dave, his former workmates. Money became short, and of course there was the dreaded mortgage. Mum decided to apply for my brother and me to receive free school meals. I was mortified, because I knew what that meant.

At my secondary school, every Monday we had to line up outside the school's administration office, where the school secretary sat as gatekeeper to the entrance hall and also to the headmistress's office just along the corridor. When you reached the window, having lined up for what seemed like hours, you would hand over five shillings and the secretary would tick off your name. Miss Nelson, the headmistress, then gave you five pink dinner tickets, which were used to get into the dining hall each day. It was a way to keep tabs on us, to make sure we were all eating, I suppose. If you were bringing your own packed lunch for dietary or religious reasons, you had to have special permission, based upon a letter from your parents with details of your nutritional or spiritual preferences. If you were eligible for free meals, you presented the letter from the local council confirming your status, and you were issued with dinner tickets of a different color, a shade of green, so everyone knew you were poor and your parents couldn't afford the five bob a week to feed you at midday.

The first time I presented my letter from the council, Miss Nelson said, in a loud voice so the entire line of girls could hear,

"Jacqueline Winspear, free school meals this week." I wanted to die of shame. The same happened the following week until I could stand it no longer and simply used money I'd saved from my summer job. It was no good taking food from home, because Mum would never have written the necessary letter to support my taking a packed lunch—as far as she was concerned, "I pay my bloody taxes, and you're entitled to this." She was right, of course, but it didn't negate the shame.

Dad went down with a very serious bout of pleurisy that winter, just as he was getting back on his feet and work was starting to come in again following the hernia operation. I remember telling Mum that perhaps she shouldn't smoke so much, invoking what I'd learned about smoking in biology at school: we were all breathing in the smoke and it wasn't doing us any good. It didn't have any effect whatsoever—she even called her cigarettes "my cancer sticks" to scare me, though she slowed up a bit when my single bed had to be moved downstairs into the sitting room so Dad could sleep there to keep warm, and I slept with her in their attic bedroom. The bedrooms had been changed around soon after John came home from the hospital, when it became clear that a girl of my age shouldn't be sharing a room with a little boy. I moved into the room vacated by my parents at the front of the house, and they moved up a floor into the attic, which was not like an attic at all, but was a lovely large room with a vaulted ceiling and views across the Weald of Kent as far as the eye could see. In some ways, I wish I'd asked for it to be my bedroom, but I was also scared in that room, because the roof beams creaked at night. I already knew the house was haunted, though Dad had assured us that all the ghosts moved out when we moved in. "Would you want to live with this family, if you were a self-respecting ghost? No, mark my words, they've moved on." Dad kept our fey Winspear feet firmly on the ground.

Money became really tight that winter and we had to be careful with the coal. One Saturday, while Mum was at work and Dad was sleeping, I came up with a plan. It was a bitterly cold day, nearing that point in the afternoon when the winter sun is low in the sky and edged with purple, a sign that dusk is just around the corner. I knew we needed logs but couldn't afford them, so I told John we were going across the field into the forest to bring back wood—and this was the right time, because we would have to return in darkness. I didn't want the neighbors to see us coming home with what was effectively filched wood. I'd remembered where some trees had been taken down the previous year and left in a great pile to season. The trunks were narrow enough to pull home, though they'd been cut to about fifteen feet long. I thought I could drag two home, resting the thinnest part of the trunks on my shoulders, and John could drag one—that would give us a lot of logs. We might have been siblings who fought a lot, but when we had a plan requiring cooperation against an outside foe, we were as tight as clams, and this year had seen us battle one enemy after another.

We bundled up in our duffel coats, boots, gloves and scarves, John wearing his woolen balaclava and me with a knitted hat pulled down so low I could just about see. Frost was already thick on the ground as we marched across Five Acres, jumping over the stile and making our way gingerly down the Burton Way into the woods. We walked on toward the wood pile, stopping to listen every few minutes. No one else was about. Not that we expected anyone to be about, but we were also used to things going wrong, so we listened to make sure. When we reached the pile of wood, I lifted one narrow tree trunk onto John's shoulder and then managed to balance two on mine. We'd walked about a quarter of a mile through the woods when, halfway up the hill that led to the field we had to drop the trunks because they were too heavy to drag up the gradient. Instead we hauled them one by one to the edge of the field, where we took up our respective loads again and began walking across Five Acres. I remember struggling with the weight of my two long tree trunks, but at the same time I wanted to keep John going. Every time I looked back at him, a boy of nine pulling a heavy tree trunk behind him, I wanted to weep—his head was down and he was puffing with sheer effort as he battled fatigue to bear his load. My shoulders were beginning to hurt where the wood was digging into me and I'd shoved my gloves into my pocket so I could get a better grip, but we had to carry on—we needed to get the wood to the house. We rested at the next stile, working together to push the long trunks over the gate. We were almost home.

The footpath alongside our house at the end of The Terrace was narrow, so once again we had to carry each trunk separately, dumping them outside the shed close to the wide tree stump we used as a base to chop wood. Mum heard us maneuvering the wood down the path and came running out of the house.

"Where have you two been? I've been worried sick about you since I got home—and you left your father on his own."

I was out of breath and pointed to the tree trunk. All I could say was, "It's already seasoned—it'll burn." Then John and I turned around to bring back two more trunks.

Mum was fighting back tears as she began sawing the wood into logs, while I split each one with the long-handled axe and John stacked them beside the shed. And while we were all tired and upset, I knew that this was our family at its best—working together against whatever might befall us. In that moment the enemy just seemed to be that year's fate, as if our ship had sailed under a very dark cloud close to rocks with no wind to be picked up by the sails.

That Monday, as I handed over my letter from the council so I could be given the green dinner tickets that showed everyone I was receiving free school meals, Miss Nelson commented upon the scratches and bruises on my hands and arms.

"What have you been doing?" she asked, her tone as snippy as ever. I could not stand that woman.

"Chopping wood to keep my dad warm—he's very ill," I replied, with a definite tone of defiance in my words.

Without waiting to be dismissed, I took up the tickets, shoved them in my pocket, and walked off. She didn't call me back to reprimand me for insolence, and I wasn't going to thank her for giving me the tickets. Perhaps she saw something in my eyes, that I was more than ready for a fight with authority and I might just win. Then anarchy would prevail, because she was not universally liked and she knew it.

Despite my father's promises, as logs burned in the fireplace that evening I wasn't at all convinced that this time next year we'd be laughing, or would even have cause for the odd smile.

But the following year even more change was in the air. Mum read about new government grants to upgrade houses without indoor lavatories or bathrooms, so she applied for the grant and in short order received word that we had not only received a grant to put in a bathroom, but to have a new kitchen installed. At that point we had an old bathtub, but it was in the kitchen, so if you wanted a bath, it had to be filled from the copper or an electric boiler that we used for the bedlinens, and you just had to make sure the family knew you needed the privacy to bathe uninterrupted. If someone wanted to use the outdoor lavatory, instead of coming through the dining room and kitchen—which you would usually do to get to the back door that led outside—they had to go out the front door and walk around the path at the side of the house.

With the new bathroom fitted—you still had to go through the kitchen and a new back entrance hall to get to it, but that was no problem when you've not had any bathroom before—next came the kitchen. The old Rayburn that had replaced the original black cast-iron stove was pulled out, and instead of a copper to heat the water, an enclosed solid fuel fireplace with a back boiler was installed in the sitting room, plus an immersion heater in the new hot water tank for backup in summer when we wouldn't need a fire. We had a new electric stove and fitted cabinetry. Dad really went to town on the house, as if the remodeling bug was nipping at him. He knocked down the wall between our sitting room and the dining room—both very small rooms—although we couldn't afford fitted carpet for the larger "lounge" for some time. Unfortunately, all this improvement meant we couldn't run to the purchase of a vacuum cleaner, so I felt like Cinderella, forever on my hands and knees brushing with a hand broom.

Then Mum bought a washing machine. It was what they called a "twin tub" in those days—a cheaper type of machine with a washer on one side and a spin dryer on the other. I think they're still made. When the wash cycle was finished, you drained the tub and pulled the laundry out of the machine and into the spinner.

There had been a previous interlude when we had a washing machine, but it was short-lived because the thing was ancient and in all likelihood possessed by a jester spirit. Dad often worked at houses that were being remodeled and people were throwing out old items they didn't want or where someone elderly had died and the place was being prepared for sale by the family, hence even older stuff was being disposed of. That's how the big green washing machine, manufactured circa 1910, had come into our possession. It comprised a large metal cylinder supported by Chippendale-style legs, with an agitator in the barrel and a wringer on the top—but it was electric powered, so no one had to do the washing by hand, though Dad had to change the plug. You had to fill the cylinder with hot water and then switch it on, whereupon an agitator thumped the laundry around until you thought it had been thumped around enough. Then you switched off the machine part and started the wringer—there was a lever to alternate power—and you fed the bedlinens, towels and clothing through the wringer, making sure you'd put a laundry basket on the other side ready to catch the clean, washed load. When you were done, you emptied the thing via a small tap at the base of the cylinder. This was what labor saving looked like before the Great War. My brother caught his fingers in the wringer once and learned a lesson—I pulled away the electric cable just in time to save his entire hand.

This ancient washing machine had its own little dance routine, because as soon as you turned it on it began to move, which meant someone had to lean against it to keep it in place. One day all hell broke loose when Mum and I went into the garden to peg out the clean laundry, leaving John to attend to the washing machine. His attention soon wandered and he ran out to play with the dog. Freed from the constraints of humans keeping watch over its behavior, the machine with the comedic turn jigged toward the kitchen door and slammed into it, so we couldn't get back into the house again—and the front door was locked. The three of us leaned against that door, shaking and vibrating as the machine on the other side was jumping up and down to a cha-cha beat. Mum had no other option than to break a window so John could climb into the kitchen, turn off the machine and drag it away from the door. It went to the dump the following week.

With this history, is it surprising that I crept out of school and came home early on the day the brand-new twin tub washing machine was delivered? I was so excited. By the time Mum arrived home from work, I'd read the instruction book from cover to cover and had four loads of laundry finished and on the washing line, drying. I'd washed bedlinens, Dad's shirts, John's school uniform, my clothes, the lot. I'd gone to each room and picked up anything that needed washing and got to work. I treated that washing machine as my own personal gift—now I wouldn't have to launder anything by hand unless it was something delicate, and I was just thrilled to bits.

Change, change, change. How much more would there be? By the time I was a few months shy of fifteen, it was clear Fate was not finished with us. Mum had asked for a raise at the dental surgery and had been turned down by Mr. Jones, the senior partner. I knew she wanted not only more money, but more opportunity. She was forty-two and more than ready to jimmy open doors that had previously shut tight in her face, from the time she'd had to turn away from a scholarship to the prestigious girls' school in London.

She applied for a job as a clerical assistant at a detention center for boys situated close to a neighboring village. Such places are often in rural areas away from public transportation, so offenders have little means for a quick getaway if they abscond. She landed the government job with ease—she already had the Civil Service exams under her belt, so it was what we might today call a "shoo-in." As soon as she was hired, I knew— we all knew—Mum was on her way, and we were so proud of her. Things were looking up again—Dad was earning decent money, Mum was on a career path, and John and I were . . . well, we were okay. The ship was on an even keel and we were out of the Doldrums. Now we were heading for next year, when we would definitely all be laughing.

22

A Social Disadvantage

I still wonder where my brain was on the day I brought home that test result informing my parents that teaching would be the best career path for me. I should have kept it hidden. They knew I wanted to be a writer. Hadn't they seen that quote on my bedroom wall, taken from the copy of *The Diary of a Young Girl* by Anne Frank I'd bought at a paperback sale at school? Anne had written, "No one who doesn't write can know how fine it is. And if I don't have the talent to write for newspapers or books, well then, I can always go on writing for myself."

But Mum and Dad thought the test result was good news, and later agreed that I should apply to college. I really didn't want to go to a teacher training college, yet I also didn't want to disappoint my parents. They knew I would be eligible for a full grant based upon their income, and the only element of cost to them would be my "spending money." While that was something to which the council expected them to contribute, I knew Mum would complain like hell if she had to give me money. I had a full timetable at college, but I'd be working through the winter, spring and summer breaks, so I knew I'd be okay.

If truth be told, my silence regarding this future I felt pushed into was due to the fact that I was still smarting from something that happened when I was close to leaving the girls' secondary school. They only offered education to O level at Mary Sheafe School for Girls, but I wanted to do my A levels, too. If you wanted to go on to higher education at college or university, you needed passes at A level that reflected your intended course of future study. Mum had done some of her "reckoning" and decreed that it would better for Dad's taxes if I did just that—remained at school to do my A levels and then go to college.

I was gearing up to apply to Tunbridge Wells Girls Grammar School when we discovered that Cranbrook School, a semi-private boys' secondary school referred to locally as "Cranbrook Grammar," would be taking a small number of girls into their sixth form as part of a gradual coeducational process. Because the school had partial government funding, it had to step into line with plans to develop coeducation in all schools receiving public money. Several girls from my school were applying, including Anne-Marie, and I must admit I liked the idea of not having to travel by bus to Tunbridge Wells each day—any mysterious anti-nausea powers in the magic penny had long ago worn off.

As soon as I applied to Cranbrook Grammar—and the application amounted to a letter to the headmaster, along with a listing of O-level results expected, plus an interview with a parent present—Miss Nelson summoned my mother to a meeting where she expressed her concern that going to Cranbrook Grammar might be a mistake for me, because I would be at a "social disadvantage" given that other pupils at the school came from wealthy families. That was definitely the wrong thing to say to my mother, who had prepared for the interview and was wearing a couture black suit with a fitted jacket and a pencil skirt that skimmed her calves. She'd handed over just a few pounds for the suit with its eye-watering price tag still attached—the bargain came via a friend of a friend, and it was cheap because it had "fallen off the back of a lorry" as the

saying went. On the day she went to see Miss Nelson, the new suit
was set off by her best black court shoes polished to a shine by my
father, and her hair was swept back in an elegant French twist. Mum
was a good eight inches taller than Miss Nelson, who was probably
sorry she had ever thought to "express concern" and was now wondering if it might have been better to just let me go without a word.
Which is effectively what happened after that visit. I can still hear
my mother saying, "She's concerned about you fitting in socially?
I'll give her something to be concerned about." Mum had just won
her first promotion and she was working in a sensitive government
department, a prison no less, so she wasn't going to take lip from
anyone, especially a headmistress whom Mum always said could
do with an afternoon in a field with a dirty old man. I know—it's a
terrible thing to say, but she said it.

In many ways I had a good time at the grammar school, I suppose because I made new friends who were a lot of fun. Our house
always seemed to be full of teenage boys who were less interested
in being my friend, I think, than in my father's massive egg, bacon,
sausage and baked beans fry-ups—for kids who board at school,
having home-cooked food was a treat.

However, I didn't care for my education there. At Mary
Sheafe, whether I liked them or not—and mostly I liked them—
the teachers knew how to teach their subject. At the grammar it
seemed as if we were just given information and had to take it
from there. Or maybe that was what growing up academically
was all about, and I just wasn't really ready. Admittedly, I'd also
made an error with my subjects, but I'd had no real advice on how
to proceed and my parents didn't discuss it with me because it
was outside their experience of education. English was an easy
first choice—it had been my best subject from primary school
onward—but as much as I loved history, I realized too late that the

kind of history I enjoyed was not being taught. Our lessons were focused more toward British political history of the sixteenth and seventeenth centuries, whereas my loves were social and modern history. Talk to me about dates and laws in the 1600s and my eyes glaze over, but tell me that Elizabeth I had black teeth, and I am all ears. I was interested in what happened to ordinary people as a result of those big political decisions, not the names of leaders and what they said at every last meeting of Parliament. I was getting bored stiff with Thomas Cranmer and Thomas Cromwell, and who was stabbing who else in the back (it's probably why I cannot bring myself to read the novels by Hilary Mantel) though I loved the fact that Oliver Cromwell said, "I can tell you, sirs, what I would not have, though I cannot what I would." I knew exactly how he must have felt.

There was another setback to deal with. As my studies advanced, the increased reading required revealed that the eye surgery I'd had as a child had not "held" sufficiently. Soon my wandering lazy eye was causing double vision and migraines, and I was finding it difficult to keep up with my work. Two more surgeries to correct my vision followed when I was sixteen and seventeen, and it was a challenge to bounce back and catch up.

In truth, though, the main problem was within me, because Miss Nelson's words echoed in my ears every single day. I became almost mute in class, afraid to speak, afraid that I was socially unacceptable. I remember in one class I was asked to describe James I of England, who was also James VI of Scotland, and in my response, I commented that being "ostentatious" contributed to his downfall because James—"the wisest fool in Christendom"— thought he was inheriting a land of riches when he acceded the throne following the death of Elizabeth I. Frankly, I was bored stiff with the words of yet another centuries-old king. I was beginning to think it would have been better had I chosen geography, a subject I had always been really good at. The teacher interrupted me with, "Do you know what 'ostentatious' means?" I gave him the correct definition and he simply said, "Continue . . ." as if disappointed that he hadn't caught out the girl who had no right to be there. Funny, the things you remember. I wish I'd had the courage to say, "Of course I know what the bloody hell it means—why else would I use the word?" That would have had me kicked out of school, which might not have been such a bad thing.

The question about my social status lingered on, affecting my time at the new school both academically and socially. My confidence was at a low ebb, further undermined by the number of times I was asked "What does your father do?" by teachers, parents of friends, parents of acquaintances and indeed by a few of my new friends. I knew very well what was at the heart of the question, and that was a process of putting a person in a specific box. It was akin to a swift assessment to discover where I really belonged, to establish the station in life where I had started my journey. Your father's job dictated the way you were seen in terms of socioeconomic class, future potential, or whether you were worth knowing at all. I had several problems with that question. First, although both my parents left school at fourteen, I knew how hard they worked. My father was a master craftsman in the home improvement business. I objected to the fact that no one asked what my mother did for a living; by that time she was an "Executive Officer" in the Civil Service. More than anything, I hated the fact that someone was willing to make a judgment about me based upon my father's job. It also grieved me that my father was worried about attending parents' meetings with my mother because he thought his Cockney accent would let me down. My mother could put on any accent, and when she went along to meet the teachers, she sounded like Maggie Smith. Dad had an accent like Michael Caine in his early films. Knowing how he felt, that was the year I chose a Father's Day card with "I don't tell everyone you're my Dad" on the front, and inside, "Just the people I want to impress." He loved it.

Years later, I was in London and in the midst of an interview for an article about my novels that was scheduled to appear in an old established magazine, when I was taken aback by the journalist's first question.

"And what does your father do?" she asked.

"Really?" I said, feeling as if someone had just hit me. "I am fifty years old and here to talk about my books, and you want to know what my father does?" I could feel my adolescent intimidation laced with fear coming back to haunt me, but this time I wasn't going to let it have the upper hand. "My father is seventy-eight years of age. He loves dancing, reading and cooking. He also makes really good wine and he hikes and does all the things a retired man of his age enjoys."

"Oh," she said.

Yes, oh indeed. At the end of the interview, I left her with a final thought, one that probably tormented her a bit.

"You should have asked about my mum," I said. "Now there's a story for you!"

Since coming to live in the United States I've been asked that question several times, yet only by a certain kind of British ex-pat. But my brother and I are like our father in so many ways—on the other side of that river pitching our tents so we don't get wet. And though we might once have cared, it's been water off a duck's back for a long time.

23

Neighbors and Other People

❧

When we moved into our house at the end of The Terrace there was just one other young family on the street and they were only there for about a year or two. They had a son, Paul, who was a little older than me, and a daughter, Anne, who was about John's age. Mr. Martin took me to Sunday school at the Hawkhurst Baptist church each week, and when they moved I went with Miss Jenner, who lived along the main road in a large Victorian terrace house with her older sister and brother, who was in a wheelchair. I believe Miss Jenner's sister had lost her young husband in the Great War—the same war in which their brother was wounded. Miss Jenner was one of the two million women considered "surplus" following that war, given the sheer number of young men of marriageable age who had been killed in the years 1914–18. Though there were a few children around, I felt that it was very much us and the old people—there certainly seemed to be a lot of elderly folk on our street.

Elsie lived next door to us with her aging mother. Elsie was a lovely lady with a broad smile who spent much time in her garden. I think she might have been about ten years older than my mother. Sometimes when I was playing in our garden she would lean over the fence and give me a flower. Her gentle kindness was magnetic and I would often go to play outside if I saw her tending her flowers and vegetables. If something went wrong in their house, Dad would go round to fix it. One day, when I was out in the garden, Elsie called out to me and asked me to come round to the front door—she had something for me. I was about seven years old and I had never set foot in Elsie's house, so I was very excited by the invitation—especially as I was asked to enter by the front door and not the back door. Only official people went into a house by the front door. Elsie and her mother met me at the door as soon as I knocked, and I was ushered into the sitting room. It was as neat as a pin. There was a desk to the right, with a series of drawers, like a roll-top bureau without the roll top. Elsie said she had something for me. Her mother stood behind her as she took a powder compact from one of the drawers. She seemed sad and turned to her mother, who nodded, as if to encourage her. Elsie smiled at me and handed me the compact, which I studied in the palm of my hand. It was silver with an insignia on the front: HMS *Hood*. It was a gift that a young navy man would give to his wife or sweetheart, a shipboard memento, a reminder that he would soon be home. HMS *Hood* was sunk in 1941 during the Battle of Denmark Strait. Only three of the almost 1,500 men on board survived. I never asked, but I believe Elsie's fiancé was one of those lost and relinquishing the compact to the little girl next door signified a final letting go. Definitely, the air in the room seemed to change when she handed me the compact. I suspect she may have wept in her mother's arms when I left, running home to show my mother my new treasure.

Mum was very quiet when I handed her the compact, telling her that Elsie had given it to me. She shook her head.

"I wondered why she'd never married," said Mum. "She lost her love on the *Hood*."

Mum told me to put it somewhere safe, pointing out that it was a very, very special gift, though I already knew that. I wish

I could say I still have that compact, but sadly I didn't hide it well enough. My very curious brother found it and just had to take it apart, pulling away the transparent cover protecting the insignia and then dismantling the compact in such a way that, try as he might, my father could not repair it. I saved the constituent parts for a long time, but at some point must have given up and discarded the pieces. It breaks my heart just thinking about it, remembering holding the broken pieces of compact in my hand. Even the insignia was shattered.

There were two old ladies on the street, sisters who were always quibbling over something or other, and they lived next door to each other. Mrs. P had her grown son living with her, a bachelor in his forties—or maybe thirties and he just looked older. The other sister, Mrs. C, had a gentleman lodger. It's funny thinking about the lodger—today it would be assumed they were a couple, and maybe they had been. But we always referred to him as her lodger. The sisters were both quite nosy, to the extent that my mother said their curtains would end up in shreds given the number of times they were tweaked as soon as anyone walked by, or a car was heard coming down the street. The older of the two— or she may have been the younger, because they both claimed to be the oldest or the youngest, dependent on what was at stake— was particularly nosy, and she also had subscriptions at the shop for about three different weekly women's magazines. If Jennifer came over while my mother was at work, we'd deliberately make a lot of noise—laughing and dancing to Radio Caroline or another pirate radio station—so that Mrs. P would just have to find out what was going on, and on the pretext of bringing a pile of magazines for my mother, she would make her way to the front door to poke her nose in. Jennifer and I would then spend hours leafing through magazines, usually reading out loud entries in the problem pages and coming up with solutions to women's dilemmas, especially the ones involving men or sex.

Polly Norris lived in a house on a street of older houses that ran along the back of The Terrace, most of which had been built in the 1700s. Polly was a very strange woman and quite unhinged. She was short, pushing seventy, and wore loud clothing—well, loud for the hamlet—and bright red lipstick. It wasn't unusual to see her making her way to the shop wearing a lurid orange beret, a color-clashing housecoat and a pair of dirty orange open-toe shoes. It was the open-toe shoes that fascinated me, because Polly Norris had a nail on one big toe that was misshapen, curling around and looking for all the world as if a large snail had taken up residence on her foot.

Polly Norris had no boundaries. If Mum was in the telephone box, perhaps calling the doctor or one of her sisters—and she only called if there was something amiss in the family, never to chat—it wasn't unusual for Polly to open the door and ask if Mum was going to be long. I remember her shoving Polly out once, and telling her to bugger off and leave her alone.

But she was obviously popular. I sometimes saw George, one of the farm workers, leaving her house—I was often over at Robin Cottage visiting Mr. and Mrs. Leech; Robin Cottage was one of the houses on the same street. And I saw others leaving Polly's house, so I imagined she must be friendly with a few of the farmworkers in the area. Years later, after Mum and Dad had moved to Sussex, to Three Oaks, a hamlet between Hastings and Rye, we were reminiscing about those years living at the house at the end of The Terrace, and I said something about old Polly Norris and how we might not have liked her much, but she clearly had friends. Mum and Dad started to laugh.

"What?" I said. Even my brother was giggling.

"Jackie," said Mum. "Polly was on the game—she was a prostitute."

I almost fell off my chair. "Never!" I said.

"Oh yes she was," said Mum. "Those men weren't going in there for a cup of tea and a chat, you know."

It was clear I didn't know and I wondered what else I'd missed.

Gentle Auntie Marion and Uncle Bryn were elderly companions who lived together in one of the Railway Cottages on Bishop's Lane. Originally built for railway staff, the cottages were on a ridge that overlooked the station from the back gardens. Uncle Bryn had once been a station manager in the west of England and had come to Kent when he was promoted after the war. Bryn was given the cottage to live in upon his retirement after more than fifty years of railway service. Auntie Marion said her Dutch surname was too complicated for children to pronounce, hence we were to refer to her as "Auntie." However, she was not Dutch but Welsh, and was fluent in the Welsh language—I know because when she told me, I asked her to speak to me in Welsh. I thought it was beautiful, so lyrical and soft, though it could have been her light voice that added to the mystery.

The story I had been told in childhood was that Uncle Bryn had known Marion and her family—perhaps her husband had worked on the railway too—but she endured such tragedy in the war, when her husband died young and both sons, who were in the army, had been killed in action. Marion stopped eating, trying to end her life by starvation. But Uncle Bryn, who was probably ten years older and a bachelor, saved her when he told her he needed help with his elderly mother and asked if she would come to the house and live in to give him a hand. Seeing that help was indeed required, Marion moved into Bryn's house and cared for the old lady until she died. Uncle Bryn never asked her to leave as they had become companions, someone to rub along with for the rest of their lives.

Aunt Marion always had a handful of sweets in her pockets, so when she saw children in the neighborhood she would never fail to give them a treat. But it was Bryn who fascinated me with his stories. On one occasion I was walking with one of my friends not far from the old station, so I decided to gather a posy of wild-flowers for Aunt Marion. They loved it when people, especially children, popped by to see them, so we were treated to a wonderful welcome with tea and cakes laid out on the table. Large portraits of the two lost sons were in pride of place in the parlor and seemed to loom large over the conversation. Uncle Bryn began to tell us about his life working on the railway and then recounted a wartime story I will never forget. He had received a call from a government office in London to inform him that two trains would be coming into the station from opposite directions—one from London and one from Devon—and he was given the train numbers. As soon as the trains were drawing near, he was to close down the line so that all up and down trains were halted for as long as the two trains were at the station. Each of the two special trains comprised only one carriage behind the locomotive. All staff except the signalman in his box along the line and Bryn were to be dismissed as soon as the message was received that the trains had passed the signal box and were approaching the station. He was reminded that in a time of war, any talk of the event would be considered treasonous. As posters on every train warned: *Careless Talk Costs Lives.* The two trains approached the station as described and Bryn shut down the lines in each direction. The staff had already been sent out to the windowless train sheds where engine and carriage repairs were carried out, and no passengers were allowed to enter the station gates. He waited on the platform to ensure the security of the station, the only person present until Winston Churchill alighted from the London train, and General "Ike" Eisenhower emerged from the other. The two visitors stood on the platform deep in conversation for over half an hour, then boarded their trains, which then left the station to return to London and Devon respectively. Bryn opened the station after their departure and no one was ever any the wiser—I suppose with the exception of a certain young girl who walked away from a cottage in Kent that afternoon knowing that she would never forget the image of Ike and Winston during the war, at a deserted railway station somewhere in deepest England, in the early summer of 1944, just before D-Day.

Pat and Ken Leech were my saviors in many ways. I believe they understood how important they were in my life. They had only lived at Robin Cottage for a short time when we moved to The Terrace, and soon I was being invited round for tea, often with Paul from along the road. At that point Pat and Ken had no children, yet clearly loved young company. In time they would have a son, but I was always welcome in their house; indeed, they treated me as if I were a daughter.

Both were teachers at the local primary school, yet in our neighborhood they were also known as rescuers of wild animals. Visiting their home was magical, as there was always a recuperating baby squirrel or two in the specially constructed cage with runs that went up into the trees. The Leeches always returned abandoned or injured creatures to the wild as soon as was safely possible, so they made sure the animal in question became used to a wilder environment while it regained health and strength.

Ken had two owls, both brought to him as abandoned young. One was successfully repatriated to the woods, but the other preferred an easy life in Ken's massive aviary and returned time and again, clamoring to be allowed back into his lair. Ken Leech was often upset when people brought animals to his door, explaining that you had to give the mother a chance to get a fallen owl back into the nest, or the opportunity to find her wayward baby squirrel. He was telling me this one day in the kitchen when it was time to prepare the owlet's food. Ken explained every step to me, how it was important to try to replicate the way a mother would bring food to the nest, and to provide the young owl with a means to regurgitate fur from, say, a mouse, or a squirrel—it was part of the creature's digestive process. He proceeded to cut up liver in pieces, and then poked small wads of cotton wool in and around the flesh, emulating the fur of a small woodland creature. Then we went out to the baby owl, who was waiting for Ken to come with his breakfast. I watched wide-eyed as the owl tucked into the mass of liver and fiber and then began to retch, finally upchucking the cotton wadding while looking very pleased with himself.

When I was fifteen I became their house-cleaner during the school holidays—they knew I needed extra money and not only was I happy to accept the work, but I enjoyed polishing their antique furniture and their lovely silver and brass. I felt at ease in the cottage and I loved the quiet it afforded me, so different from our boisterous household, where someone always seemed to be shouting, usually my mother. Mid-morning, Mrs. Leech—it took me until I was about forty to call them by their first names—would make fresh coffee and toast with her home-made strawberry jam. I wasn't a coffee drinker when I first came to Robin Cottage to clean, but their fresh coffee was nothing like Mum's instant coffee at home. They bought Santos coffee beans—Mr. Leech's favorite coffee—from Importers coffeehouse in Tunbridge Wells—and then ground the beans at home each day before using a special filter to make the beverage. I had never seen anything like it—it was amazing to me. Sometimes Mrs. Leech would play the harpsichord for me, because she knew I loved the sound it made—she was our music teacher at the primary school, and an accomplished musician.

I was driving up to Los Olivos in California's Santa Ynez Valley when Mum called to say that Ken had died, and I grieved for a long time. Several years later, Pat contacted my parents to break the news that she was dying of pancreatic cancer; she asked if they would let me know. I returned to England shortly after that call, heartbroken to hear the news, yet blessed to be able to spend precious time with her before she died.

Lennie Robertson played a significant part in my teenage life, though unlike the Leeches she never realized it. The Robertsons moved into a local manor house—a grand home close to The Terrace—when I was in my early teens. They were very wealthy, and not only from inherited money. Mr. Robertson was a lawyer in London for a very powerful man, the sort of business mogul you might see depicted in a television series. The Robertsons also had a flat "in Town" where he stayed during the week. They had two young daughters, Pammie and Ella.

Lennie Robertson—real name Leonora—was not universally liked when she arrived in the hamlet, and I'm not sure why. She was forthright, yes, and if truth be told, she might have found rural life just a bit tedious, though she certainly had a lot of friends, other "country set" mothers with children attending local private schools. She was in her early thirties and she was hip—that might not have gone down well with the neighbors, either; mothers were not supposed to be hip.

I was fifteen when the local shopkeeper passed on a message that Mrs. Robertson wanted to speak to me about looking after the girls, who were seven and four, during the summer months and other school holidays. He was quick to say, "As long as we don't lose you," because I was also working at the shop on Saturdays and I had to juggle any other work with cleaning at the Leeches'. I was instructed to go to the Robertson's house at five o'clock on Friday.

I put on my best dress and knocked on the back door—no answer. I knocked on the front door, ambled around the garden and even took a look at the swimming pool, but the house seemed deserted. Now I remember why people didn't like Lennie much—the manor's previous owner had built a large walled rose garden in memory of his wife when she died following a diagnosis of cancer. There was an engraved plaque set into the wall in her memory. The Robertsons bought the house when the man moved away, and soon after had the rose garden ripped up, though they kept the wall as it provided a surround for their new swimming pool. People said it was disrespectful. I thought, well, they didn't know the previous owners and they kept the wall and the plaque—why shouldn't they have a swimming pool?

I tried knocking a second time and was walking away from the front door when Lennie pulled it open and called out to me. She was wearing a snug white blouse, pink jeans and gold flip-flops. A mass of dark curls framed her face.

"There you are!" she said. "Sorry—I was upstairs in the sewing room sorting out school uniforms, so didn't hear you until the dogs started. The girls are at a party—come in."

Sewing room? Lennie Robertson looked as if she had never threaded a needle in her life.

I went in and very quickly accepted the summer job offered. I would be looking after her daughters, Pammie and Ella, three days a week, nine to four, and two days noon to four, so I could keep the job cleaning for Mr. and Mrs. Leech. I worked for Lennie Robertson until I went away to college and occasionally until I was twenty-one and about to start my first full-time job. The path was not always a smooth one, though not in terms of my relationship with Lennie, because I really liked her and we got along very well. But I had to be careful what I said at home about Lennie, because my mother didn't care for her, and although Mum liked me having a job, she would rather I made up my working hours with someone else. It took a while to realize that my mother was probably jealous of Lennie and hated the fact that I looked up to her.

Caring for the girls was easy, even though the younger could be a bit of a drama queen. I was pretty much free to keep them occupied in any way I saw fit, as long as they were entertained. I took them on the bus to other villages, I took them to their parties, and to the cinema—always on the bus, which they really liked because it was different for them, until I learned to drive. When I turned up for work that first summer with a driving license, Lennie threw her car keys at me to catch and said, "Be a dear and take the girls over to Benenden, to this address—it's easy to find. Drop them off for the party, and then could you run some errands for me in Cranbrook?"

No problem, except that my parents would not let me drive their car, though I was allowed to drive Dad's ancient blue van to my job at the local doctor's office, where I was the evening receptionist two nights a week. Lennie had a brand spanking new posh car. So, off I went, dropped the girls at their friend's house in

Benenden, and then went into Cranbrook to pick up dry cleaning, collect a meat order from the butcher and do some grocery shopping—Lennie had pushed a good amount of folding money into my hand as I left the house. I was driving back to the manor when I passed my father in his van, so I waved out to him. And as I looked in the rearview mirror, I saw him almost careen into a ditch, such was the shock of seeing his seventeen-year-old daughter in a new flash car blithely driving in the opposite direction. My mother was snippy that evening at home, after she learned that Dad had seen me driving a very, very nice car. I didn't care, because in a way driving that car made up for what had happened the previous summer.

I was sixteen and looking forward to leaving the Mary Sheafe School for Girls and starting my A-level studies at Cranbrook Grammar, when Lennie left a message at the shop for me to go around to the house to talk about plans for the summer. I had been working for her for a year by this time and I was looking forward to another summer's work keeping an eye on the girls—I'd become fond of them and Lennie paid me well and on time. Lennie opened my world in many ways. She treated me like an adult, telling me stories about her life as an airline stewardess with British United Airways, a job she gave up when she married—oh, the places she had been. She had grown up overseas because her father was a diplomat. When she left finishing school, Lennie's father landed her a job as a messenger—for the CIA. She took small packages and envelopes from one Asian city to another, her travel paid for by the US government. Lennie whetted my appetite for travel, because she'd been everywhere and she took time to tell me about all those places. She was so fashionable and had lovely expensive clothes.

One afternoon she was scheduled to meet her husband in London and would be staying at their Chelsea flat, so I was going to sleep overnight at the house to look after the girls. Lennie was running behind when I arrived in the afternoon, and was in a hurry to get to the station. She had showered and was dressed in a bathrobe as I entered by the kitchen door, wrangling my way in past the Old English Mastiff puppy and the elderly spaniel. Lennie was holding a crumpled wad of navy blue silk on one hand, which she threw across the kitchen to me.

"Be a dear and put the iron over that for me—I'm incredibly late, and I must get something on my face."

I set up the ironing board and plugged in the iron, moving the dial to "silk" before double-checking the label. The word "Chanel" seemed to leap out at me. I sweated buckets ironing that cocktail dress, making sure the pleats were just so and that there was not a single crease. Fortunately, I had been trained by years of having to iron clothes at home, and more recently by Mrs. Musgrave, the new needlework teacher at school who had previously worked in "couture." I don't think I took a breath until I had that dress on a hanger outside Lennie's dressing room, ready for her to wear to an important event in London. I wish she'd gone to London a lot more, because by that time her husband was having an affair with his secretary.

But on this occasion, the summer after I'd turned sixteen, Lennie had a proposition for me. I'd start work for her when school ended and then after two weeks the Robertsons would be driving down to the south of France, to Antibes, to meet another family at their villa. Lennie showed me photos of a massive property overlooking the Mediterranean Sea. Now I knew why it was known as the "azure" Mediterranean Sea. The image of the house could have made a stunning a postcard, if billionaires had their own postcards. The two families would be staying at the villa for a month. Lennie wanted me to come, too, so I could look after the children if the adults wanted an evening out, or to take the kids to the beach. I wouldn't have to do the journey by car because I would join their friends who were flying to Antibes on their private jet.

I had never been abroad and I had never been on a plane. I was beside myself. In fact I am sure my heart stopped beating for a while because I remember feeling a bit dizzy, but with a calm voice I said I would love to come, what a wonderful opportunity, though I would have to ask my parents. Lennie said that if they had questions, she would be happy to answer all of them—and I would be paid double time. After all, there would be four children and the other family would be contributing to my employment, and of course I would have days to myself. Oh my goodness, I think my feet hovered above the ground as I ran home. Mum and Dad were not back from work, but I ran to the telephone box at the end of the street to call Anne-Marie—I had to tell somebody my news. I was effervescent with excitement—I was going to Antibes, for heaven's sake, and in a private jet! I blurted it all out to Anne-Marie.

Anne-Marie was silent as I recounted the whole story, and then said, "Jack—don't get your hopes up. You'll only get hurt."

"What do you mean?"

"Your mum won't let you go. I know it. She won't let you go."

"But she has to—this is my chance to go abroad."

"I know your mother, Jack. I love her, but I know what she's like. Don't get your hopes up—she won't let you go." Anne-Marie has always been wise.

I tried not to worry as I waited at the end of the road for Mum to arrive home from work. As soon as the bus stopped and she stepped out, I could not stop talking, telling her about the summer job as we walked toward the house; about the south of France and the private jet and how I would be getting paid double time and it would be for four weeks, and . . .

"No. You're not going."

"But Mum—"

"The answer is no. Don't bother asking me again, because you're not going."

"Why?"

"I don't have to give you reasons, but seeing as you asked, I don't want you to be a slave for those kind of people."

Those kind of people. There it was again.

"She's not those kind of people. Lennie's good to me."

"Well, then *Lennie*—Mrs. Robertson—will understand why I've said no."

I stayed in my room that evening and didn't come down to eat, to talk, to say goodnight. Anne-Marie was right—she knew my mother and she'd done her best to warn me. But I was devastated.

I went to the Robertsons' house the following evening and told Lennie that I couldn't go to the south of France. I think she saw the big tears in the corners of my eyes. "Oh, not to worry, Jackie," she said. "Another time, perhaps."

A couple of weeks later after school ended for the summer, I was at the house helping Lennie orchestrate a pool party for about twenty children when she turned to me and said, "We deserve a drink." I thought she'd come back with lemonade or ginger ale, but instead, as I sat on the patio watching the children—and perhaps I should have told her I couldn't swim—Lennie sat down next to me and handed me a tall glass with a clear sparkling beverage over ice with a slice of lemon.

"And you, especially, deserve this," she said, clinking her glass against mine.

That evening I toddled home slightly tipsy, having tasted my first gin and tonic. No one noticed. I went straight to my room, which was becoming a regular occurrence anyway. The following week after the Robertsons left for Antibes, I started a summer job at the local egg packing factory. The supervisor was supposed to pick me up at the top of the road each morning—the factory was well off the bus route—and then go on to Cranbrook to collect several other female workers. After repeatedly having to shove his wandering hand off my knee during the first couple of days, I discovered that another woman drove from Cranbrook each day, so I arranged to meet her there in the mornings and be dropped off after work, when I would walk the two miles home, alone. I hated the job, hated the supervisor, hated the smell of broken eggs, was sick when I found half-rotting mice or rats around the storeroom, and I was earning less than Lennie Robertson would have paid me. But Mum loved my working there because I was given two-and-a-half-dozen eggs free each week, and she liked getting something for nothing. Except it wasn't really for nothing, not in my mind. I didn't touch an egg for three years. Or was it four? I know it was a long time before I could face seeing an egg on my plate, though I can still pick up ten eggs at once.

I worked for Lennie Robertson for a few more years, though I hardly saw her after the divorce, which came a few years later. I remember reading in a local paper that she'd married again, so I bought a card and sent it to her, care of an address I'd found for her in another Wealden town. I wished her well and hoped she was happy. I truly hoped she was happy, because I'd always thought she was wonderful.

Now that I've made my home in the USA, I think I should write about the Americans who came to live in our small hamlet when I was about ten. The family comprised an African American couple and their two young boys, who both attended the local primary school. I think about that family every so often and I wonder what they made of us. The man was a teacher on a three-month exchange program at another private boys' school in the area. Each morning the woman would walk from their house on the hill with her boys, neat as pins in their new school uniforms, both carrying American book bags that were nothing like our old-fashioned school satchels. And she was so beautiful—everyone commented on it. I remember going into the shop for some groceries, clutching the list Mum had scribbled on the torn open back of a cigarette packet, and the neighbors were talking about the American family.

"And she's so lovely," said Jean, who lived up the road.

"Oh, isn't she," said Ivy. "She looks just like that Jackie Kennedy."

She reminded everyone of Jackie Kennedy, with her elegant suits and pill-box hat. Women in our community wore headscarves, sometimes over curlers that seemed to be in twenty-four hours a day.

One winter's morning some local boys were skylarking around as I was waiting at the bus stop—they were pulling thick ice from puddles and throwing it around. One boy missed his friend and the ice, sharp as a freezing cold windowpane, hit me across the knees. Muddy ice and blood oozed down my legs onto my clean white socks and I tried to clean them with my gloves, determined not to give in to the pain. The American lady rushed over, pulled a starched white handkerchief from her black leather handbag, and began to clean my knees.

"Oh dear, oh dear, oh dear," she kept saying, and I remember I just wanted her to carry on speaking to me, because her voice was so smooth and velvety and dignified.

I kept thanking her and saying sorry, and I said I'd take home the handkerchief to wash and return it, and she said everything would be okay. Then she smiled at me and put her hand on my shoulder, and I thought then that the women were right about her—she was just like that Jackie Kennedy.

I've often wondered if the family knew that when we all stared at them as they went out in their car on a Saturday or to church on Sunday—and they always went to church—it wasn't because of their color, but because they were Americans and we all knew they were used to driving on the wrong side of the road. When she went into the shop, the beautiful American lady with the pillbox hat might never have known that people were interested in what she was buying because we knew they had big refrigerators in America, and we wondered how much food they could get in theirs. They were our first—and only—foreigners and Americans into the bargain, and we were all quite in awe of them.

24

Leaving

⟋⟍

With zero knowledge of how, exactly, I might escape the career locomotive steaming ahead in a direction that didn't interest me, I was soon training to be a teacher. I left for college after a final summer working on local farms. I'd spent a few weeks following A levels looking after Pammie and Ella, so when they went off on holiday for the summer, my brother and I managed to land a job together apple- and pear-picking at farms in Horsemonden and Brenchley, typical Kentish villages not so far away. We were taken there by van, which meant we didn't have to catch a bus. In the early 1930s, artist and writer Clare Leighton traveled around England to complete *The Farmer's Year*, a series of wood engravings depicting farm life. Of apple-picking in Kent she wrote of September, "It is the month of ripeness— a golden, crimson and russet month. Here in Kent the orchards offer themselves to stage the drama of the year."

I loved that last golden summer working with my brother, as we moved our ladders—wide at the base and narrow at the top—from tree to tree picking Worcesters and Bramleys, big, tart apples mainly used for cooking, and sweet Cox's Orange Pippins, and my favorite Kentish apple, the crispy brown Russet. Time and again we'd fill our picking aprons—formed of two voluminous deep canvas bags joined by a strap that went around the neck so the opening of each bag was at hip height and the base almost to the ankles—then we'd clamber down the ladders to pour our apples into bushel boxes. With our load lighter, we'd rush up to the top of the tree again, working hard to weigh ourselves down with apples picked, and money earned.

I'd chosen a college in South London that was situated in a large park filled with trees—many later lost to the Dutch Elm disease epidemic that ravaged Britain's open spaces. I knew I wanted to be in London, but I also liked the idea of getting out into the country; the location offered me reasonable access to both. I've done that ever since—chosen to live in places where I can have my cake and eat it. Now I live just twenty miles north of San Francisco, so I can get into the City with ease, traffic notwithstanding, and yet from my home I can walk up through a redwood grove and out onto protected land from the Marin Headlands and on to Point Reyes National Seashore and beyond.

From the time I started college, I couldn't wait to leave. In one of my first English literature classes, the instructor handed back my essay and in a throwaway comment said I had a very journalistic style to my writing and maybe I was in the wrong place. I should have upped sticks right there and then, seeing it as a "message"—but I couldn't stand the thought of what might ensue when I called to tell my parents that I'd left college before I'd even really started. Fortunately, I have something of my father's patience about me. I could sit at the riverbank with my fishing rod, the fly bobbing in the water and the hook ready, and I could wait and wait all day for something to bite. I never became a teacher, though I completed my training and did very well at college, earning distinctions for my academic work and praise in my teaching practice.

Despite the doubts I had about college even before it began, I met Judy on the first day, and she became one of my dearest lifelong friends—and I can tell the tale about the time Judy and I were knocked flying by Mick Jagger and he didn't even stop to apologize, or even help us up from the floor. His dad was an instructor at the college and we just happened to be walking along the empty corridor when Mick came careening out of his father's office, making a run for it before a few hundred students found out he was in the building. That lasting friendship was something I cherished far more than the college experience, which I just got on with.

I'd been at college for only a short time before I knew I had made another error. It wasn't just that I didn't really like what I had chosen to study, but I also missed being in the true country. A park with a lot of trees wasn't quite cutting it for me. Yet college was made bearable by Judy and another friend, Sue. The latter's boyfriend had a grocery shop and would leave big baskets of fresh fruit from his weekly trips to Covent Garden Market, so we all liked him. Judy's boyfriend—later husband—worked for Mars, so chocolate was often plentiful. And there was Ann, a tall, stunning redhead who loved books as much as me and who also wanted to be a writer. To this day I look out for her name, and am sure that one day I will see it on the side of a book. Or maybe she's a best-selling author writing under a pseudonym.

By the end of my first year I was going home almost every single weekend, having snagged a ride from a fellow student who lived in Hawkhurst and made the long journey back and forth to college daily because he had a family.

At the close of my second year I had saved enough money to visit Jenny in Canada and I had a blast. I knew I only had another year of college to endure and had put by enough money not only for the trip, but to get me through the final leg of my studies. I loved Canada and loved finding my way around Toronto alone while Jenny was working for a travel agency. Her parents took us to Ottawa, Quebec and over to Vermont and upper New York state, before looping back into Toronto again—it was an amazing trip. Then Jenny came home from work with a special treat—tickets for us to fly to Bermuda. She had received complimentary rooms for a week at one of the best hotels on the island. Life was changing almost too rapidly for me to keep up, and I felt my naivety keenly—Jenny seemed so worldly and sophisticated and I was still a country bumpkin.

As if presaging my future, my flight was delayed out of Toronto to London—I was returning home just a week before college started again. The airline accommodated the stranded passengers in a new five-star hotel overlooking Lake Ontario. My room was enormous and I felt like a movie star, yet I had a deep sense that there would be more experiences like this, though I wasn't quite sure what might come next.

Mum and Dad met me at Gatwick Airport, rushing toward me as I came through customs.

"You're home," said my mother, pulling me to her. "Oh, you're home."

By the time I left college, I wanted only to travel. I didn't want to teach, and there was a glut of new teachers anyway, so many of my fellow students had to look for jobs outside the profession. A year after leaving Canada and having graduated from college, I was back in that same Toronto hotel, working for the airline that had taken me across the Atlantic to see Jenny. I was a penniless graduate who had found a way for someone else to pay my way as I collected labels from around the world that I would slap on the side of my suitcase over the next two years.

I might have taken a circuitous route to the end goal, but at the age of thirty-six, twenty years after a vocational test funneled me into teaching, I signed up for a journalism class at the University of California in Los Angeles, and I began writing for magazines while at the same time holding down a day job. I was a bit late to the game and I was definitely too old to try to become a foreign correspondent reporting from war zones—just as well as I'd probably be dead by now—however, I became the US correspondent for two educational journals in the UK and recorded a few essays for radio broadcast. With the all-important clips to my name I was able to extend my reach and began writing for other magazines, cobbling together the career I'd wanted from the very beginning.

One thing led to another until a day some nine years later when, in a moment of artistic grace, I wrote a war story that slipped into my imagination while I was stuck in traffic on a rainy day in California. *It never rains in California, it pours.* I was living almost six thousand miles away from the land of hops and apples, of farms and fields, of wild garlic and celandines, and of London in darker times, but it was as if the voices of those elderly women and their secret loves echoed down the years, along with the images of young men lost to war and the sweethearts left behind. The story became a manuscript, and the manuscript became my first novel.

And the rest, as they say, is history.

But this memoir is a glimpse at a certain place and a certain time, traveling back and forth across the years before my birth and lingering upon the stopping places of a country childhood that framed who I might become.

Dad's business went very well for some years, until he was in his mid-fifties, when not only did repetitive motion injuries caused by his work and arthritis in his elbows begin to give him great pain, but he was losing jobs to men who charged less, men who didn't have the same training or level of craftsmanship, but were cheap. And to be fair, he liked coming home early to watch cookery shows on TV—sometimes with a little regret that he hadn't taken up that place at the army catering college. But then he wouldn't have met Mum.

Mum's career had gone from strength to strength. By the time I was working in academic publishing, Mum was chief administrator at a men's prison, and on one occasion, on Boxing Day, was called out in an emergency because there was a riot. Knowing my mother, she probably arrived on the scene and told everyone to get back to their bloody cells and stop their sodding nonsense. In time she moved on, taking up the chief administrator position at a women's prison, while at the same time involved in management training at other prisons and at the Home Office in London. As her standing grew in the department, she began to be offered plum jobs, and at one point the position of chief administrator of one of Britain's most notorious high security prisons was on the table. The government paid for my parents to visit the area to look at properties and the local community, and they were very positive about it—Dad knew he could get work there, and both my brother and I had left home so they considered themselves free agents. Then came time for Mum to visit the prison and she told me that the hair stood up on the back of her neck the moment the big gates slammed shut behind her—she knew she would have to turn down the job. Had she accepted the position, she would have been the first woman promoted to the position of chief administrator of a British high security prison.

A friend recently asked me if I'd watched *Orange Is the New Black*. I shook my head—I'd heard enough stories of prison life.

In the mid-'70s there had been a successful drama on British TV called *Within These Walls* about a women's prison, starring the classic British actress Googie Withers. Whenever it came on we quickly changed the channel before Mum could shout, "Oh no—I have enough of that all day!"

I was almost thirty and Mum fifty-seven when she was again contacted by a senior Home Office official and formally offered another plum job, one that was only ever offered to staff of high regard when they were three years away from retirement. The role would be to represent her Home Office department—prisons—in the Prime Minister's office, and would mean a lot of travel away from home on those occasions when she joined the government entourage during the PM's official journeys overseas. Her remit was to ensure her department's interests were taken into account in the drawing up of any international agreements. If a given trip required an early morning departure, she would stay in a government house near the PM's residence. Who knew that there were many such representatives in a PM's entourage, acting in the interests of not only every government department, but sections within that department?

Mum called me as soon as she was offered the job—typical of the position, she had only twenty-four hours to make up her mind. She wasn't sure what to do. On the other hand, I was absolutely sure what she should do.

"Go for it, Mum. Think of the travel! Think of the things you'll see and do! And it's so important! I mean, they said you'd be going to China next month! What does Dad say?"

"He says whatever I want to do, he's right behind me." My father had retired a year earlier at fifty-six.

"Well, there you go. Call them back and tell them you're in."

She turned down the job.

"What do you mean, you turned it down?" I could not believe my ears when she called to let me know her decision. I was working my own way up the career ladder and this was the 1980s. We professional women all had our linebacker shoulder pads and we knew where we were going, shoving doors open to get to where we thought we'd like to be. I discovered a few years later that I didn't want to be there at all.

Mum was firm. "I just didn't want to be away from your dad for that long, Jack."

"And?"

"And I had this terrible vision of Margaret Thatcher running into my bedroom at four in the morning and saying, 'Quick, Joyce, you've overslept. Get up,' and me still in my curlers, saying, 'Oh, just give me another five minutes, would you, Maggie.'"

I laughed. "I suppose it's for the best," I said. "And you never did like dung-spreading, did you?"

In their mid-forties, my parents had taken up ballroom and Latin American dancing. It was Mum's idea—Dad had to be dragged along to the first class. Mum decided that they should make new friends, because I was at college and John would be going off on his own at some point. Yet my father took to dancing like a duck to water, and soon they were joining dance clubs and were off dancing every night of the week, either in lessons or with new friends they'd met. They became dance instructors, winning medals and competitions. I went home for my twenty-first birthday, for some crazy reason thinking my parents might have organized something special for me, but as I walked into the house, they rushed past me, my mother telling me that they were off dancing and I'd find my cards on the kitchen table. Then my brother went out with his mate Pete, and I spent my twenty-first birthday alone watching *Starsky & Hutch*. Birthdays never had been a big thing for my parents, though we usually had a decorated cake. They forgot my twenty-second birthday altogether, but the following week I was in Toronto again on a four-day layover, so Jennifer's parents put on a special dinner for me, presenting me with a birthday cake iced with the words, "Happy Birthday, Jackie—from your Canadian Mum and Dad."

Mum was about seventy years of age when she saw an advertisement in the local paper, "Apple Pickers Wanted." The farm was only a mile away from the house, so she told Dad that she was going to call the farmer and apply. Dad rolled his eyes and said she was welcome to it, but no, he was not going back to farm work after all these years. "Please yourself," said Mum. She called the farmer, who asked her a few questions then told her she could start the following Monday. On her first day, Dad packed up her sandwiches and a flask of tea, just as he had when they were young, and waved her off to work. At the end of that week, when Mum opened her wage packet and counted her earnings, Dad changed his mind. Friends and relatives thought they were crazy, but every year for the next ten years they picked apples as summer turned to autumn and they had a great time doing it. The farmer maintained they were his best workers. As Mum said, "We've gone back to our roots." They would work in the orchards until late afternoon, come home, have a bite to eat and then go out dancing. Their zest for life knew no bounds.

I've often wondered how it was that both my brother and I live in California. Yes, of course I know the details, the events that led each of us to decide to leave the UK to try something new, but it's interesting that we chose the west. I've put it down to early conditioning—all those Westerns that my dad so loved, and the idea that there was a place for the individual in the west, for loners and those who didn't quite fit in. Neither of us intended to remain in the USA forever—we were just off on our own adventures. Without doubt, Mum and Dad missed us, but I know they were proud that we'd each done something akin to them leaving London in an old Gypsy caravan.

My parents loved California, loved the United States, and I think they would have moved, too, had it not been for the abysmal American healthcare system. Even if they could get insurance, it would have taken only one accident or hospital stay and we would all have been in the poor house. They visited often, many times with a group of their dancing pals who came to Palm Springs for a month every December. Mum and Dad just tagged on another month to spend two weeks with my brother and two weeks with me. And of course, I went back to England, traveling more each year as they grew older—once a year became twice, became three times.

Then, in the early part of 2012, everything changed.

My cousin Martine succumbed to leukemia in February that year and the entire family was devastated. She was a light, a joy, the wittiest of the cousins, just lovely—her passing affected everyone, especially as she was not the first of our cadre of girls to die. Tall, beautiful Stephanie died of cancer at the age of forty-two in 1996, shattering the fabric of our extended tribe. In her later months, Stephanie would sometimes call me when the pain was such that she could not sleep—given the time difference, when she was awake in the middle of the night in London, it was only late afternoon in California and I was someone she could talk to. On my father's side, my cousin Rita had also passed away at age sixty due to something they call "Sudden Adult Death" syndrome. At eighty-five, both my parents were as fit as fiddles, or that's what the doctor said when Dad had his annual physical after returning from two months in California at the end of January 2012.

Not long after Martine's funeral had taken place, my mother noticed that Dad seemed to bleed at the slightest knock. At first the doctor was not keen to do more blood tests as Dad had only recently had a full work-up and had been deemed one of the fittest men among his patients. But my mother insisted, and as soon as the results came back, Dad was rushed to hospital. Neither my brother or I were told anything for a while, though in mid-March, Mum called to tell me that Dad was having a blood transfusion, and it was nothing to worry about. *Nothing to worry about?* A blood transfusion? As Mum was giving me the details, telling me it was no more than a bit of anemia, I jotted down the name of Dad's hematologist.

I started a book tour in the second week of March, and at the end of the first week traveled to Sacramento, where I was a guest of honor at Left Coast Crime, a convention for mystery readers and writers. It was a great honor and I was excited about it. At the end of the convention, I would be flying on to Chicago, Boston and Washington, DC. A car came to collect me on that Friday to take me to Sacramento. I was clutching a book about grief, as I had been so downcast since Martine's passing. I had wanted to go to the funeral, but my mother said no, there was nothing I could do and it was a long way to come for something that would be all over in an hour. As children and teens, Martine and I had been all but inseparable, but had drifted apart after she married and became a mother and I forged a different kind of life.

The driver was holding open the door for me as I approached the car, but I asked him to wait, just a minute, as I'd forgotten something. I rushed into the house, grabbed my passport and green card, and ran back to the car—a strange move, as I had no need of a passport; my travel schedule was purely domestic.

At a cocktail party that evening, I was chatting to Toby and Bill Gottfried, two very respected mystery fans who were involved in organizing conventions and were always staunch supporters of writers. Both were retired doctors, Toby having worked at the forefront of AIDS research years earlier, and Bill a well-known pediatric oncologist at UCSF Medical Center.

"How are your folks?" asked Bill. They knew I tried to get back to the UK as much as possible to see my parents, and my most recent book was dedicated to my father.

"Good, though Dad's not been well."

"What's going on?" he asked.

I tried to explain, but without my scribbled notes could only remember one word: "Thrombocyto-something."

Bill's manner changed. "When are you next going back, Jackie?"

"After my book tour, in May."

"Oh Bill, don't worry her," said Toby.

"No." He held up his hand, looking at his wife. "I'm going to say what's on my mind—" He turned back to me. "Jackie, I think you need to find out what's going on, and you should plan to get over there as soon as you can. I don't like the sound of this."

I cannot remember the rest of the evening. I ran to my hotel room as soon as I could and waited out the hours until I knew the Conquest Hospital in Hastings would be open. I had the hematologist's name in front of me, hoping he wouldn't respond to my call with talk about doctor-patient privilege—that's if I managed to speak to him. The secretary was brilliant, telling me when to call back, while in the meantime she would see if she could squeeze me in between patients. It took three calls back and forth, but finally, at three in the morning in California, which was eleven in the morning in England, my father's hematologist came on the line. It was a forty-minute call and one I am eternally grateful for. He understood my predicament, as had his secretary—I was almost six thousand miles away and I hadn't a clue what was happening to my father.

"I think my mother is lying to me," I blurted out.

"Your mother is lying to herself, Jackie. Here's what's going on with your dad. He's very, very poorly."

I asked him how soon I should come home, knowing that if I turned up too soon, my father would be suspicious, and my mother even more worried.

"You don't have to come back tonight, but I would like to think you'd be here in the next couple of weeks."

It was that bad.

"I'll be there for his next appointment."

I was about to thank him and end the call when he stopped me.

"Before you go, and before you come home, there's one more thing. When you get here, I don't want you wrapping your father in cotton wool. If he wants to go dancing with your mum, let him. If he wants to go out to dinner, let him. I don't want him handling sharp knives or tools, but let him be himself." He paused. "Your father has something I cannot prescribe, and it is something incredibly powerful—your father has an amazing spirit. Don't crush it. And Jackie—it's a privilege to be his doctor."

I thanked him, ended the call, then I broke down and wept. I couldn't imagine losing him.

I think I must have been a terrible guest of honor, though I did my best, aided by writer Rhys Bowen, who was my rock. She buoyed me up every time I thought I would falter. My literary agent, Amy Rennert, along with the team at HarperCollins, especially Katherine Beitner and Jennifer Barth, pulled out the stops and rallied round to make sure everything was done to make my departure easy. As I walked into my parents' house the following Saturday, having flown into Heathrow from an event in Washington, DC—bringing that passport with me had been a godsend—my mother all but fell into my arms.

"You're home. Oh, thank heavens. You're home." The words seemed to echo down the years.

Within minutes she was on the telephone to my aunts with the news: *Jackie's home.*

I set up my office in the dining room and remained in England until a month after my father passed away in July, and I returned again in October, and then December, when I brought Mum back to California for a month. In the years between my father's passing in 2012 and Mum's in November 2015, I was in England as much as California. I think I might have broken some ex-pat residency laws, but what the heck.

In the year following my father's death, my mother lost almost every hair on her head. She had reached the age of eighty without a single grey hair—certainly by the time I was forty, I had more grey hair than she had when she died at eighty-eight! But despite crippling grief, she put her best foot forward, joining lunch clubs for seniors and making some new friends. She tried going back to one of the dance groups, but it was too upsetting, so she never went again.

My relationship with my mother was always a challenge. She never stopped wanting a fight, and as much as I tried, there were times when I just felt so bullied, I snapped back. Yet amid those highs and lows, she could be so lovely and warm-hearted, so funny, so entertaining—and of course, I loved her more than words could describe. But it was when she was in the hospital in

June 2015 following a hip replacement, that I had to put a final stop to the discord. I had taken to leaving a room whenever she began sniping at me, which was usually in company, an attention-seeking ploy I'd been used to since childhood. The final straw came when my brother, cousin Celia and I were seated around Mum's bed in the hospital, and she snapped at me with all the sarcasm she could muster. I must have let so much go over my head, because I can't even remember what it was about. I said nothing in return, but simply told my brother and cousin I would meet them outside later and to just text me when they were ready to leave because I was going to the cafe. I leaned over and kissed Mum on the cheek, told her I loved her and walked out of the ward.

Celia recounted to me that my mother said, "I think Jackie's upset."

"Well, of course she is," Celia responded. "What do you expect, after what you just said?"

The following day, on the pretext of taking clean pajamas into the hospital for Mum, I left the house early. I'd probably always had trouble finding my voice with my mother—to be sure we had words, but there's a difference in finding your voice, expressing what you really want to say in a measured tone, and being "on the defensive" against an incoming verbal missile. The issue of voice was something I'd struggled with since childhood and I dreaded being on the receiving end of what might at first appear to be witty repartee on my mother's part, but was really a cutting com-ment. Perhaps I had been too sensitive on occasion, not able to see the joke.

And there had been the devastating critique of my voice when I was about eight or nine. I had started singing along with my mother while we were both in the kitchen—she would often sing as she worked. I was peeling vegetables and Mum was standing near the stove. She stopped singing, turned to me and said, "Jack, can you sing solo?"

I nodded and smiled, pleased that she'd asked, and began to sing the song with all my heart, stopping only when she held up her hand and shook her head.

"No, Jack—I mean, can you sing *so low* that I can't hear you?"

She didn't smile or laugh, so it didn't sound like something said in jest.

I never sang again.

I mimed in music class and I mimed in school assembly, moving my lips so no one knew I wasn't singing. I left the choir at the Congregational Church because I was sure I had the most terrible voice. I still don't sing, and I don't know if I'm really dreadful or just moderately bad.

But on this day, years later, I knew I had to find my voice and speak from my heart. Even though visiting hours had not started, the nurses said it was okay to go along to see Mum. She looked up as I approached her bedside.

"What are you doing here? It's not visiting time."

I sat down and reached for her hand. "I can't do this anymore, Mum. I can't do this fighting. I can't take the nastiness, and I just cannot have any of it any more. I'm fed up with the highs and lows—it's gone on my whole life. I'm exhausted and I'm done with it."

She said nothing, just stared at me. Then she nodded. She had heard my voice, and she hadn't told me to shut up.

So much more happened that summer. Before her hip replacement, Mum had decided to leave the house in Sussex where they had lived since 1982, when they moved away from the house at the end of The Terrace. Having lived in the "new" house for over thirty years, she was now on her way to an apartment in an "independent living" complex for the over-sixties in a local village. It was a lovely apartment, with views across the country-side and just a short walk from the local pub with its big roaring fire in winter, a comfort I came to be very thankful for as events unfolded. How often I sat by that fire with just a hot chocolate cupped between two hands.

John returned to England to be with us while Mum was in the hospital, so together we cleared the house ready for her move—it was a massive task as my parents were pack rats who kept sixty-four years' worth of "stuff" in the house and garage. They had not discarded a thing prior to leaving The Terrace—they had just brought everything with them to the next house. It was during this time of packing and sorting and trips to the dump that I found one of my brother's old composition books from school. Though he later trained in landscape gardening, design and estate management at college, and with the National Trust and Royal Horticultural Society, my brother's disregard for school had never been in doubt. But upon finding the book, I stopped clearing and started reading stories he'd written as an eleven-year-old. I was stunned—this was very good storytelling. His handwriting was not the best—Dr. Wood's had been much worse—and the spelling was a bit iffy, but I've known people with doctorates who couldn't spell. This was a boy who used metaphor, who could weave a descriptive sentence that put you right there in the action.

The most searing essay was his story about putting down our dog, Rex. Rex was a great dog, a massive retriever/Border collie mix; what he could sniff out he could round up. He was a bored dog, though, and had followed either John or me to school on occasion. I was screamed at by the headmistress and made to walk the two miles home with Rex on a makeshift leash of string, then two miles back again, where I received another telling off for missing lessons, whereas at my brother's school, both John and Rex were brought home by one of the teachers who thought it was just hilarious. Among other transgressions Rex had taken to escaping the house and sheep worrying, so my parents said he had to be put down before the farmer shot him—and the farmer had every right to shoot him. We were country folk, so we knew the stakes. John cried so much he became ill, and in his composition book he had poured out his heart's pain at losing Rex. It was good reading. But the teacher had crossed out his poor spelling with her nasty red pen and given him a C-minus.

I walked over to my brother, who was putting aside a pile of my father's old tools ready to be shipped back to California.

"This is great," I said, holding up the exercise book. "You deserved much more than the mark the stinky teacher gave you."

He shrugged. "Chuck it out—it's just more crap."

I put the book to one side, and later I saw my brother slip it into his suitcase.

That same afternoon, I received an email from friend and fellow writer Hallie Ephron, asking me if I was going to be at a certain conference in August. I replied that I wasn't, told her what I was doing and then recounted the story of my brother's composition.

"Take notes," said Hallie. "Take notes about everything."

Mum was only in the new apartment a few weeks when she began having breathing problems. In the early hours of a mid-October morning in 2015, she called to let me know she was being admitted to hospital, and that she would leave the heating on in the flat for me. I flew home that day and by the time I walked into the ward at the Conquest Hospital, she had been diagnosed with small cell lung cancer, usually associated with smoking. My mother was eighty-eight years of age and had given up smoking thirty years before—but she had been a heavy smoker for forty years and these things can come home to roost. Hadn't she bragged about her "cancer sticks"?

One of the questions the doctor asked her was, "Have you ever been exposed to asbestos?" And that made her laugh.

"Of course I have—I was a kid in London during the war. Bombs were dropping, buildings were falling, so we were all exposed to asbestos."

I shared that story with Aunt Ruby, who told me, "In the war, everyone was given these asbestos mats. They were about twelve inches square, and the idea was that you were supposed to use them to put out incendiary devices if you saw them dropping in the street, or to help put out fires in the house when a bomb dropped. But we thought they were just great for making toast— we'd put a slice of bread on top of the asbestos and then heat it up over the gas ring. Everyone did it."

There are moments of grace at times of keeping vigil. They come in as if to counter fear in the face of a most dreaded outcome. I was tired and jet lagged, not only from the rush across the Atlantic, but from months of anxiety about my mother's future and from moving her to the new apartment, selling the old house, and sorting out so much clutter. And I'd raced to meet a manuscript deadline. On my second day back in the UK, I stepped outside the ward when beckoned by my mother's doctor, who was completely honest with me. "We're talking weeks, not months," he said. Then I had to call my brother, who couldn't get his head around the prognosis. When he said he'd come back in a couple of weeks, I'd lost my temper, telling him that he didn't have a couple of bloody weeks. I ended the call feeling just terrible and so alone. I returned to the ward and sat down next to my mother's bed; she was dozing. I rested my head upon her lap, and as fatigue enveloped me she began to stroke my hair. At once I was a back on the bus from Tunbridge Wells, soothed in my weary sickness by my mother's hand.

My mother died in the hospice in November 2015, one hour after telling the nurse, "I want to die. I've had enough, and I want to die." She was given pain medication and I watched her every breath until she passed away. Every one of those breaths was on her terms.

My brother and I were fortunate to be with both parents when they died—it could have been so different considering we lived thousands of miles away. Mum and Dad each left us with, dare I say it, memories of their passing that are quite comical—a gift in the very worst of times, I think, that are ours to remember and smile about.

Dad was in the hospice, cared for by medical staff not only expert in palliative care, but with hearts perfectly attuned to the vulnerable family. He had been due to return home on a Monday following the period of respite care, but after a fall the day before, the sister in charge called me to say that they were keeping him in. I phoned my brother in California and told him to get on a flight as soon as possible. Dad was upset at not being allowed home, but we told him that John was on his way, so that elevated his spirits.

John's flight the following day didn't get in until Tuesday morning, so I left instructions at the house—in an envelope stuck to the door—that we were with Dad at the hospice, and to call me as soon as he arrived and I would come back to pick him up. I will never forget the look on my father's face as the call came in and I said, "John's coming—Dad, John's coming . . ." and the broad smile when his son finally arrived. My big tall brother strode into the room and leaned over the bed, almost lifting my frail father as he held him close. I knew then that Dad would be gone soon, that he had waited for John. He died two days later with John and me at his bedside. The nurses in attendance left the room after my father departed this world. They had been there supporting us, gently rubbing our backs as my father passed, John and I saying the words, "I love you" over and again. We sat for some time before we no longer felt his presence within the physical form that remained before us. As we were about to leave, I realized my brother was perturbed about something.

"Are you okay? Do you want to stay longer?" I asked.

He shook his head. "No—but aren't we supposed to open the window, so his spirit can fly free? Aren't you supposed to do that when someone dies?"

"You're right," I said, turning to the window behind me.

I slid back the catch and pushed against the window, which wouldn't move. It was almost dark in the room with only one small light illuminating my father, so I couldn't quite see what I was doing. I pushed again. The window wouldn't budge. I gave it a thump, and nothing happened. I covered my hand with a sweater and gave it a good shove—still nothing, so my brother came around the bed and whacked the frame.

"Shhhhh," I said. "You'll have Sister running in here to tell us off." And we began to giggle. I looked around at my father, at rest. "You know, John—he's done this deliberately to give us a laugh. And we know Dad—if he wants to get out, he'll put a cosmic sledgehammer through this window."

My mother maintained that, once married, a woman should never remove her wedding ring—it was unlucky. Even during various hospital stays, when patients were supposed to remove all items of jewelry, my mother refused to take off her wedding ring.

However, she had one stipulation for us—when she died we had to remove her ring so no one else would get it. She was adamant because she'd once read an article about unscrupulous undertakers stealing jewelry left on the bodies of dead people. After she passed away, the nurse who came to the room to confirm the death opened the window before she left us. At least we wouldn't have to thump a window frame again. When we were ready to leave, my brother reminded me of one last thing we had to do.

"You've got to take off her ring, Jack."

"Why is it always me that has to do these things?"

"Because you're older." He grinned at me.

I sighed and lifted her left hand. As I suspected, the ring would not budge.

"John—"

"Use some baby oil," he suggested.

I found baby oil among my mother's things in the bathroom and began massaging it into the third finger of her left hand. The ring still would not come off.

"If you don't get that ring off, she'll come back and haunt you," said my brother.

"Okay, okay, I know that. I'll give it a pull."

I've often wondered if the nurse who walked in at that moment thought Mrs. Winspear had a right pair of heartless adult children, because the image of me tugging at the ring on a dead woman's finger and my brother saying, "You're not pulling hard enough," must have given her a story to tell time and again. I dropped my mother's hand and I know we must have looked like a couple of guilty grave robbers.

"Everything all right?" she asked.

"Yes, we're just leaving," I said.

As the nurse nodded and left the room, a wry grin on her face,

I turned to John. "The undertaker can get the ring off—I'm not doing it."

Mum may have given us a laugh, a bit of black comedy as she left the stage, but we wept all the way home.

In the days following her passing I came to a profound yet so simple understanding about my relationship with my mother. I knew she loved me—her love for her family was deep and intense. Then why did she hurt me so much? While walking alone across the fields, once again seeking solace in nature, I asked that very question aloud: "Why did she hurt me so much?" The answer came to me in an instant, as if a dear friend were walking beside me offering counsel.

"Because she knew you would always love her, that you would never falter."

And she was right. I would always love her. As those words settled in my heart, a comfort entered my aching soul.

There's one more story to tell about my father's final breath—that the very moment he left this world, there seemed to be the fragrance of roses in the air around us. Even when we returned to the house, I could still smell the roses. I had taken my mother home earlier in the evening because she was exhausted, and John and I had planned to remain at Dad's bedside throughout the night; the staff had brought in pillows and duvets for us. I knew Mum wanted to wait at home, because she believed that when my father died his spirit would return and she didn't want him to come home to an empty house. As we pulled into the driveway late at night, with headlights signaling our arrival, Mum knew he was gone and came to the door, weeping as we encircled her with our arms. Once inside I turned to my brother.

"John, can you smell that fragrance?"

"You mean the roses? I smelled it as soon as he died."

"Me too—what do you think it is?"

"It's the sweet smell of heaven, Jack, the sweet smell of heaven."

My mother finally went to bed—I was to listen to her terrible keening all night—so I looked up "smell of roses at time of death" on Google. Of course there was a raft of scientific explanations. I prefer my brother's answer. *The sweet smell of heaven.*

So what if we Winspears are a bit fey? It's worked for us.

"Take notes," instructed Hallie. "Take notes, Jackie."

So I made notes, recorded my memories and gathered them together in a collection of stories about a family at a certain time and in a certain place. Even as a child I felt as if I were caught in a time warp, because my cousins had such modern lives and mine seemed so old-fashioned.

I wrote a few of these stories at Hedgebrook, a retreat for women writers on Whidbey Island, just off the coast of Seattle in Washington state, with a landscape so much like southern England I felt as if I were at home. On the first day at our orientation, when we were shown our individual fairytale-like cottages, each with a cast-iron log stove, the manager offered to teach us how to light a fire. I can remember smiling, because I couldn't imagine not knowing how to light a fire—I had been doing it since childhood. After all, it had been the only way to heat our home and cook our food.

When my mother was admitted to hospital for her hip replacement, she took pains to inform the doctor that, "I was a dancer, you know." It was probably the accomplishment of which she was most proud—same for my dad. So I think of them as dancers, tap-dancing their way through life, quick-stepping over the bumps and cracks, cha-cha-ing around the odd dark abyss and then jit-terbugging their way forward, laughing. People would stand back and watch when they hit the floor. It was a lesson for me and my brother—though neither of us can dance, not like our parents could dance.

I feel privileged to have lived that childhood, in that place at that time. Whatever came along in between, the good and the bad, and sometimes very ugly, everything now is just icing on the cake—perhaps it took writing this memoir to realize it. Perhaps that's what I was searching for, a way to come home to myself. And hadn't Dad always promised, "This time next year, we'll be laughing."

It helps if you're quick on your feet, a dancer.

EPILOGUE
This Mas-cure-ayd

❧

I know when my extended family reads this memoir, they'll ask why I didn't tell this story or that story. My cousins will wonder why I didn't mention the Big Climbing Tree in the woods at the back of our house at the end of The Terrace, or the time John and Larry found the site of a black magic ritual while we were on holiday in Cornwall, or at least mention the fact that Linda was baptized in a hop garden by the village vicar, who happened to be making a pastoral visit to the hop pickers from London. And someone will ask why I didn't write about the Wendy house my dad built in the garden, or the big dressing up trunk we had in the attic, or the time Auntie Dot made us walk in single file along the beach, pretending she was our teacher and saying, "Come along children, this way . . ." And I will be asked how I could have missed Auntie Ruby coming home from Canada for the first time since she'd emigrated, along with Janice and Christine, whom we'd never seen before. My brother chased them around the garden brandishing a rounders bat yelling, "You're in England now and we're not playing your rotten baseball here—we play rounders!" Or what about Uncle Joe, on his first visit back from Canada after he and Auntie Alma emigrated with Josie and Sharon, and how he drove up the wrong side of the road and all us cousins in the back of the car yelled, "Uncle Joe . . . other side!"

My brother will say I should have written about Dad sneaking off on a mid-December winter's night to snag our Christmas tree from the pine plantation nearby, and he may wonder why I didn't write about our final party, just the four of us coming together to say goodbye to the house at the end of The Terrace a few days before my parents moved to their new home in Sussex. We each thought we had the original idea of buying a bottle of champagne for our special supper, and Auntie Dot gave me a twenty-pound note to buy another bottle, so we'd have a really good time— which is why the four of us imbibed five bottles of champagne that evening. My brother was loathe to leave the house he'd been born into, and even after the removal lorry had taken everything in that house to my parents' new home, John remained behind, bedding down in a sleeping bag for several nights, making tea on a camping stove and not leaving until the new owners came rumbling down the street in *their* removal lorry.

Remember when? Remember when? Remember when? And the list will go on. I will be treated to more family stories and I will be drawn back into the past on a tide of nostalgia. Re-memory making even the bad times good. But my big boisterous extended family will also look for this part, for an honest paragraph or two where I say something more about my mother and her stories— the truth of the matter, if you will. Her *mass-cure-ayd*. And I know they will read this, because my family will read what I write even when they don't like it. As one of my cousins said, "Your kind of writing isn't really my thing, but it's nice to see your books published." If that's as good as it gets, I'll take it.

A couple of years before my mother's death, I was in Devon visiting my cousin Gillian and her family, and while I was there, Uncle Charlie came over for dinner—he lived in the area and it was great to see him. I'd always really loved Uncle Charlie, my mother's youngest brother. We were talking about the past, about my Dad, who had died the year before, and I mentioned my mother's claustrophobia, and how it probably started when she was buried under the rubble when that bomb landed in the street outside the house.

"What are you talking about?" said Uncle Charlie. "Your mother was never buried under any rubble."

"Oh she was, Uncle Charlie—she's told me all about it since I was a child." I recounted the whole story to him, every single detail.

He shook his head and we dropped the subject. It seemed the best thing to do.

As soon as I arrived back at my mother's house, I told her what Uncle Charlie had said. She rolled her eyes. "What does he know? He was evacuated at the time—he wasn't even bloody well there!"

I accepted that.

Aunt Sylvie shrugged when I asked her about Mum's experience, and Aunt Ruby said, "Oh well, you know how your mum could weave a story."

After she died, so many people took pains to tell me how much they loved Mum, and especially how much they loved her stories. But there was a dark side.

"She used to tell really scary stories," said Celia. "When we were little she made up ghost stories where terrible things happened, and we'd really believed her, she was so good at it. But they gave us all nightmares."

Time and again, I heard the same refrain. *Your mother was a great storyteller.*

And so as I embarked upon writing my memoir, I started checking, where I could, and found that most of her wartime stories were true—but one big one was not. Or was it? I had to do some digging.

As a child I had been shocked by a certain story my mother recounted about Uncle Jim's experience during the Normandy Landings in 1944, and what ensued as he went ashore and moved inland, part of a special unit tasked with a dangerous job. It had a devastating outcome and involved a dreadful decision on the part of someone in his unit that culminated in the death of a local child. Whenever Mum told this story there was always the unspoken suggestion that it was Uncle Jim who'd had to make that decision. According to Mum's story, the men were moving into a Normandy town where it was known there were German snipers in the taller buildings, waiting to pick off Allied soldiers. The marines had to move with stealth, but their position was about to be revealed by a little boy who had seen them and was running toward them—and much depended upon this special unit breaking through the enemy line. Someone made the decision to take the child's life in order to save more local people. I remember asking her once, "Did Uncle Jim shoot the little boy?" and instead of saying "No" she looked away, and left the question hanging in the air. I went to bed and wept for that little French boy. Now, with doubt in my mind as I recalled the conversations with Uncle Charlie and my aunts, I decided to ask Jim's daughter, my cousin Linda, about it. In an email message I wrote down the whole story as told to me by my mother, and clicked "Send." I didn't receive a reply and started to worry. Perhaps I'd told Linda something she didn't know. What if I'd touched upon a family story that was painful for my cousins to hear?

I was still concerned when, several days later, Linda's reply popped into my inbox—the delay was due to the fact that she'd sent my message along to her brother, my cousin Jim, the family historian who was coming up with all sorts of interesting bits and pieces about our ancestors. It was Jim's discovery of our great-grandmother's name—Kezia—that inspired me to name a character after her in my WWI novel, *The Care and Management of Lies*. Through Jim's research, I also discovered that my grandfather was born in Bedford Square, in the Bloomsbury area of London—I had worked in Bedford Square for several years and had never known the old man was born just on the other side of the square.

In response to my email, Jim sent me official reports of his father's service on the beaches of Normandy, and it was harrowing. Uncle Jim had been a stoker and driver on one of the landing craft—it was his job to keep the landing craft going toward the Normandy beach while under fire, not only steering it but making sure it was fueled. After an attack that killed so many of the men on board, my uncle had floated unconscious in the bloodstained water for a long time until rescued. He had been like Charon, the archetypal ferryman taking departed souls across the River Styx to the next world. He had ferried young men to their deaths—what a terrible memory to live with. But this recounting of events was nothing like my mother's story, about a task that would have been carried out by a commando unit, and my uncle wasn't transferred to the Royal Marine Commandoes until he reenlisted after the war.

I read the official account twice, reconsidered my mother's out-of-whack story, then sat back and thought, "She lied." Never mind being good at storytelling—she had lied to me. I had not only been deeply wounded by it, but it had left me scarred. Where had the story about the little boy come from? Mum's stories were generally founded on truth, never mind how much she might have embellished them. But this one had gone too far. I was upset about it and felt foolish because I had never doubted her. I'd believed every word of every story, and now I felt humiliated, as if I had been played for a fool. But there was a niggle of doubt—there had to be more.

I called my brother and asked him if he had ever heard the story of Uncle Jim in Normandy in 1944. I went through every detail of the story as told to me by our mother.

"Sure I've heard it—just like you've described. But I never heard it from Mum," said John. "No, it was Uncle Charlie who told me about it when I went to Amsterdam with him."

"I give up!" I said aloud and began to laugh. It was a nervous laugh. I didn't know what to think. We talked some more, and when the call ended, I began to imagine what might have happened to inspire Mum's story.

I know my mother put her older brother on a pedestal and I am sure the younger siblings did too, especially the boys. I wondered about Uncle Jim's later service, when he transferred to the Royal Marine Commandoes—the division that would undertake more covert operations—and whether he served with men who had indeed been in smaller units during the Normandy Landings, their remit to seek out and destroy the enemy, especially snipers. Sitting in my upstairs home office on a sunny day in California, I speculated whether one of Uncle Jim's new buddies might have told the story of those dreadful events that happened as a result of being targeted by a German sniper. I could imagine Uncle Jim coming home on leave and, when asked to tell his siblings about what he'd been doing, recounting a story heard from another marine commando. Had my mother and Uncle Charlie been mistaken in their listening, and absorbed the story as something their older brother was involved in? Mum always told me how close she was to Jimmy, that she would walk with him to the station when he returned to barracks following a couple of days' leave, and how he would talk to her about his life in the Marines, what he was doing and his mates. She adored him—he was her hero.

Do we absorb stories told by our family and make them our own, so they become a sort of genetically encoded myth ingrained in our cellular memory? The story goes through another wash cycle, and our re-memory is changed. I decided to let it go—but perhaps not for long, because I'm a storyteller too.

There's still a big question mark in my mind regarding my mother's epic recounting of being buried in the rubble when a bomb hit the street. The details were so raw, so specific, and I'd witnessed her claustrophobia, which was real and terrifying. I suppose I don't want to believe she would willfully burden a child with a tale so horror-filled and vivid. But while talking to my aunts to corroborate some of her stories, more emerged, and I learned how brave she could be—and so were her siblings—but then, everyday bravery by ordinary people is what happens in a time of conflict. Everyone has their stories.

"We were walking home from work through the blackout," said Aunt Sylvie. "Just your mum and me, and it was pitch black, but the bombers were going over, and I was scared. So your mum said, 'Come on, Sylvie, let's sing—sing with me and you won't be scared.' And she started to sing. Your mum made me sing and dance along the street through the blackout until we reached the shelter."

"It was during an air raid," said Aunt Ruby. "I was terrified, so I ran down into the cellar and all I could hear was shrapnel hitting the metal dustbins outside, and the bombs falling. I was a little girl and I had only just come back to London—Sylvie, Rosie and me had been brought back from evacuation by our dad when he came home on leave and discovered our foster mother was feeding us a slice of bread and dripping for each meal and nothing else. As soon as he left after his leave, our mum had us evacuated again, so we were sent away. I was so scared all alone in the cellar, I clapped my hands over my ears and closed my eyes and started to cry, but my Joycie came to find me. Everyone else had gone down the shelter, but your mum stayed to look for me. She grabbed me by the hand and made me run with her through the bombing to the shelter, so we'd be safe." My mother would have been about fifteen or sixteen at the time.

In reconsidering her stories, at first I wanted to discover the facts. Did this happen? Did that happen? I started to dig a bit more, then I realized it just wasn't worth it. Whatever the facts, my mother had shared her truth—she had woven compelling stories wrought by her memories and she not only entertained people with them, but she inspired them, touched their emotions, and yes, she sometimes scared them in the way that a good thriller can have you on the edge of your seat at the movie theater. As soon as she had told me her stories, they were inside me and there was no taking them back. I couldn't un-know them, so it was up to me to decide what I would do with them—and there's only one route ahead for a teller of stories. The image of that little French boy was too sharp, too defined in my mind's eye. It's a piece of fabric I'll work with, probably sooner rather than later, the needle threaded with whatever my imagination comes up with to create another story.

I completed the first draft of this memoir over three days spent in a cottage on the northern California coast, just south of Mendocino. It was a wonderful personal writing retreat, to finish something I think I began writing in my mind when I was a child, sitting at the desk Fred Cooke had given me, a treasure I accepted with such gratitude so I could pretend to be a real writer. On my last morning before driving home I was walking my elderly Labrador along a deserted beach when I saw a whale just off the coast. Not unusual in northern California, but always magical. And at once, I could hear my father's voice, as if he were with me.

"See that, Jack? See it? Look where I'm pointing—follow my hand. There you go. Look at that! Not a lot of people get to see something like that—a whale! It's what they call a 'cetacean'—and we've seen it! I bet no one will ever believe us—we've seen a whale! We're very lucky. Very lucky, aren't we, love?"

I sat down on a washed-up tree trunk, a massive piece of driftwood worn by the sea and time, and recalled a radio interview I'd heard while on the long drive from San Francisco down to Ojai in southern California. It featured the British singer-songwriter Dido, and she had just been asked how coming to the United States and touring across the country had affected her work. A few seconds of silent airtime passed while she considered the question, and then she replied, "There was something about the openness of America that made me feel limitless." Remembering those words, I felt my throat catch and my eyes fill with tears, grateful I was alone on that beach as I rested my head on my knees and began to weep.

My parents left the bombsites and memories of wartime London for an openness they found in the country and on the land—they were a couple of kids in search of that feeling of being limitless, and through good times and bad, fair weather and foul, they not only found it, but they created it. They challenged us to look forward, to take their example and create something bigger for ourselves. So again I wondered if it should be any surprise that both my brother and I would be drawn to America and the promise of limitlessness in her wide open spaces.

I looked up and squinted, wiping those tears from my eyes as I focused on the ocean again, and watched small waves cresting the whale's back as she spouted once more before moving off across the limitless sea. I stood up and clapped my hands—the only sound my old dog can hear now—summoning her to my side so we could make our way back across the sand. It was time to go home.

Yes, Dad, we were very lucky. More fortunate than we ever knew.

ACKNOWLEDGMENTS

It was a class on writing the personal essay with Bay Area writer Adair Lara that started the memoir ball rolling for me almost thirty years ago. I abandoned the project and stashed it in a drawer so I could concentrate on publishing my essays—but Adair also encouraged me to write fiction. She read the first fifteen pages of *Maisie Dobbs* and pressed me to continue, though she asked if I was planning to revisit my memoir. It took a few years, but thank you, Adair, for helping me set out on the path.

I bit the memoir bullet again when I attended Barbara Abercrombie's workshops at UCLA Extension, delving into memories and family stories while searching for truths among the facts. In Barbara's class I met writer Monica Holloway, who became a dear friend. Sixteen years after that first meeting, Barbara and Monica both read *This Time Next Year We'll Be Laughing* and I am ever grateful for their encouragement.

Attending Hope Edelman's 2018 memoir master class at Hedgebrook, the retreat for women writers on Whidbey Island, Washington, helped me focus more deeply on my memoir's underpinning, giving me the confidence I needed to delve into the childhood relationships and events that defined my life. Her suggestion to remember points of tenderness touched me deeply—thank you, Hope, for your sensitive, focused modes of inquiry.

My literary agent and dear friend, Amy Rennert, has been a rock for me since, as a first-time author, I sent her an unsolicited letter and sample pages for a novel I'd written called *Maisie Dobbs*. At our first meeting, Amy asked me a question that has remained with me: "Who do you want to be as a writer?" Whenever I tried something new, Amy encouraged me even when I doubted myself. From the moment she read my memoir, she was enthusiastic and supportive on a personal and professional level. My deepest gratitude for your wise counsel and lovely friendship, Amy.

I adore my big, giant-hearted and sometimes rather crazy extended family, some of whom have answered my questions with patience and compassion. My cousin Susan Noonan graciously read the manuscript and shared some of her own memories—thank you, Sue, for your love and support. And thank you to my cousins Linda Willmott and James Clark for providing crucial information about your dad's role during the Normandy Landings. To my cousin Larry Iveson—as always, thank you for offering your perspective on aspects of our family history. To my beloved aunts Sylvia, Ruby and Rose—thank you for answering questions about my mum and for sharing your own stories, even when the remembering was difficult. I now have enough material for another book! To my entire family, thank you for tolerating my putting a few of our collective experiences through the wash cycle of remembrance.

To my friend Holly Rose—thank you for reading my manuscript, Hol. As always your comments were direct and much appreciated.

The late Laura Hruska, co-founder of Soho Press, was my first ever editor. After a few welcoming words regarding the *Maisie Dobbs* manuscript, she warned me, "I am your worst idea of a strict high school English teacher. Every manuscript I touch is returned to the author hemorrhaging red ink, but we will find out if you have what it takes to be a professional writer." From that moment I was determined to gain her respect—she was wonderful, a true publishing pro. Now my deepest gratitude goes to Laura's daughter, Bronwen Hruska, Publisher at Soho Press for her enthusiastic response to *This Time Next Year We'll Be Laughing*, and to Associate Publisher and Editor, Juliet Grames, for such insightful editing. My thanks to Dan O'Connor for his sensitive copyediting. Writers are solitary storytellers, but when a book goes into production, the author becomes part of a team— and I would be remiss if I did not thank the entire team at Soho, including Managing Editor Rachel Kowal; Director of Sales and Marketing, Paul Oliver; and Sales Manager Steven Tran. At time of writing there are people I have not yet worked with, but their enthusiasm is already evident, for which I feel blessed.

When I asked my brother, John, if he wanted to read my memoir, he declined, adding, "It's your memoir, Sis, your memories. I'll read it when it's published." His response could not have been more trusting and respectful—mind you, let's see what he says when he has the book in his hand.

To my husband, John Morell, thank you for listening to my stories, for encouraging me to write *This Time Next Year We'll Be Laughing*, and for your support throughout the process of bringing it to fruition.

The two people who deserve my most profound gratitude are my late parents, Albert and Joyce Winspear. More than anything, this book is for them.